THE FIGURE OF NATURE

STUDIES IN CONTINENTAL THOUGHT
John Sallis, editor

CONSULTING EDITORS

Robert Bernasconi James Risser
John D. Caputo Dennis J. Schmidt
David Carr Calvin O. Schrag
Edward S. Casey Charles E. Scott
David Farrell Krell Daniela Vallega-Neu
Lenore Langsdorf David Wood

The Figure *of* Nature

ON GREEK ORIGINS

JOHN SALLIS

INDIANA UNIVERSITY PRESS
Bloomington & Indianapolis

This book is a publication of

Indiana University Press
Office of Scholarly Publishing
Herman B Wells Library 350
1320 East 10th Street
Bloomington, Indiana 47405 USA

iupress.indiana.edu

© 2016 by John Sallis
All rights reserved

No part of this book may be reproduced or utilized in any form or by any means, electronic or mechanical, including photocopying and recording, or by any information storage and retrieval system, without permission in writing from the publisher. The Association of American University Presses' Resolution on Permissions constitutes the only exception to this prohibition.

The paper used in this publication meets the minimum requirements of the American National Standard for Information Sciences—Permanence of Paper for Printed Library Materials, ANSI Z39.48-1992.

Manufactured in the United States of America

Library of Congress Cataloging-in-Publication Data

Names: Sallis, John, 1938- author.
Title: The figure of nature : on Greek origins / John Sallis.
Description: Bloomington : Indiana University Press, 2016. | Series: Studies in Continental thought | Includes bibliographical references and index.
Identifiers: LCCN 2016010955 (print) | LCCN 2016029601 (ebook) | ISBN 9780253022882 (cloth : alk. paper) | ISBN 9780253023124 (pbk. : alk. paper) | ISBN 9780253023360 (ebook)
Subjects: LCSH: Philosophy of nature. | Philosophy, Ancient. | Plato.
Classification: LCC B118 .S25 2016 (print) | LCC B118 (ebook) | DDC 113.0938—dc23
LC record available at https://lccn.loc.gov/2016010955

1 2 3 4 5   21 20 19 18 17 16

αἰεὶ παπταίνουσα πρὸς αὐγὰς ἠελίοιο
"Always looking toward the light of the sun."
—Parmenides, Fragment B15

CONTENTS

Acknowledgments   ix

PROLOGUE   1

1 THE REIGN OF ARTEMIS   3

2 OPEN AIR.
   ON PHILOSOPHY BEFORE PHILOSOPHY   13

3 ENSHROUDED NATURE AND
   THE FIRE OF HEAVEN   26

4 RADICAL GATHERINGS.
   THE IMPERATIVE OF PHILOSOPHY   42

5 MONSTROUS WONDER.
   THE ADVANCE OF NATURE   58
   (a) Openings, Chronology, Topology   59
   (b) Appearings   73
   (c) Ventriloquy, the Protagorean Λόγος,
       and the Scene of Φύσις   86
   (d) The Scene of Philosophy   112
   (e) Parerga   138

6 EARTHBOUND. THE RETURN OF NATURE   158
    (a) Theseus   158
    (b) Down to Earth   170
    (c) Mythologizing   192
    (d) Remembrance   201
    (e) Ascent   212
    (f) Second Sailing   227
    (g) Song of the Earth   241

English Index   249
Greek Index   253

ACKNOWLEDGMENTS

I am grateful to the editor of *Internationales Jahrbuch für Hermeneutik* for permission to draw on previously published material.

All translations are my own, though I have consulted available translations, especially that of the *Theaetetus* by Seth Benardete and that of the *Phaedo* by Eva Brann, Peter Kalkavage, and Eric Salem.

For their very generous and able assistance during production of this book, I am grateful to Nancy Fedrow, Ryan Brown, and Stephen Mendelsohn. The support of my editor and friend Dee Mortensen has been indispensable, and I am especially grateful to her.

Boston
May 2016

THE FIGURE OF NATURE

PROLOGUE

To return from nature to φύσις is not merely to substitute for a modern word or concept its ancient equivalent. Rather, it is to reverse a history of translation that, beginning with the Latin rendering of φύσις as *natura*, has distanced what is said in the translation from what was once said in the word φύσις. In the modern designation there is borne a sedimented history of interpretation, which has both deposited senses alien to that of φύσις and rendered imperceptible much that originally sounded in the word, not least of all the echoes of mythic discourse.

To return from nature to φύσις is to venture to suspend this history so as to retrace the figure that oriented philosophy in its Greek beginning. It is to venture the attempt to write again περὶ φύσεως, to span the distance in such a way that it might become possible from this distance nonetheless to reinscribe such discourse.

In orienting the discourse to the figure of nature, to its σχῆμα, the intent is to free *nature* from the weight of the concept. For φύσις is neither a concept abstracted from the many natural things (τὰ φύσει ὄντα) nor itself one such thing alongside others. In certain respects it resembles a geometrical figure as distinct from both the corresponding concept and the visible trace that can be drawn of such a figure. This resemblance is what motivates to an extent the focus on the figure of nature, which is not something apart from nature, not something simply other than nature.

The intent is also to distance nature from anterior determination—indeed, in a double sense and manner: in such a way that, on the one side, it is not construed simply as an anterior determinant, as a nature beyond nature; and, on the other side, in such a way that, its incessant flow having been granted, its resistance to preconstituted forms and conditions is acknowledged.

Yet, even if the things of nature flow just as a flow of olive oil flows without a sound, all things whatsoever—being itself, λόγος, even their character as things of nature—depend on their somehow being brought

2 THE FIGURE OF NATURE

back, on their being retrieved, even if in the process they undergo mutation and appear in a very different guise. There are many ways in which their retrieval can be accomplished; and these ways as they are progressively laid out constitute a *fil conducteur* running through the history of Greek philosophy from the Milesians up through Plato. The things of nature may be gathered into what come to be called elements, which serve to delimit nature itself; thus they may be gathered up in air or fire or in four elements intertwined like the roots of a tree. Or their flow may be interrupted by bringing a sounding to bear on them as they flow and otherwise would remain without a sound; then it is speech—or rather, λόγος—that conveys and, at once, evokes the stable look of things. The same capacity is displayed in thinking, the silent dialogue carried on with oneself. Memory too retrieves what is otherwise lost, bringing into the present, into presence, what has flowed away into the past.

In these ways natural things come to be manifest as what they are, as, in releasing them into presence, nature itself withdraws its very figure.

1
THE REIGN OF ARTEMIS

She reigned with such sovereignty that her rule extended even into the beginning of the Christian era. It is reported that when Paul came to Ephesus, the site of the great temple of Artemis, he encountered such resistance that he dared not enter the theatre where the Ephesians were assembled. A surrogate named Alexander was thus put forth to offer a defense to the multitude assembled there. Yet when the crowd recognized that he was affiliated with Paul, then "for about two hours they all with one voice cried out 'Great is Artemis of the Ephesians!'"[1]

Her reign extended throughout Greece, from Ephesus, Miletus, and Samos, the three sites where what would be called philosophy had its beginning, to the Greek mainland and on beyond to Magna Graecia. In the μῦθος recounting the deeds through which she exercised her sovereignty, her bond to φύσις, to what would come to be called nature, was paramount. In this μῦθος the figure of nature was already drawn before philosophy came onto the scene and set about interrogating nature as such. When philosophy appeared on the scene, it took up this figure in which a certain sense of nature was already gathered. Even though the name Artemis goes largely unmentioned by the early Greek thinkers, the disclosure of nature sustained by her μῦθος remained directive for Greek thought from its beginning on.

Homer calls her "Artemis of the wild, the mistress of wild beasts,"[2] thus declaring her reign in the sense both of her sovereignty, her rule,

---

1. Acts of the Apostles 19:34 (Revised Standard Version of the New Testament).
2. Homer, *Iliad* 21:470. Burkert elaborates: "This *Potnia Theron* is a Mistress of the whole of wild nature, of the fish of the water, the birds of the air, lions and stags, goats and hares; she herself is wild and uncanny and is even shown with a Gorgon head" (Walter Burkert, *Greek Religion*, trans. John Raffan [Cambridge, MA: Harvard

4 THE FIGURE OF NATURE

and of the domain over which she rules, her kingdom or realm. She may seem to be a kind of goddess of nature, and yet, at best, the genitive expression only defers a proper characterization of the bond between Artemis and nature, of the manner in which she carries out her reign. Her rule bears little resemblance to that of a human monarch: whereas a mortal queen will always be intent on displaying herself in all her glory before those whom she rules, Artemis, as a goddess, is never to be directly beheld. Even her most devout follower, Hippolytus, declares that he cannot see her face to face.[3] Though indeed he has the unique privilege of hearing and answering to her words, for all other humans she appears only from within her realm, only in and through what she effects in the wild places over which she reigns, but in which, nonetheless, she remains withdrawn from the sight of mortals. Yet precisely as reigning—while remaining withdrawn—over the domain in which things are begotten and come to be born (φύομαι), Artemis is set apart as one who does not give birth. She is ἁγνή, pure, chaste. She is an inviolable virgin.

She reigns over the wild regions beyond the cities and beyond the cultivated fields. When her ardent disciple Hippolytus returns from her meadow and approaches her altar, he declares:

> My Goddess Mistress, I bring you ready woven
> this garland. It was I that plucked and wove it,
> plucked it for you in your inviolate meadow.
> No shepherd dares to feed his flock within it:
> no reaper plies a busy scythe within it:
> only the bees in springtime haunt the inviolate meadow.[4]

Her reign takes two forms, which, though apparently opposed, are in fact intrinsically connected. First of all, she is a huntress. Vase paintings portray her as the beautiful virgin huntress clad in a short tunic and carrying a bow and a quiver of arrows; often she is accompanied

---

University Press, 1985], 149). On the other hand, Vernant and Vidal-Naquet regard Artemis as located in frontier regions such as the mountains that bound and separate states. Thus, she would be positioned "at the intersection of the wild and the tame." They relate this positioning of the goddess to various rituals associated with her (Jean-Pierre Vernant and Pierre Vidal-Naquet, *Myth and Tragedy in Ancient Greece* [New York: Zone Books, 1988], 195–201). While indeed Artemis' deeds are on occasion portrayed as mirroring the intrusion or domestication of φύσις, most of the pertinent writings appear to position her at a farther remove from the fields and cities of humans.

3. Euripides, *Hippolytus* 87.
4. Ibid. 72–77.

by a stag or a doe. The Homeric Hymn dedicated to her describes her in these words: "I sing of Artemis, whose shafts are of gold, who cheers on the hounds, the pure maiden, shooter of stags, who delights in archery, sister to Apollo with the golden sword."[5] Along with her twin brother, Apollo, she was born on the island of Delos, the daughter of Zeus and Leto. In the *Odyssey* there is a more extended portrayal of her, which provides the context in which the beautiful maiden Nausikaa is compared to her:

> As Artemis, the archer, roves over the mountains,
> along the ridges of Taygetus or on lofty Erymanthus,
> delighting in the pursuit of boars and swift deer,
> and the nymphs, daughters of Zeus who bears the aegis,
> share her sport and Leto is glad at heart—
> high above them all Artemis holds her head and brows,
> and easily may she be known, though all are beautiful—
> so this one shone among her handmaidens,
> a virgin unwedded.[6]

Ranging across Taygetus, a high range of mountains on the western border of Laconia, or climbing to the top of Erymanthus, a lofty mountain in Arcadia that was the haunt of the Erymanthean Boar, Artemis and her nymphs pursue their wild prey. Yet it is not only to wild beasts that she is a threat, not only at them that she aims her arrows, but also at women. The passage in the *Iliad* in which she is described as "Artemis of the wild, the mistress of wild beasts" tells of an episode in which she scolded her brother for having yielded in a quarrel with Poseidon. Though—as the account continues—Apollo said nothing in his defense, Hera, full of anger, set upon Artemis with these words:

> It will be hard for you to match your strength with mine
> even if you wear a bow, since Zeus has made you a lion
> among women, and given you leave to kill any at your pleasure.
> Better for you to hunt down the ravening beasts in the mountains
> and deer of the wild, than try to fight in strength with your
> betters.[7]

---

5. Homeric Hymn XXVII: *To Artemis* 1–3.
6. Homer, *Odyssey* 6:102–9.
7. Homer, *Iliad* 21:482–86.

Whatever the measure of her strength against the likes of Hera may be, Artemis is—by Zeus' decree—a lion among women, and as such she can inflict sudden death upon them with her golden arrows.

And yet, as she can bring death, so also can she offer protection to all creatures who are born and aid to those who bear them. She reigns not only as huntress among animals and lion among women, but also as one who gives succor to the young of wild beasts and comfort to women in childbirth.

In Aeschylus' *Agamemnon* the chorus sings of her reign:

> Beautiful you are and kind
> to the tender young ravening lions.
> For sucklings of all the savage
> beasts that lurk in the lonely places you have sympathy.[8]

As protector of wild beasts, Artemis vents her anger when an animal is killed within her sanctuary. Especially loathsome to her is any slaying that interrupts the natural course of nativity. Thus the chorus tells also how her anger was provoked when a hare bearing its unborn young was killed and devoured.[9]

In the story of how, on its way to Troy, the Hellenic fleet commanded by Agamemnon was detained at Aulis, Artemis is identified as the one responsible for summoning the strong contrary wind that prevented the ships from sailing on. When Agamemnon consulted Calchas the soothsayer, the words he heard announced that the ships would be allowed to sail only if Agamemnon's daughter Iphigenia were offered as a sacrifice to Artemis. There are at least two accounts of the reason this sacrifice was demanded by the goddess. One is found in Euripides' *Iphigenia in Tauris*. At the outset of the drama, Iphigenia herself repeats the words that were addressed to Agamemnon when he brought his inquiry to Calchas:

> Agamemnon,
> Captain of Hellas, there can be no way
> of setting your ships free until the offering
> you promised Artemis is given to her.
> You had vowed to render in sacrifice to the light-bringing goddess
> The most beautiful one born each year.[10]

---

8. Aeschylus, *Agamemnon* 140–43.
9. Ibid. 133–37.
10. Euripides, *Iphegenia in Tauris* 18–23.

The sacrifice that is demanded by the goddess is to be carried out in belated fulfillment of a vow geared to natality. In this instance again what comes to light is the reign of the goddess over the domain of all that comes to be by way of birth, by being born (φύομαι), that is, the domain that also bears the name φύσις. As her reign comes thus to light, she is herself given the epithet "light-bringing" (φωσφόρος).

The other account of Artemis' demand is found in Sophocles' *Electra*. The words are those of Electra, also a daughter of Agamemnon:

> My father, as I hear, when at his sport,
> started at his feet an antlered dappled stag
> within the goddess' sanctuary. He
> let fly and hit the deer and uttered some boast
> about his killing of it. The daughter of Leto
> was angry at this and therefore stayed the Greeks
> in order that my father, to compensate
> for the beast killed, might sacrifice his daughter.[11]

As the protector of wild beasts, as the goddess who grants them the refuge in her sanctuary, Artemis demands recompense from anyone who, like Agamemnon, violates that sanctuary.

Powerless against the demand of the goddess, Agamemnon had wily Odysseus bring Iphigenia to Aulis under the false pretense that she was to marry Achilles before the fleet sailed. In Aeschylus' story of the events that followed, the sacrifice of Iphigenia was actually carried out. According to Euripides, however, she was snatched away at the last minute by Artemis, who substituted a deer for her. As she herself recounts it:

> When I had come
> to Aulis, they laid hands on me. The flame
> was lit. The blow would have been struck—I saw
> the knife. But Artemis deceived their eyes
> with a deer to bleed for me and stole me through
> the azure sky.[12]

Borne off to Tauris, Iphegenia became Artemis' priestess, even—as some have declared—a second Artemis.[13] Thus, in Euripides' version of the story, there is a peculiar reversal. Having demanded the sacrifice of Iphigenia, Artemis then becomes her protector, whisking her away from

---

11. Sophocles, *Electra* 366–73.
12. Euripides, *Iphigenia in Tauris* 25–30.
13. Burkert, *Greek Religion*, 152.

8   THE FIGURE OF NATURE

the scene of death to the sanctuary of Tauris, where as priestess she is entitled to deliver to mortals the words of the goddess. This reversal is indicative of just how intrinsically connected the two forms of Artemis' reign are.

Though a lion among women, Artemis was also often portrayed as coming to the aid of women, especially to those in childbirth. In such instances her intervention is not unlike that in the case of Iphigenia: at the very time when pain and the threat of death in childbirth are most intense, Artemis can be called on to bring aid and relief. Thus, in *Hippolytus* the chorus intones words that tell of the misery and helplessness of childbirth to which women are subject and of the aid that can be brought by Artemis:

> My body, too, has felt this thrill of pain,
> and I called on Artemis, queen of the bow;
> she has my reverence always
> as she goes in the company of the gods.[14]

Artemis is the maieutic goddess who brings her reign to the confluence of pain and deliverance, of the threat of death and the promise of new life. She is the goddess whose name invokes the realm of φύσις and who, herself unseen, reigns over all creatures that are born (φύομαι) and that accordingly belong to the domain of φύσις.

The two opposed directions in which Artemis exercises her sovereignty inscribe the primary lines around which the figure of nature takes shape. Her dual reign as both huntress and protector, as both demanding sacrifice and providing escape from it, and as both lion among women and comforter of those in childbirth mirrors in the figure of the goddess the ambivalent force of φύσις, that it both threatens and nurtures, that it both imposes deprivation and grants abundance, that it is the scene both of death and of new life.

Artemis is also light-bringing (φωσφόρος) and is portrayed as bearing torches in both hands. It is precisely as light-bringing that, in Euripides' dramatic presentation, she is promised the most beautiful one born each year. Yet the beauty, the radiance, the resplendence of one who, in being born, has come to behold the light of the sun can shine forth only in that light or, in its absence, by means of torches brought to light up the darkness. The light-bringing capacity of the goddess whose realm is φύσις corresponds to the elemental bearing that light has in

---

14. Euripides, *Hippolytus* 165–68.

φύσις, that it is what allows all things to shine forth, each in its own distinctive way.

The word φύσις commands to a large degree the writings of those whose thinking moves within the orbit of the beginning of philosophy. Indeed, in the formulation Περὶ Φύσεως, it provided what is said to have been the title borne by many of these writings. According to the authors of late antiquity by whom what remains of these early Greek writings was transmitted, this title was used by Anaximander, Anaximenes, Xenophanes, Heraclitus, Zeno, and Empedocles. While it is not certain whether in all cases the title came from the authors themselves and not, rather, from Alexandrian editorial practices,[15] its pervasiveness attests nonetheless to the prominence that discourse on φύσις commanded in these writings. For those who wrote in proximity to the beginning of philosophy, the primary focus and animating theme of their thought was, with only few exceptions, φύσις. Even later, when the venture is launched to set thinking apart from the beginning—as in Socrates' second sailing—φύσις remains the reference point from which whatever might be projected beyond would be determined. Among the writings of the ancients, there are few that interrogate φύσις so insistently as does the *Theaetetus*, despite—yet also perhaps because of—its critical detachment from almost all earlier writers from Homer to Empedocles.

Yet when early Greek thinking brings φύσις into focus, it is its figure as already gathered in the figure of Artemis that is most readily discerned. In this regard the deeds of the thinker are most revelatory: to Heraclitus, above all, there are attributed deeds that reveal the bearing of the thinker who, precisely in his engagement with φύσις, is borne toward the goddess. Diogenes Laertius' report regarding Heraclitus' alleged book Περὶ Φύσεως is explicit: "He dedicated it in the temple of Artemis" (A1). The report also tells of how, convinced that his native city of Ephesus was governed by a bad constitution, Heraclitus refused to take part in writing laws and instead set himself entirely apart from the politics of his fellow citizens. In the words of the report: "Retiring into the temple of Artemis, he played knuckle-bones with children" (A1). Even though in Heraclitus' extant writings the name Artemis does not occur,

---

15. Modern scholars have observed in this regard that Alexandrian writers tended to supply titles where they were lacking or missing; in particular, they seem to have assigned this title, Περὶ Φύσεως, to major works of nearly all those whom Aristotle designated as φυσικοί. See G. S. Kirk, J. E. Raven, and M. Schofield, *The Presocratic Philosophers*, 2nd ed. (Cambridge, UK: Cambridge University Press, 1983), 102.

the figure of the goddess sustained no doubt a certain openness to what came to be thought as φύσις. Indeed, in the figuration of the goddess as remaining withdrawn from sight at the very scenes of her interventions, the Heraclitean declaration regarding the self-concealing propensity of φύσις can already be discerned.

And yet, it is not as if the thinking of φύσις simply leaves the figure of the goddess behind. More generally, it is not as if Greek thinking utterly abandons the mythic, simply forsaking whatever might have been given a degree of manifestness by it. The writings of Heraclitus and Empedocles abound with the names of the gods, of Zeus, Apollo, Aphrodite, and others; and these mythic names are closely configured with terms denoting moments seemingly remote from everything mythic, moments such as the natural elements or the recurrent cycles in nature. The Platonic dialogues are manifestly infused with mythic moments, with moments so thoroughly interwoven with the seemingly non-mythic λόγοι of the dialogues that they cannot be suppressed. Even when the portrayal of the Homeric gods is submitted to criticism, these figures continue to play a role in Platonic discourse, as do also such legendary figures as Theseus and Heracles. When, in the *Phaedrus*, Socrates is asked about such matters, the very formulation of the question incorporates the name of a mythic figure: "By Zeus, Socrates," says Phaedrus, "do you believe this mythic tale [μυθολόγημα] to be true?" (229c). Though the question refers specifically to the tale of Boreas and Oreithyia, Socrates' response is more general. Ironically setting himself apart from those who explain away such tales, Socrates tells Phaedrus that he has no leisure (σχολή) for such alleged explanations but rather accepts the current beliefs about them. Declaring that it would be ridiculous (laughable—γελοῖον) to concern himself with devising such accounts when he does not yet know himself, he then goes on to describe the task of self-knowing by referring to a mythic figure and then finally to nature: "I investigate not these things but myself, to discover whether I am a monster more complicated and more furious than Typhon or a gentler and simpler animal to whom a divine and modest fate [μοῖρα] is given by nature [φύσει]" (230a). Thus, over against those who explain away mythic figures, Socrates describes his stance by invoking the mythic figure of Typhon, the hundred-headed monster who rose up against the gods and finally was killed by Zeus' thunderbolt. Though Socrates leaves undecided whether he belongs on the side of the monster or on the gentler side of nature, it is evident that mythic tales such as that of Typhon are woven into his discourse of self-knowing, and indeed that even monstrosity—that is, divergence from nature within nature—may have significant bearing on this endeavor.

Artemis makes two appearances in the Platonic dialogues.[16] In the first of these, it is the name of the goddess more than she herself that is the theme. This appearance, in the *Cratylus*, is very contextual: it occurs in the course of the etymological comedy, specifically in that part in which Socrates allegedly—or ironically or comedically—inquires about the opinions that mortals had in giving the gods the names by which they call them, the names that are pleasing to the gods, in distinction from the names, the true names, by which the gods call themselves. Within this highly comedic context, Socrates' etymology of the name of Artemis refers mainly to her virginity. He first offers a direct and laudatory formulation: she "is named for her wholesomeness [ἀρτεμές] and orderliness [κόσμιον], on account of her passion for virginity" or because she is "skilled in virtue [ἀρετή]." Then he adds another that, though it says much the same, gestures toward comedy: "maybe the one who gave the goddess her name was calling her . . . one who abhors the sex act of a man upon a woman" (*Crat.* 406b).[17]

The second appearance of Artemis is immeasurably more significant, for it is not immersed in a context having no specific orientation to her. This appearance occurs in the *Theaetetus* at the juncture where Socrates rather abruptly informs Theaetetus that he practices the art of the midwife (149a–c). Invoking Artemis as the goddess to whom childbirth is allotted for her protection, he portrays ordinary midwives as likenesses of Artemis. Thus, as himself a midwife, if of another sort, he carries out his own practice in imitation of Artemis' maieutic reign. It is, then, in the very context in which he compares his practice with the reign of Artemis as midwife that Socrates launches the thoroughgoing and radical interrogation of φύσις that occupies the greater part of the *Theaetetus*.

Although her name is directly invoked only in these two instances, Artemis and all that is gathered into her reign are seldom entirely absent from those contexts in the dialogues in which questioning is directed at φύσις. Even the event of sacrifice and of its reversal as in the case

---

16. The name Artemis is also mentioned in passing in the *Laws* at 833b.

17. For the full context, see my account in *Being and Logos: Reading the Platonic Dialogues*, 3rd ed. (Bloomington: Indiana University Press, 1996), 232–62.

12 THE FIGURE OF NATURE

of Iphigenia come to be taken up and mirrored in Platonic discourse. Though it resonates throughout the entire *Phaedo*, the most powerful and consequential enactment of sacrifice occurs near the end of the dialogue. The scene is very brief: once the executioner has handed him the potion, Socrates "looks up from under his brows at the man with that bull's look that was so usual with him" and proposes a libation or at least a prayer to the gods (117b). The scene simulates a sacrifice, and yet, as with Iphigenia, the outcome would appear to be escape, deliverance, a recovery for which, as his final words declare, Socrates owes a cock to Asclepius. Everything hinges on whether these final scenes portray a deliverance from φύσις, a flight to a beyond (μετά) of φύσις, like that of Iphigenia borne off to Tauris by Artemis; or whether, even as death impends, the issue remains that of the mortal bond to φύσις.

2 OPEN AIR.
ON PHILOSOPHY
BEFORE PHILOSOPHY

Beginnings are rarely simple. Seldom is there a point marking a single, unique beginning, a point entirely discrete and determinable. Rather, in most instances any alleged point of beginning will prove to extend into an interval or even into a more complex figure. Furthermore, the operation that determines beginnings is not only geometrical in structure but also linguistic: at some point, perhaps undecidable, perhaps multiple, a name, a distinctive, definitive name, comes to designate that which at that point can perhaps most properly—if still improperly—be said to begin. Yet at that point it will also almost certainly already have begun, already before the beginning. Seldom can anything simply have begun.

There was, then, a beginning before the beginning of philosophy, a time of philosophy before philosophy. According to ancient testimony, it was Pythagoras who first called himself φιλόσοφος. Yet it is equally attested that he was not the first philosopher, that there were others who could have been—but were not yet—called philosophers, not even by themselves. Theirs was a thinking before philosophy: before the name, but also, therefore, before the unity of sense that the word would come to bear.

Only later, when this name had been firmly established and its complex signification had become thoroughly determinative, did the thinkers of ancient Miletus come to be designated as philosophers. This entirely retrospective designation no doubt opened a way of access to their thinking, especially to the degree that the primary sense of philosophy continued, as with the Milesians, to be determined by an orientation to φύσις. On the other hand, there is good reason, even at a purely formal level, to suspect that the projection—or rather, retrojection—of the signification of philosophy back upon the Milesians may also have had the effect of distorting and concealing the genuine concern and the decisive accomplishment of their thinking. There is also good reason to suspect that this effect became ever more forceful and itself more concealed in the wake of the basic shifts, the growing complexity, and the multiple differentiations that emerged in the course of ancient Greek philosophy. It has been said that even Aristotle's account of φύσις—as in *Physics* B1—is no more than an echo of what was thought in the beginning of Greek philosophy.[1] If such is the case, then there is every reason to expect that only a still fainter, more remote echo can be heard of what was not even yet quite this beginning in its full compass—but only a beginning before the beginning. By the time discourse on φύσις comes to be confined to a single discipline along with others within philosophy as a whole, the echo of philosophy before philosophy will perhaps have died out entirely. Or rather, it will have been silenced by the force of such concepts as μορφή and ὕλη, concepts quite foreign to Milesian thinking.

What would be required, then, in order to let these discourses on φύσις sound again on their own rather than, at best, only as transposed into Aristotelian concepts? How can they be brought to sound otherwise than as a kind of echo of Aristotle before Aristotle?

The difficulties are enormous. For in turning back to early Greek thinkers, especially to those whose thinking belongs to the time before philosophy, we continue—for the most part unknowingly—to operate largely within the legacy of Aristotelian concepts, long since wrapped in the disguise of common sense and obviousness. Furthermore, the difficulty is compounded by the fact that nearly all the pertinent reports and citations on which we must rely are mediated through Aristotelian sources. Most significant in this regard is the work of Aristotle's student Theophrastus, whose massive history of Greek philosophy became the ancient world's standard authority. Most later authors who cited or reported on the early Greek thinkers relied heavily on Theophrastus' work, either directly or indirectly. As in Aristotle's own accounts of those whom he regarded as his predecessors, so likewise Theophrastus brought to bear on earlier Greek thinking an Aristotelian discourse and conceptuality that is less than appropriate to most previous thinkers but that is most suspect when applied to those whose thinking was

---

1. Martin Heidegger, "Vom Wesen und Begriff der Φύσις. Aristoteles, Physik B, 1," in *Wegmarken*, vol. 9 of *Gesamtausgabe* (Frankfurt a.M.: Vittorio Klostermann, 1976), 300.

not yet governed—or, alternatively, restricted—by the signification of philosophy.[2]

It is proverbial to suppose that, among the Milesians, Thales was the first, though the doxographic evidence for determining the dates of and the relations between the three preeminent Milesians is very slight, quite inconclusive.[3] It is proverbial also to attribute to Thales the view that the material principle of all things is water; Anaximenes, so it is said, simply identified another element, namely, air, as the principle, while Anaximander is supposed to have identified it not with any definite element, but rather as the indefinite. Supposedly there is little more to be said about these early thinkers and about what cannot but appear to be their empty speculations about nature. At most, they might be accorded the honor of having been forerunners—though among the most primitive—of the natural scientists of later eras.

And yet—

Behind almost every word that occurs in the proverbial account of these allegedly empty speculations, there lie presuppositions that have inadvertently been read back from philosophy into this thought before philosophy. Each of the three Milesians is alleged to have held a *view*. And yet, is it self-evident that what arises in and from thinking can be appropriately characterized as a view or that the thinker's comportment to a view—if indeed it be a view—is one of *holding* the view, of keeping it in one's grasp, of keeping it constantly in view? If construed objectively, a view of something is its look; and in this connection the question cannot but arise as to whether the sense of *view* can be determined independently of what the Greeks designated by the word εἶδος. But then, is it not Plato who first undertook to think φύσις by recourse to εἴδη? Is this not the outcome—even if mediated by recourse to λόγοι—of the strategy that Socrates articulates in the *Phaedo* as his second sailing

---

2. Kahn is explicit about the character and effect of Theophrastus' reports on the earlier Greek thinkers. He writes: "It must be remembered that Theophrastus' motive in reporting the views of earlier Greek philosophers is by no means purely historical. The documentary concern with the past is for him above all a tool in the creative search for truth." As regards the effect of Theophrastus' report, Kahn adds that he "tends to distort the original form of the doctrines under consideration. And the gap between Theophrastus and his historical subject matter naturally widens precisely at those points where the Aristotelian school is in possession of an essentially new doctrine and a complex terminology of its own" (Charles H. Kahn, *Anaximander and the Origins of Greek Cosmology* [Indianapolis: Hackett, 1994], 18f.).

3. See Kirk, Raven, and Schofield, *The Presocratic Philosophers*, 143.

(δεύτερος πλοῦς) and contrasts with the approach to φύσις taken by the earlier thinkers? But in this case, if *view* is inseparable from εἶδος, then the supposition that the Milesians held certain views proves to be utterly anachronistic.

The views that they are anachronistically said to have held supposedly had to do with the *material principle*. Yet prior to Aristotle there is no concept of matter. Before it was theoretically delimited and rendered fundamental in Aristotle's *Physics*—and then eventually translated as *materia*—the word ὕλη hardly even alluded to the philosophical signification that it would come to have. In Homer, ὕλη means forest or firewood that has been collected from the forests; and even in its infrequent occurrences in the Platonic texts, the word remains limited to this quite mundane sense. The Milesians have no word for what will come to be called matter—not, however, because there is some lack in their language, some preconstituted meaning they cannot express, but rather because they do not think φύσις in this way at all; that is, they do not think it as involving a constituent for the expression of which the word ὕλη would be required.

Still, it will be said that each of the Milesians proposes a *principle* of all things, that each identifies such a principle. Yet even if one sets aside the sense of *principium* as a theory or discourse about things and takes it instead in its objective sense, as the beginning or origin of all things, this construal still falls short of the full sense that the word ἀρχή had in early Greek thought, a double sense that, quite remarkably, is still operative in Aristotle's *Physics*. An ἀρχή is, first of all, that from which things arise, that by virtue of which they come forth into the open; but furthermore, it is that which has sovereignty over things, that which commands their coming forth, not merely at a point of origin but throughout their entire course.

It is in this double sense, then, that the Milesians identify the ἀρχή of all things. Yet what they identify as ἀρχή cannot, without further ado, be called an *element*. For prior to Plato the word στοιχεῖον, which the Romans translated as *elementum*, was not used to designate the constituents of things; even when, in the *Timaeus*, the sense of the word is extended so as to designate not only, as up to then, the constituents of λόγος (syllables, for instance) but also the constituents of things, this move is carried out with extreme hesitation and with serious reservations as to its appropriateness.[4]

---

4. *Timaeus* 48b; see also *Theaetetus* 201e.

Even if the generic designation is suspended, as it must be for the Milesians, the names for what will eventually be called the στοιχεῖα or elements remain, from a modern perspective, elusive and difficult to delimit with precision. It goes without saying that the modern conceptions of chemical compounds or mixtures are entirely inapplicable. But other differentiations are more subtle and more difficult to mark in recognizable terms. For instance, the sense of ὕδωρ, which Thales is said to have identified as the ἀρχή, expands in certain contexts beyond that of water. In the *Timaeus* metal is regarded not primarily as earth, as one might suppose, but rather as ὕδωρ that is fusible.[5] Yet something that can be fused into a solid would presumably have been itself intrinsically fluid, and thus the sense of ὕδωρ exceeds, in this context, that of mere water: it acquires the sense of fluid, of something intrinsically prone to flow, though certain conditions serve to congeal the fluid and fuse it into something solid such as bronze or ice. Only the slightest extension of this sense would be required in order, bonding the sense of ὕδωρ more rigorously with that of flowing, to bring to light an otherwise invisible affinity between Thales and later Greek thinkers such as Heraclitus and the Plato of the *Theaetetus*. And then the ludicrous assertion that Thales thought everything was water would long since have proven to be, at best, a fit subject for a comedy still to be written. It would perhaps prove an apt counterpart to the comedy narrated at the very center of the *Theaetetus*, the comedy of his falling into the water of a well.[6]

Among the three Milesian thinkers, priority is sometimes accorded to Thales as chronologically the first. Sometimes, on the other hand, Anaximander is awarded the prize, since in identifying the ἀρχή as the indefinite, he appears to have surpassed the concreteness of his fellow Milesians and thus to have achieved a higher, more abstract level of thought. In either case, Anaximenes would seem to deserve no more than third place in this ancient ἀγών.

Yet many of the ancients regarded Anaximenes as most deserving of the laurel wreath. For he was the one with whom the inaugural advent of what would come to be called philosophy reached its culmination and

---

5. See *Timaeus* 59b–c.
6. There is also a certain drift of the word πῦρ from meaning simply *fire* toward signifying *light*, and conversely. This drift between *fire* and *light* can be detected in Anaximenes' declaration that the sun, moon, and stars are fiery (πύρινον) (A15, DG356, A14; cf. Plato, *Laws* 865b). Kahn points out that for Heraclitus, πῦρ has also the sense of "shared daylight" (*Anaximander and the Origins of Greek Cosmology*, 215).

was passed on, its spirit migrating from Miletus to Ephesus and Samos. The testimony of the classicist John Burnet is significant in this regard, even though his philosophically reductive, indeed naive, approach obtrudes in virtually every word. Burnet writes: "It is not easy for us to realize that, in the eyes of his contemporaries, and for long after, Anaximenes was a much more important figure than Anaximander. And yet the fact is certain. We shall see that Pythagoras, though he followed Anaximander in his account of the heavenly bodies, was far more indebted to Anaximenes for his general theory of the world. We shall see further that when, at a later date, science revived once more in Ionia, it was 'the philosophy of Anaximenes' to which it attached itself. Anaxagoras adopted many of his most characteristic views, and so did the Atomists. Diogenes of Apollonia went back to the central doctrine of Anaximenes and made air the primary substance."[7]

Hegel, too, declares Anaximenes the winner of the Milesian ἀγών. Hegel's decision is based on the fact that Anaximenes carried out the advance by which a natural element and an indeterminate principle were brought together, submitted to synthesis. Hegel writes: "In place of the undetermined material of Anaximander, he again posits a definite natural element (the absolute in a real form)—but instead of the water of Thales, that form is air. He found that a sensible being was necessary for the material; and air has, at the same time, the advantage of having greater formlessness. It is less corporeal than water; we do not see it, but feel it first in movement. Everything comes forth from out of it and dissolves again into it. He determines it as infinite, as well."[8]

This description is incomparably more perceptive philosophically. Two points stand out as especially significant. The first consists in Hegel's setting air apart from water, and by implication from all the other elements. Air is virtually unique among the elements in that it is invisible. In this connection Hegel calls attention to the Fragment in which Anaximenes posits a connection between air and πνεῦμα, that is, wind, breath, or, as Hegel translates it, *Geist*. The second point is broached in Hegel's observation that everything comes forth from out of air and dissolves again into it. Here Hegel makes it virtually explicit that the coming forth of things is not a matter of simple origination, as if things were composed from air, but rather is a process of coming forth

---

7. John Burnet, *Early Greek Philosophy* (New York: Meridian Books, 1957), 78f.
8. G. W. F. Hegel, *Vorlesungen* über *die Geschichte der Philosophie* I, vol. 18 of *Werke* (Frankfurt a.M.: Suhrkamp, 1971), 214.

OPEN AIR   19

into the light, of coming forth into the open, from which, then, in their self-obscuring, they withdraw. It is less a matter of generation and dissolution than of advancing into the open and receding from it.

Though embedded in a modern—and to that extent alien—context, Hegel's remarks about Anaximenes are not so very remote from what is expressed in a Fragment from Empedocles, the thinker with whom, in a decisive sense, early Greek thinking oriented to φύσις reached its culmination. The Fragment provides an appropriate directive by which to approach the thought of the Milesians, especially that of Anaximenes. Despite its decisiveness, there is nonetheless an irresolvable uncertainty about the Fragment, since the text in which it was handed down was written more than six centuries after the original passage that is allegedly quoted, and it sets the passage in a context quite different from that of early Greek thought. With such a passage, as with those linked to Anaximenes, not even the utmost caution, not even the most patient and careful reading, can compensate entirely for this uncertainty.

Account need not yet be taken of its precise diction and its full context. Rather, at this point it suffices to cite the imperative with which the major part of the Fragment begins. These are the first words: "But come, consider by all means how each thing is manifest" (B3). Thus the passage enjoins the one to whom it is addressed to consider each thing in its manifestness, as it is manifest, in its way of being manifest (δῆλον).

But can one suppose that such an attentiveness to things in their manifestness was operative already in sixth-century Miletus, when even the name *philosophy* was still lacking? Can one suppose, in particular, that such a bond of thought to the manifestness of things was operative in the thinking of Anaximenes? To be sure, he is reported to have been an astute observer of certain natural phenomena. For example, he is said to have declared that "a rainbow is produced when the rays of the sun fall on thickened air" (A7). And again: "a rainbow is formed by the illumination of the sun falling on a dense, thick, dark cloud, when the rays, which are not able to penetrate to the other side, are gathered together on it" (A18). Yet, when Anaximenes' thinking surpasses such observation and comes to bear on φύσις as such, does it remain bound to the manifestness of things?[9] Would such a supposition not be thoroughly at odds with what Diogenes Laertius says of Anaximenes, namely, that

---

9. It is not entirely irrelevant that Anaximenes focused on the rainbow. For in the case of the rainbow, its manifestness is all that counts. It is not as if the rainbow somehow *is* and then becomes manifest; rather, it *is* only as it is manifest.

according to him, everything is or comes from air, or, more precisely, that the ἀρχή is ἀήρ? What could be less attentive, less bound to things in their manifestness, than such a theory, if it can be called a theory? And yet, if even the minimal clue provided by Hegel is brought to bear, then the sense of Anaximenes' identification of the ἀρχή as ἀήρ begins to shift: the ἀρχή names neither the hidden identity of things (what they "really" are) nor the element from which they are composed. Rather, Anaximenes can be taken as setting forth ἀήρ as that from which all things come forth into their presence, into their manifestness. To posit ἀήρ as ἀρχή would be, then, a decisive way of pondering things in their manifestness, in their way of becoming manifest.

Yet how is it that Anaximenes thinks the ἀρχή as ἀήρ? What is to be understood by ἀήρ? It goes almost without saying that it does not mean air in the sense determined by modern science, namely, as a mixture of gases; neither can it be identified with the element that Aristotle designates by this name and links to his conception of ὕλη. In Homer and Hesiod the word often refers to mist, vapor, or cloud.[10] Sometimes the reference is to the underworld, and to the obscurity that prevails there. But more often—and later almost exclusively—ἀήρ refers to the so-called lower air, the denser atmosphere from the surface of the earth up to the clouds; thus it is distinguished from αἰθήρ, the shining upper air, above the clouds, beyond which there is only οὐρανός, the heaven. For example, there is a passage in the *Iliad* where it is declared that "the fir-tree reached through ἀήρ to the αἰθήρ";[11] in this case, either sense—or both—may be operative. Yet it seems that by the sixth century the word had come to refer primarily to the openness and transparency that the English cognate conveys, though the older meaning, not entirely effaced, could still allude to an obscuring of the otherwise illuminated openness. The phenomenal connection with wind and breath remained intact.

When, as we proceed, it proves expedient to let the word ἀήρ be replaced by its English cognate, it is imperative that this configuration of senses remain still intact and be kept constantly in mind.

---

10. On this basis Kahn insists that Anaximenes' conception of ἀήρ is not derived from Homer (*Anaximander and the Origins of Greek Cosmology*, 152f.). While granting this dissociation, the question remains as to whether a trace of older meaning continues to be operative in Anaximenes' thought.

11. *Iliad* 14:288. See also Kirk, Raven, and Schofield, *The Presocratic Philosophers*, 10; and Burnet, *Early Greek Philosophy*, 74.

It is in relation to this semantic configuration that the relevant Fragments are to be read. The utmost care as well as a sense of tentativeness is necessary, not only because of the heavy overlay of Aristotelian language but also because the number of reports about Anaximenes' thought is exceptionally small; indeed, there is only one Fragment—in fact a fragment of a Fragment—that can with some justification be taken as a quotation of his actual words. The five main Fragments are all traceable to Aristotelian sources: Diels-Kranz A4 comes directly from Aristotle's *Metaphysics*. A5 comes from the sixth-century AD commentator Simplicius, who based his account on Theophrastus, as he himself grants; in fact, in reporting on Anaximenes' conception of certain generative processes, he refers explicitly both to Theophrastus' *Studies* (ἱστορίαι) and to a statement from Aristotle's *Physics*. A7 derives from Hippolytus, a third-century AD Christian writer in Rome, who authored a work entitled *Refutation of All Heracies*, in which he ventured to show that all heresies derived from Greek philosophy; not only was he less than sympathetic to the texts he cited, but also his primary source was, if more indirectly, the work of Theophrastus. Both A10 and B2 are transmitted by Aetius, a first- or second-century AD writer, who relied also on Theophrastus, though his reports are mixed with certain Stoic and Epicurean motifs; in B2 certain distinctively Aristotelian terms such as ὕλη occur.

The first of the five Fragments, Diels-Kranz A4 from Aristotle's *Metaphysics*, reads: "Anaximenes and Diogenes place air [ἀήρ] prior to water and as in the highest degree the ἀρχή of the simple bodies [τῶν ἁπλῶν σωμάτων]." It should be noted that Aristotle does *not* ascribe to Anaximenes the thought that everything comes from air. Rather, according to Aristotle, Anaximenes posits air as the ἀρχή of the simple bodies. Since, for Aristotle, at least, air is itself one of the simple bodies, Anaximenes' thesis would be, more precisely, that air is the ἀρχή of the *other* simple bodies. Aristotle does not say, however, what Anaximenes took to be the other simple bodies, except that he mentions ὕδωρ, presumably to mark what he takes as the contrast with Thales. Nothing whatsoever is said as to how *all other* things come to be.[12] Though Aristotle would have taken all other things to be composed of simple bodies, even he considers accounts of things in terms merely of their composition to be limited; the determination of the being of such things is ir-

---

12. See Heribert Boeder, *Grund und Gegenwart als Frageziel der Früh-Griechischen Philosophie* (The Hague: Martinus Nijhoff, 1962), 45f.

reducible to their mere decomposition into constituent elements. There can be little or no assurance that Anaximenes would have relied on such a decompositional account. Whether even the expression *simple bodies* (ἁπλὰ σωμάτα) is appropriate to his thinking is open to question.

The second of the Fragments, Diels-Kranz A5 from Simplicius' *Physics*, begins with the link to Anaximander. Anaximenes, so it reads, "says that the underlying φύσις is one and unlimited...." In Aristotle's *Physics* the word ὑποκείμενον (*underlying*) is integrated into the distinctively Aristotelian account of change. But if it is kept detached from that conceptuality so that the focus is on the most direct sense of the word, then the Fragment can be read as saying: when other "simple bodies" come about, there is an underlying φύσις, a φύσις that persists—a φύσις that the Fragment will go on to identify as air. This underlying φύσις is said to be one and unlimited. To say that it is unlimited (ἄπειρον)—like the ἀρχή of Anaximander—is to say that it has no πέρας, no limit or extremity at which it would end or from which it could begin. If, in this connection, we were to translate ἀρχή simply as *beginning*, then we could say that it is a beginning that has no beginning, a beginning before beginning.

The Fragment continues by differentiating between Anaximenes and Anaximander: Anaximenes considers φύσις "not indeterminate [ἀόριστος] but determinate, calling it air." Thus, the underlying φύσις, the φύσις that underlies what will eventually be called the other simple bodies, is one—that is, presumably, one kind of body and one that exhibits a certain oneness, a continuity. As such it is something determinate; it has a determinate identity; it is something delimited (ὡρισμένος—from ὁρίζω)—namely, air. On the other hand, it is unlimited: there is no limit beyond which or before which air would *not be*. Hence, wherever anything *is*, there is also the underlying, determinate φύσις *air*. Wherever anything *is*—be it fire, earth, or stone—there will be not just one, but *two*: fire or earth or stone *and* air. Except perhaps where there is simply air, there will always be two—that is, a dyad.

Doubling, the formation of a dyad, can always be expressed, reciprocally, as division or differentiation. Thus, it could just as readily be said that with respect to each so-called simple body that comes forth, there is a differentiation: there is air, and there is something else differentiated from air. Thus it is that Fragment A5 says that air is "differentiated in its being [διαφέρειν ... κατὰ τὰς οὐσίας]." This differentiation is said to be determined by rarefication and condensation: when air becomes rarer, then there is also fire; in the other direction, when air becomes denser, then there appear clouds, water, earth, or stone. Fragment A7 expresses it, all too cryptically—indeed, in a manner that perhaps best exemplifies the testimony that Anaximenes "used simple and unadorned Ionic speech" (A1—from Diogenes Laertius). It reads: "When denser or rarer, appearance [φαίνεσθαι] occurs differently." In other words, the condition of the underlying φύσις, the degree of condensation or rarefication of air, determines the way in which whatever appears with it, in it, actually appears; its condition determines what the appearances appear as, how they show themselves. Thus—and here the cautiousness and degree of reservation must be proportioned to the indecisiveness of this as well as the other Fragments—it is not a matter of mere transformation of each element into another (as though water could simply turn into stone); rather, it is a matter of the way in which their appearing is released and governed by air as their ἀρχή. It is a matter of how their self-showing—and Fragment A7 uses the middle voice form φαίνεσθαι—takes place.

Both Fragments A5 and A7 name the so-called simple bodies: fire, wind, cloud, water, earth, stone. Both Fragments then extend the process of manifestation beyond these. Thus, after naming the simple bodies, Fragment A5 simply continues with these words: "And the rest from these." The implication is that all additional appearances, that is, the appearances of things that are not simple bodies, come about from the blending of these primary appearances. Thus, these Fragments can be taken as outlining the full range of manifestations.

And yet, most remarkably, Fragment A7 indicates that there is a discontinuity in this range, indeed a kind of zero-point of non-manifestation. In the words of the Fragment: "Whenever air is most uniform [or equable—ὁμαλώτατος], it is not manifest [ἄδηλόν] to sight." It is said even that this is the look (εἶδος) of air, that when it is most equable, it is not manifest to sight. The conclusion is that insofar as air can be manifest, it is so only in its differentiation from something else. As long as it remains simply by itself, as long as it stays entirely to itself, as long as difference does not intrude, it does not show itself. Its look as such is no look at all. Its εἶδος is to have no εἶδος. Thus is measured the distance, the differentiation, from Plato, for whom being most equable, being utterly selfsame, defines the very sense of εἶδος and conditions entirely the shining forth of the εἶδος. For Anaximenes, on the other hand, air never shows itself *as itself* but rather is operative only in the manifestation of something differentiated from it. In such manifestation it remains air;

it does not undergo change into something else but only becomes rarer or denser. Thereby it originates and governs the appearance, the self-showing, of water, of earth, of stone, and indeed, as indicated by several other ancient reports, of the stars as they revolve in the heaven, appearing as such to us only through the air (ἀήρ and αἰθήρ) opening to the heaven (οὐρανός). The idiom, if not yet the full sense, of these Fragments can begin to sound in simple expressions, as in saying: "in the refined air spreading upwards from the earth, the fire of heaven, the stars raised on high, shine forth" (A7). Or again: "From the broad earth, embraced and sustained by air, the sun, moon, and other heavenly bodies too are sustained in the breadth of their visible manifestness" (A7).

Yet still, we need to consider more precisely how air as such is operative in letting things come forth into the open. In what way does it, while not itself manifest as such, belong to the event of manifestation?

Fragment A10 consists of a report in which the author Aetius comments on Anaximenes' declaration that air is a god. According to the report, this declaration is to be taken as referring to "the powers [δυνάμεις] that pervade the elements or bodies."[13] The question is, then: What does air empower in its pervading the elements and bodies that entitles it to be called god? The answer could not be more direct: it empowers the very appearing of things themselves. It empowers the appearance of the elements and bodies and all the other appearances blended from these. Air empowers the coming forth of things into manifestness. Its very invisibility, its transparency, its never showing itself as itself, is precisely what renders it capable of providing the site where things can come forth and be manifest. Air is what grants the transparent opening in which all other things can appear. As it becomes rarer or denser, things appear differently, and different things appear. But it is anterior to all appearance, the beginning before the beginning, the archaic ἀρχή. For it is there, in the open air, that all things come to light.

It is because of the gigantic spread of open air that the profusion of things, gathered into their manifestness, are gathered to us and we to ourselves. It is to this spread and these gatherings that the words are addressed in the sole Fragment that has some claim to presenting the words of Anaximenes himself. Fragment B2 reads: "As our soul, being

---

13. There is a related passage in *The City of God* in which Augustine says that Anaximenes "attributed all the causes of things to infinite air and did not deny that these were gods or pass them over in silence; yet he believed not that air was made by them but that they arose from air" (A10).

air, holds us together, so do wind [or breath—πνεῦμα] and air enclose the whole cosmos."

In denoting air in the form of breath, the word πνεῦμα serves to extend the entire configuration in the direction of λόγος. For air in the form of breath can sound, can be brought to sound in certain ways, and thus to evolve into voice and speech. Through λόγος we gather to ourselves what appears, while also raising its manifestness to a higher level, broaching the advent of knowing in an originary sense.

It would have to be said of air that it belongs and yet does not belong among the elements (as they will come to be called). On the one hand, it remains largely out of sight, withholding itself in order that things can appear. And yet, it is nothing apart from the elements and indeed can show itself only in its dyadic, differentiated connection with them. It is an ἀρχή withdrawn from the elements, which nonetheless belongs with them. Its figure is mobile, both extending to the elements (and thereby to all things) and, at once, withdrawing. It is a figure that resembles that traced by a dancer more than that of a rigid shape or form. It is, then, not a condition of possibility set entirely apart from that which it makes possible. Rather, it is the open air *of the elements* in which they—and indeed all things—can shine forth in the brilliance of their manifestness.

3 ENSHROUDED NATURE AND THE FIRE OF HEAVEN

In the word *nature* almost everything will already have been said. This word, translated back into Greek, commands almost everything, as it says the one that is almost all things. In the words that Aristotle attributes to Heraclitus: "From all, one; and from one, all [ἐκ πάντων ἓν καὶ ἐξ ἑνὸς πάντα]" (B10). The one that is from all and from which all are—this one is thus such that, even as one, it nonetheless includes differentiation. As also in certain other Fragments attributed to Heraclitus, one saying is made to include a saying of all, setting out differentiation, even between extremes, while marking the mutual engagement that gathers all into one. Thus in Fragment B62: "Immortals mortals, mortals immortals: living the death of these, dying the life of those."

In the word translated as *nature*, almost everything is said, everything but the differentiation that nonetheless belongs to it so integrally that this one can be properly said only by retracing the differentiations of the all as they are marked in the Fragments attributed to Heraclitus. Beyond the single, all-commanding word, there is little to be said, only the differentiations within the all. Yet, in the end, these differentiations all come back somehow or other to nature, just as the Fragments, according to later reports, all once belonged to a single book (βιβλίον) entitled *On Nature* (Περὶ Φύσεως).[1]

Everything comes back somehow or other to nature. All things return to it along some way. For every thing is, if not nature itself, nonetheless a thing of nature, a natural thing; nothing is completely apart from nature, not even the gods. Indeed, it is primarily in and through

---

1. Numbered as A1 in Diels-Kranz, this report comes from Diogenes Laertius, *Lives of Eminent Philosophers* 9:5.

nature that the gods make their presence known, to such an extent that their very presence is inseparable from the manifestness of nature. Zeus reigns from the sky (οὐρανός) and announces his presence in and through the thunderbolt. Such confluence of nature and divinity appears most fully realized in the reign of Artemis, and nothing could have been more fitting than for Heraclitus to have dedicated his book in the temple of Artemis.[2]

Yet in the word *nature*, the name of the goddess is no longer to be heard. This is one reason that even when we continue to write *nature*, its translation back into φύσις must be constantly borne along and allowed to determine what sounds in it. For the thinkers who wrote in proximity to the beginning of philosophy, φύσις never designates, as *nature* often does, a region of things, the totality of so-called natural things. Even still in Aristotle it is necessary to distinguish nature from natural things, even from the totality of natural things; or, translating back into Greek, it is necessary to distinguish between φύσις and τὰ φύσει ὄντα, those things that are determined in their being by φύσις, those things that arise from φύσις, that begin from it, that have φύσις as their beginning, their ἀρχή. Yet, in distinction from Aristotle, with whom the reduction of τὰ φύσει ὄντα to one region among others has begun, Heraclitus' Fragments teach that all beings are of nature, that all arise from or through nature. After Aristotle, especially with the Stoics, such reductive divisions are extended and rigidified, and finally the utmost anachronistic confusion is fostered when, in the third century AD, Diogenes Laertius projects back upon Heraclitus' book the Stoic division between discourse on the universe, politics, and theology, declaring these to be the three parts of Heraclitus' alleged book Περὶ Φύσεως. If indeed Heraclitus' writings actually formed what could be called a book (βιβλίον), an assumption that is much less than certain, such division of the alleged book is quite foreign to what is said and to the manner of composition of the Fragments.[3] And yet, on the basis of the Fragments, there is more than good reason to say that his writing, however elusive,

---

2. Diogenes Laertius reports that Heraclitus dedicated his book in the temple of Artemis (Diels-Kranz A1; Diogenes Laertius, *Lives of Eminent Philosophers* 9:6).

3. Kirk, Raven, and Schofield note that the title Περὶ Φύσεως may have been attributed by later authors and "cannot be regarded as necessarily authentic." Furthermore, they observe, "the division into three sections is unlikely to have been original, and suggests that Diogenes or his source was thinking of an edition or collection of sayings, probably made in Alexandria, which followed a Stoic analysis of the parts of philosophy" (*The Presocratic Philosophers*, 184).

as if imitating φύσις itself, could not have been more appropriately titled than with the title Περὶ Φύσεως.

As all things come back to nature, the one commands all. Yet, in the return to nature, it is a matter not only of the one and all as such but also of appearance, of the enabling of appearing. Thus, Fragment B28 reads: "Those who are most esteemed understand, that is, guard [or: preserve, keep watch over—φυλάσσει] appearance." Even they, however—indeed, they above all—submit to the supreme commander and guardian of appearance. This is none other than the sun itself, as is declared in Fragment B100: "The sun is commander and guardian, delimiting, governing, showing forth, bringing to light the changes and seasons that bring all things." In this declaration the enabling of appearing is thought in utmost proximity to the bringing forth of things: being brought forth consists in being brought into the light. Or, in the saying often repeated in Homer and echoed in Greek tragedy: "To live is to behold the light of the sun."[4]

The question that imposes itself perhaps most forcefully concerns the difference between nature and natural beings, the difference across which all things return to nature in such a manner that their appearing is enabled. It is a question of whether this difference is one of sheer precedence. Is φύσις to be regarded as constitutively apart from natural beings in the sense of constituting a condition for those beings that is in no way reliant on them? Is φύσις thus apart from natural beings, or do natural beings somehow bear on φύσις, drawing it to them? Do they in some respect determine φύσις precisely as in another respect they are determined by it? This question is not unrelated to another, to a question aimed at bringing Heraclitus' guiding thought into relation to concrete experience. Granted that φύσις cannot simply be rendered as *nature*, that an entire history of interpretation must be deconstructed in order that *nature* say what is said in φύσις, the question is whether, even perhaps short of such deconstruction, that which sounds in φύσις is so utterly remote from what one can experience as nature, especially when a kind of deconstruction in deed is ventured, as when one sets out into the wilderness, withdrawing from most of the products of τέχνη, which otherwise distort and veil what would be experienced. For the goddess to whom Heraclitus is said to have dedicated his book on φύσις, the goddess whose name is the other name of φύσις, was named by Homer

---

4. ζώειν καὶ ὁρᾶν φάος ἠλίοιο (Homer, *Iliad* 18:61, 442; 24:558; *Odyssey* 4:833, 10:498. See also Euripides, *Hippolytus* 3, 56–58).

"Artemis of the wild, the mistress of wild beasts," and was described as roving across mountains and forests in pursuit of boars and deer, that is, as reigning within expanses of wilderness.[5]

In order to formulate and develop the question of the difference between nature and natural things, and thereby to begin forging a connection to the experience of nature, consideration needs to be given to the four Fragments by Heraclitus in which the word φύσις occurs. In these considerations it will be necessary to leave aside many other questions, enormous questions, that are prompted by these Fragments. The sole concern is to begin hearing from these Fragments what is sounded in the word φύσις.

In two of the Fragments, the word occurs in the form κατὰ φύσιν, according to φύσις; in both cases the expression is used to describe the way in which an exemplary thinking proceeds. In a passage in Fragment B1, Heraclitus describes his own thinking: "I distinguish each thing according to φύσις and declare how it is." Minimally this says: things are considered—that is, are to be considered—not just in any way, for instance, not just as they appear, but rather by referring them to φύσις: by means of this reference to φύσις, things are distinguished, each from the others, so that it becomes possible to declare of each thing how it is. One could say: it is precisely *from* φύσις that each thing comes forth as itself, that it comes to light as it itself is, so that one can then declare of each how it is. The connection of the word φύσις to the verb φύω is thus broached: it is from φύσις that things are brought forth, brought into the light of day, coming thus into their being, each into its being.

The second Fragment in which the phrase κατὰ φύσιν occurs, Fragment B112, needs to be considered in its entirety, though, even so, it is imperative to focus on the question of φύσις and to forgo pursuing the other, also far-reaching questions prompted by the Fragment. Regarding this Fragment, there are also significant philological questions on which there has been debate since the time of Schleiermacher. Even the authenticity of the Fragment has been put in question by some,[6] though it is vigorously defended by others.[7] What makes both translation and

---

5. See the account in chap. 1. The most important passages in Homer concerning Artemis are found in *Iliad* 21:470 and *Odyssey* 6:102–9.

6. For example, G. S. Kirk, *Heraclitus: The Cosmic Fragments* (Cambridge: Cambridge University Press, 1954), 390f.

7. For example, Charles H. Kahn, *The Art and Thought of Heraclitus* (Cambridge: Cambridge University Press, 1979), 120.

interpretation of the Fragment especially difficult is that both depend on the punctuation, which cannot be determined with complete certainty.⁸ The Fragment names two virtues, calling one or both of them the greatest virtue (ἀρετὴ μεγίστη). One of them is σωφρόνειν—let us say: *sound thinking*, keeping in view the link to σωφροσύνη (moderation, discretion). The other is σοφίη, the Ionic form of σοφία—let us say: *wisdom*. Here, then, is how the Fragment might be translated following one possible punctuation: "Sound thinking is the greatest virtue, and wisdom is to speak and act the truth, apprehending things according to φύσις." The alternative punctuation would yield the following: "Sound thinking is the greatest virtue and wisdom: it is to speak and act the truth, apprehending things according to φύσις." What remains uncertain is whether it is sound thinking or wisdom that is specifically described in the last part of the sentence. However this may be, the description is the same: to speak and act the truth, apprehending things according to nature.

What does it mean in this connection to speak the truth (ἀληθέα λέγειν)? Kahn notes that speaking the truth in the sense of telling the truth, of not holding it back, is not a virtue that the Greeks admired without qualification; recall that Telemachus' discretion, his σωφροσύνη, consisted in not telling the truth, in not revealing Odysseus' true identity. In this regard Kahn proposes, then, that ἀληθές be given its etymological value, and thus be rendered, not just as *true*, but as *not concealed*.⁹ Thus ἀληθέα λέγειν would consist in speaking of things as they would show themselves when brought forth out of concealment. It would consist in speaking of things as they, unconcealed, show themselves in their proper being, as what they are, each of them in its distinctness. Of anything that, as in the case of Odysseus' identity, lay still—in some regard—concealed, there could be—in that regard—no such speaking.

But what, then, about acting or doing the truth (ἀληθέα ... ποιεῖν)? Does this simply mean acting in accord with the unconcealed, with things as, in their unconcealment, they show themselves to be? Does

---

8. Ibid. The problem is compounded by the fact that ancient Greek manuscripts did not have punctuation marks. In the *Rhetoric* (1407b), Aristotle mentions that "it is difficult to punctuate Heraclitus' text because it is unclear whether a word goes with what follows or with what precedes." Aristotle cites the initial words of Fragment B1 as an example.

9. Kahn, *The Art and Thought of Heraclitus*, 121f.

it mean simply—or even not so simply—acting in the way called for by the configuration of persons and things as they unconcealedly show themselves to be? Does it mean conforming one's deeds to what that configuration calls for? Probably it does mean this. Yet another, more originary sense can be discerned if ποιεῖν is taken not to mean acting or doing, but, as is equally possible, to mean bringing forth, as, for instance, one brings something forth by making or producing it; or, more to the point, as one may bring something forth out of concealment so that it is brought to show itself as it properly is. Now it becomes clearer that and how such ποιεῖν belongs together with λέγειν: by bringing something forth so that it shows itself as it is, one can then speak of it as, in its unconcealment, it shows itself to be. One may even bring it forth to an extent in and through speaking, intertwining ποιεῖν and λέγειν so as to bring things unconcealedly to show themselves. It is by bringing things thus to show themselves unconcealedly that one can then act in the way called for by the configuration of unconcealed things, that is, do the truth.

But then, in turn, it becomes evident why the Fragment concludes with the participial phrase "apprehending things according to φύσις." Consideration of Fragment B1 showed that apprehending things according to φύσις consists in referring things to φύσις so that each might come to light as it is. More precisely, it consists in letting things come to light as they are brought to light from and through φύσις. Thus, the phrase "apprehending things according to φύσις" says precisely how it is that one can speak and bring forth the truth [ἀληθέα λέγειν καὶ ποιεῖν]. By apprehending things according to φύσις, by letting things come to light as they are brought to light through φύσις, one can speak of them as they unconcealedly show themselves to be; and one can bring them forth—even make, produce, certain kinds of things—as they, brought to light from and through φύσις, show themselves to be. Such apprehending, speaking, and bringing forth constitute what the Fragment calls—depending on punctuation—either sound thinking or wisdom.[10]

---

10. The interpretation of this Fragment would not be significantly affected if one took ἀληθέα to be the object only of λέγειν and so connected ποιεῖν with κατὰ φύσιν. For, as the above interpretation of the passage from Fragment B1 shows, to bring forth κατὰ φύσιν is precisely to bring each thing forth so that it shows itself as it itself distinctly is; that is, it is to bring things forth into unconcealment. It is indeed remarkable how the sense of this Fragment remains largely invariant regardless of how one divides the words with punctuation or groups them into units. It is as if Heraclitus' writing had secured or sealed within the passage that which the passage was to say.

Thus, interpretation of the two Fragments in which the phrase κατὰ φύσιν occurs (Fragments B1 and B112) allows one to say: φύσις is that which grants a space of illumination, which lets things come into an expanse in which they can shine forth as they distinctly are. It is because φύσις lets illumination happen that sound thinking or wisdom must, as it were, detour through φύσις: it must apprehend things according to φύσις, must refer them to φύσις, in order to be capable then of bringing forth and saying things as they distinctly are. Recall that Artemis is represented with torches in both hands and that she is called φωσφόρος, light-bringing.

Yet, granted the bearing of φύσις on things, granted that sound thinking or wisdom must approach things by way of φύσις, what about φύσις itself? Granted that it is by detouring through φύσις that one can come to be able to speak of things as they are, how does one come to speak of φύσις itself?

In contrast to the two Fragments considered thus far, which direct that one speak according to φύσις, there is another Fragment that speaks directly of φύσις, that speaks of what one could call φύσις itself. Yet this Fragment speaks directly of φύσις itself in precisely such a way as to put in question any direct speaking of φύσις. This Fragment, the third in which the word φύσις occurs, is numbered B123 and reads: φύσις κρύπτεσθαι φιλεῖ. The conventional, seemingly straightforward translation is: φύσις loves to hide. Yet nothing—perhaps least of all translation—is straightforward here, for this Fragment says nothing less than the interruption of any straightforward appearing that one might otherwise ascribe to φύσις. Regardless of how one settles the difficult question of how to translate and interpret φιλεῖ in this Fragment—one could say, at the very least, *loves* or *is wont to* or *is inclined to*, all these in multiple senses—the hiding, the self-concealment, that somehow goes with φύσις serves to set φύσις apart from the things that, through φύσις, come to be illuminated. Precisely as φύσις lets things come to light so as to reveal themselves in their distinct being, it conceals itself, either withholding itself from the very light that it lets illuminate the expanse of things or hiding itself in the very brilliance of that light, shining with such brilliance that, as it instigates visibility as such, it itself borders on invisibility.

Like the day. One hardly sees it as such. Indeed, one hardly knows even what seeing it would involve. Yet it is in the expanse of the day that the manifold things on the earth shine forth as they are and thus as they can be said in their distinctness.

The fourth of the Fragments in which the word φύσις occurs speaks of φύσις and of the day. Handed down by Plutarch and not entirely undisputed,[11] the Fragment—numbered B106—is presented as a criticism of Hesiod, who is said not to have known or to have recognized that—and these are supposedly the words of Heraclitus—"the nature of the day is one" [φύσιν ἡμέρας μίαν οὖσαν]. Here it is imperative to forgo construing *nature of the day* in the way that comes into play only with Plato, namely, as the ἰδέα or essence (as will even later be said) of the day. In these four words that constitute the Fragment proper, it is perhaps more important to focus not on the genitive construction but on the juxtaposition of φύσις and ἡμέρα, regarding the day, not as something that has a φύσις (a nature, an essence), but rather as nothing other than φύσις, as one of the ways in which φύσις, though concealing itself, can be seen and said to happen. It is a way in which φύσις happens as the one by which the manifold things come to be illuminated in their expanse. An echo of this thinking of the day is to be heard later in Plato's *Parmenides*. The passage is one in which Socrates is defending against Parmenides the thesis that a whole εἶδος, being one, can be in each of the many. What Socrates says is: "It might be like the day, which is one and the same, is in many places [πολλαχοῦ] at once, and yet is not separate from itself."[12]

The question is, then: what is φύσις as it is said in these four Fragments? This question requires a certain precaution: its sense must be kept open so that in asking about the *what* of φύσις, one does not inadvertently assume the *what* to have the sense determined for it from Plato on, the sense of ἰδέα or εἶδος, which comes also to define the very sense of sense. Holding the sense of the question, then, in a certain detachment, one can say that φύσις is that from and through which things are brought to light as they are, in their distinct and proper being. Φύσις is what lets illumination happen—a *what*, therefore, that is prior to those *whats* that Platonic discourse will call εἴδη and regard as that which preeminently comes to light, which gets illuminated. More determinately, φύσις is that which grants a space of illumination in which things can shine forth as they distinctly are. Φύσις is that which lets things become distinctly perceptible within an expanse opened by φύσις itself; indeed,

---

11. See Kirk, *Heraclitus*, 157–61.
12. Socrates' example of the day stands out especially by contrast to the example with which Parmenides immediately replaces it, that of a sail that is spread over many persons (*Parmenides* 131b–c).

this spacing belongs to the letting become distinctly perceptible. Even though Heraclitus grants a certain privilege to sight and, presumably for this reason, says the operation of φύσις primarily by reference to visibility,[13] the coming forth of things into unconcealment is not to be simply identified with their becoming visible. In order that they be able to sound and so to be heard, a space must be opened up across which they can sound. The spacing of φύσις—as, at the same time, it makes things perceptible—is required for the operation of all those means by which access is had to things, those means that will later be gathered under the word αἴσθησις: even touch requires the expanse of a surface and the distance that is abolished in touching that surface.[14] It requires also, even more manifestly than do vision and hearing, a span of time in which to take place. As it opens a spatial expanse, the spacing of φύσις plays out a temporal span (αἰών).[15]

Φύσις spaces things in their distinct perceptibility. Yet φύσις hides itself—indeed, loves to hide itself—letting things come to light as it withdraws or otherwise remains concealed. This hiding, if one is attentive to it, cannot but impart a certain reticence to the discourse—any discourse—that would speak of φύσις. In speaking of φύσις, one will, as in speaking of the day, be at a loss for words. Even as one says that one of the ways in which φύσις happens is as the day.

The difference can be expressed thus: while φύσις lets things appear as they distinctly are, φύσις does not itself simply appear but, even insofar as it may in some measure appear, remains unapparent. This difference is expressed in Fragment B54: ἁρμονίη ἀφανὴς φανερῆς κρείττων. A conventional translation would be: the unapparent harmony is better than the apparent. Yet ἁρμονία does not mean primarily harmony but rather that which may produce, form the basis for, something like

---

13. There are highly significant exceptions, especially when it is a matter of ὁ λόγος—as in Fragment B50, conventionally translated as: "Listening [ἀκούσαντας] not to me but to the λόγος, it is wise to agree that all things are one." Presumably a complementary discourse that proceeded from ὁ λόγος rather than (as with the present text) from φύσις would be no less oriented to listening than discourse on φύσις is to vision.

14. Heraclitus addresses the question of smell in Fragment B98, conventionally translated as: "Souls have the sense of smell in Hades." See my discussion of this Fragment in "Hades (Heraclitus, Fragment B 98)," in *Delimitations: Phenomenology and the End of Metaphysics*, 2nd ed. (Bloomington: Indiana University Press, 1995), 186–93.

15. Fragment B52 begins: αἰὼν παῖς ἐστι παίζων, πεσσεύων [αἰών is a child playing draughts]. On the meaning of αἰών, see my discussion in *Chorology: On Beginning in Plato's "Timaeus"* (Bloomington: Indiana University Press, 1999), 79.

a harmony between things or even between musical sounds. The verb ἁρμόζω means to fit together, to join, so as to set in order or arrange. Thus, ἁρμονία designates a fitting together or arranging, as a composer arranges sounds, fits them together, so that they sound in harmony; and ἁρμονία designates also what results from such fitting together, an arrangement or array. Diels-Kranz translates ἁρμονία as *Fügung*,[16] as does Heidegger, who also translates κρείττων as *edel*, *noble*, thus excluding the vague moral connotations of the word *better*.[17] It should be noted that κρείττων also means *mightier, superior to, master of*. If one translates κρείττων as *noble*, the word needs to be construed broadly enough to include also these senses.

Because it loves to hide, φύσις is unapparent. It is an unapparent ἁρμονία in that it lets things be arrayed in their distinctness, grants the space in which they can shine forth in their array. As shining forth they appear and are apparent, manifest (φανερός); they make up an apparent array. What Fragment B54 says is that φύσις itself, the self-concealing arraying, is nobler than the manifest array of things that it governs. In short, the unapparent arraying is nobler than the apparent array.

A provocation is produced if this Fragment, declaring the nobility of φύσις, is juxtaposed to Fragment B55. In Fragment B55 Heraclitus writes of sight, of hearing, and of learning directly from things. His reference is specifically to all that comes from sight, hearing, or direct learning—that is, to what is seen, the look or appearance of things, to what is heard either from them or about them, and to what one learns directly of them from them. Fragment B55 says: "Whatever comes from sight, hearing, and direct learning I esteem most highly." The esteem for what will later be called the senses or sense perception (αἴσθησις) is not without its condition. It is this condition and not a denigration of seeing and hearing that is declared by Fragment B107: "Eyes and ears are bad witnesses for men if they have barbarian souls." If one takes *barbarian*

---

16. "Unsichtbare Fügung stärker als sichtbare." The word ἁρμονία has much the same sense in Fragment B8: τὸ ἀντίξουν συμφέρον καὶ ἐκ τῶν διαφερόντων καλλίστην ἁρμονίαν (conventionally translated: "What is opposed comes together, and the most beautiful harmony comes from things at variance"). Here too Diels-Kranz renders it as *Fügung* ("Das widereinander Strebende zusammengehend; aus dem auseinander Gehenden die schönste Fügung"). Note also its occurrence in Fragment B51 in the phrase παλίντροπος ἁρμονίη (conventional translation: "back-stretched harmony" or "back-turning connection"), which Diels-Kranz renders: *gegenstrebige Vereinigung*.

17. Martin Heidegger, *Heraklit*, vol. 55 of *Gesamtausgabe* (Frankfurt a.M.: Vittorio Klostermann, 1979), 141–42.

in its usual sense as referring to those who do not speak Greek, then one can conclude that the condition under which seeing and hearing become good witnesses and are thus to be esteemed most highly has to do precisely with speech. Here again, then, Heraclitus alludes to a connection between speech and what later will be called αἴσθησις, a connection that in turn alludes to a certain complementarity between λόγος and φύσις.[18]

There are other Fragments that serve to supplement Fragment B55 in various ways. One of these is Fragment B101a, which grants a certain privilege to sight: "Eyes are more precise witnesses than ears." Sight yields higher precision, it seems, not only because of its superior power to discriminate but also because hearing may rely either on what is heard from things or on what is heard about them, that is, on opinion. A further supplement is provided by Fragment B17: to the attestation in Fragment B55 concerning the esteem to be accorded to sight, hearing, and direct learning, Fragment B17 adds the critical observation that many fail to understand things from what they learn directly about them, from those things themselves as they are come upon. The Fragment reads: "Many do not think things as they come upon them, do not understand what they learn directly, but believe their own opinions."

The provocation is evident: how is the nobility of φύσις in its distinctness from things to be granted (in accord with Fragment B54) if what is esteemed most highly is that which is seen and heard of things and learned directly from them? How can unapparent φύσις be more noble if apparent things, as revealed to the senses, are the most esteemed? In other words, what must be the relation between φύσις and the things of sense in order that appearance and what appears might be most highly esteemed without φύσις being thereby denied its nobility? Clearly the relation cannot be such as simply to set φύσις apart from appearing things; the figure of nature cannot be one of sheer bifurcation. On the contrary, φύσις must be such that in letting things come to light so as to shine forth to sense, it too shines forth to sense, even if also in some respect remaining unapparent in its very appearing. Φύσις cannot, then, operate as an invisible ἀρχή distinct from all that would begin

---

18. This complementarity by which each of the two, λόγος and φύσις, would be—though differently—all things is most directly addressed in Fragment B1. Along with the passage considered above ("I distinguish each thing according to φύσις and declare how it is"), Fragment B1 also includes the following: "All things come to be according to this λόγος" [γινομένων γὰρ πάντων κατὰ τόν λόγον τόνδε].

from and through it. It must, rather, operate precisely at the site that it opens for the illumination of things; and, as itself taking place in this place, it must itself be illuminated, even if differently from the things it lets come to light. Its figure must be such that it belongs together with the things for which it opens a space of illumination yet is distinctively other than these things.

How, then, is φύσις to be thought and named? It must be thought as operating in and as certain elements that belong to the place where things are illuminated but that are not simply reducible to things. What is required is that φύσις be thought as what will later be called—or rather, translated as—elements: not the στοιχεῖα of Aristotle's *Physics*, not even quite the ῥιζώματα of Empedocles' work reportedly entitled Περὶ Φύσεως. A very direct rendering of and reference to Fragment B47, rendering it as "Let us not heedlessly throw together those that are greatest," could support the supposition that Heraclitus avoided a common name by which earth, sea, and the fire of the heaven would have been—and later were to be—thrown together. Yet if φύσις is to be thought thus and is to be named γῆ, ὕδωρ, πῦρ, it is utterly imperative that we put aside the assurance that we know what is meant by these words, the assurance—an assuredly false assurance—that these words can without further ado simply be replaced by *earth, water,* and *fire*. This imperative is no less imperative with regard to Heraclitus than it proved to be previously with the Milesians. It is perhaps not so very difficult to forgo thinking of these as the material substances of least determinacy, as the terms eventually reached by a process of decomposition. What is much more difficult is to begin to sense these as they show—as they once showed—themselves before the onset of such conceptuality: fire showing itself in the thunderbolt, water stretching forth as the sea, earth granting secure ground, yet as closed off, sealed off like the dead buried in it. And yet, as difficult as it may be to regain a sense of what we call the elements or the elemental, is there not still a trace of it in what we experience of nature, in what we can still experience as nature—even if it is only rarely that we succeed in opening our senses to what is elemental in nature?

Φύσις is, above all, to be thought as and named πῦρ. One can say *fire*, but only if one suspends later conceptualities and orients the word to the elemental in nature, that is, to the fire of the heaven, preeminently the sun and the thunderbolt. Yet φύσις as fire involves not just these, the sun and the thunderbolt, which serve to bring all things to light; it involves also the opening of the region in which fire takes place as φύσις, the spacing of fire in the upper region from which is illuminated the scene, the surface of the earth, where all things come to appear as what they distinctly are. This region the Greeks sometimes called αἰθήρ. To a degree it coalesces with the ἀήρ that Anaximenes declared to be the ἀρχή, that is, φύσις itself.

The spacing of fire as φύσις is perhaps said most directly in Fragment B66. A possible translation is: "Fire, coming upon all things, will differentiate them and detect them." This says: coming upon all things, shining upon them, the fire of heaven illuminates them in such a way that they are revealed; it lights up a region of illumination within which they can shine forth in their differentiations, their distinctness, from one another. Thus, in this Fragment *fire* says φύσις as the illuminative spacing that lets things become manifest as they distinctly are. Even with the thunderbolt—as in Fragment B64: "The thunderbolt steers all things"—what is thought therein as φύσις is the momentary brilliance of the expanse lighted up in the name of Zeus. Though fire may, especially as the thunderbolt, reduce to ashes, it is not primarily its power of conflagration but rather its expansive brilliance that enables *fire* to say φύσις. The conflagration that the Stoics import into Heraclitus, indeed on the basis—or rather non-basis—of Fragment B66, this world conflagration that the Church fathers conceive as the fires of hell[19]—all of this is—needless to say—worlds apart from what Heraclitus said in saying φύσις as *fire*.

Heraclitus also says κόσμος as *fire*, says this as another way of saying φύσις as *fire*. Yet when in Fragment B30 he writes of the κόσμος, one should avoid simply equating it with the universe (τὸ πᾶν) or even directly with the heaven (οὐρανός). The tradition is that Pythagoras was the first to use κόσμος to designate what had up to that time been called οὐρανός; presumably Heraclitus, too, contributed to setting in play the equation of κόσμος with οὐρανός and with τὸ πᾶν. Yet even much later, in Plato's *Timaeus*, these equations can still not be taken for granted. In Homer, on the other hand, κόσμος designates the ordered battle array of an army; only subsequently did it come to designate any ordered array and then finally that of the heavenly bodies.[20] The corresponding verb κοσμέω means not only to order or arrange but also to embellish or adorn; thus κόσμος also designates an adornment, ornament, or

---

19. See Hans-Georg Gadamer, "Heraclitus Studies," trans. Peter Warnek, in *The Presocratics after Heidegger*, ed. David C. Jacobs (Albany: State University of New York Press, 1999), 212; and Kirk, *Heraclitus*, 318ff.

20. See my *Chorology*, 53f.

decoration. Hence, the word itself carries a reference to visibility, to an ordered array that is distinctively visible, that is to be beheld primarily with the eyes. The word κόσμος is thus especially suited for saying φύσις as fire, for saying the illuminative spacing through which things can become manifest in their visible array.

Fragment B30 says that this κόσμος, "the same for all, was not brought forth [ἐποίησεν] by any gods or humans, but it always was and is and will be ever-living fire [πῦρ ἀείζωον], kindling measures [μέτρα] and extinguishing measures." The κόσμος *is* fire: this does not mean that the κόσμος is made of fire. On the contrary, the κόσμος is not made at all, not brought forth either by gods or by humans; here the κόσμος—and hence φύσις—is not thought through reference to ποίησις or τέχνη (as in the *Timaeus*, at least in the first of Timaeus' three discourses). Rather, it is thought as fire; yet this does not mean that Heraclitus thought the universe to be made of fire as a primary material. Since it is not made at all, any reference to a material taken over and shaped through a process of making is utterly inappropriate. Most certainly fire is not taken as the matter of which the universe consists, for prior to Aristotle there is no such concept of ὕλη.

That the κόσμος is fire means that the heavenly fire is what illuminates and spaces things in such a way that they can come to show themselves in their visible array. Yet this spacing-illumination itself belongs, if with a difference, to the visible: the array of the heavenly fire, of stars, planets, sun, and moon, is itself visible. Thus Heraclitus calls fire ever-living, not only alluding to the temporal spanning (αἰών) effected by the fire of heaven but also indicating that, like those beings that are normally called living beings (ζῷα), the heavenly fire itself comes forth into a certain visibility. As plants open to the sunlight, as humans and animals seek the light, so does the heavenly fire itself come to light: with the rising of the sun and of the moon, with the nightly appearance of the stars. In its comings and goings, the heavenly fire lays out and withdraws an expanse of illumination, kindles and extinguishes the lighted expanse in which any kind of measure (μέτρον) in the ordinary sense becomes possible.

Because φύσις is thought as the heavenly fire, preeminently as the sun with its expansive brilliance, and because φύσις also is thought as the day in which from their luminous expanse things can shine forth, the sun and the day can be yoked together, said together. Thus Fragment B6 reads: "The sun is new each day." Minimally this says: the very operation of the sun as φύσις is so thoroughly linked to the luminous expanse of the day—the luminous expanse as which the day takes place—that, as the day is other, so also is the sun, so also is it new each day. The same could be said of any temporal span, that is, of any ὥρα, whether the word is taken to mean season, springtime, the whole year, or even a time of day such as morning. Though indeed in Fragment B100 ὥρα is linked to the sun—at least provided one takes the definitively Heraclitean phrase together with the context in which it is presented by Plutarch—within the Heraclitean phrase proper, ὥρα is yoked instead to the things that are brought forth into the lighted expanse of solar φύσις: it is the ὧραι that bear along, present, bring, all things [ὥρας αἳ πάντα φέρουσι].

Nonetheless, in thinking φύσις as fire, Heraclitus was compelled also to think the other two elemental regions, that of water (ὕδωρ), primarily as the expanse and transparent depth of sea (θάλασσα), and that of self-closing earth enclosing the souls as well as the bodies of the dead.[21] Yet these elemental regions are thought not just as others alongside the fire of heaven; they are thought, rather, in an orientation to the fire of heaven, to the region from which all things are illuminated and which is itself, in a distinctive sense, limited by the other two regions. In Fragment B36 Heraclitus writes of all three regions: "For souls it is death to become water, for water it is death to become earth; out of earth water arises, out of water soul." What is decisive here is the soul's departure from and return to the site of illumination. To depart to the region of water and, even more, to that of earth is to depart from the space of illumination, from the site where things shine forth in the light of the fire of heaven. To depart from this light and its expanse is for the soul to depart from itself, from itself as open to the light in such a way that, seeing and hearing the things that appear, it can learn of them, come to distinguish them and to speak of them as they are. For to live is to behold the light of the sun.

There are Fragments that venture to say, in quite different ways, how the three elemental regions belong together. For instance, Fragment B22: "Seekers of gold dig up much earth and find little." This says: the noblest of metals, the most brilliantly shining, can nonetheless be found

---

21. See Fragment B31, which speaks of the exchange between fire, earth, and sea (not ὕδωρ but θάλασσα). In Fragment B76, air (ἀήρ) is added so as to yield the four that will become common in post-Empedoclean thought. But Fragment B76 is merely a Stoic reformulation of Fragment B36 (see Kirk, Raven, and Schofield, *The Presocratic Philosophers*, 204n1). For Heraclitus there are only the three: fire, sea (or water), and earth.

in minute quantities—though only in minute quantities—in earth, in the region of darkness and closure, which thus, even as such, is not utterly apart from the region of the fire of heaven.

Yet there is perhaps no Fragment in this regard more provocative than Fragment B15, in which, referring to the Bacchic revels with their processions and phallic hymns and declaring that they would be most shameless (ἀναιδέστατα) were they not in honor of Dionysus, Heraclitus then writes that Hades and Dionysus are the same [ὡυτὸς δὲ Ἀίδης καὶ Διόνυσος]. To be sure, many would-be interpreters have been content with regarding this strange identification as just another instance of some vague principle that Heraclitus is supposed to have held regarding the unity of opposites. But if one recalls that the very birth of Dionysus was by means of Zeus' thunderbolt, one will perhaps begin to wonder otherwise. Or at least to ask how it is that the destructiveness of the fire of heaven, its power to reduce to ashes, even if in such a way as also to birth a god—how it coincides with the utterly closed region of the dead, the region of a darkness entirely without promise of light, everlasting night. One will then perhaps wonder and ponder how it is that φύσις as the fire of heaven is limited, as from itself, properly limited, by the secluded region of shades. One will perhaps wonder and ponder how it happens that the question of nature and its limit brings one back to the question of the earth.

4 RADICAL GATHERINGS. THE IMPERATIVE OF PHILOSOPHY

Although the development that began with the Milesians was hardly linear or homogeneous, it reached nonetheless a certain culmination in the thought of Empedocles. In his thought much of what his predecessors had ventured was gathered up, rounded out, and brought to a certain fulfillment. In this fulfillment there were two primary moments, the first having to do with the character of the thinking that had by then begun to be called philosophy, the second pertaining specifically to the scope and articulation of φύσις. As with many of his predecessors, Empedocles too is reported to have applied to certain of his writings the title Περὶ Φύσεως.[1]

As to the character of thinking, Empedocles' achievement consisted in formulating explicitly what had indeed been carried out from the beginning. Empedocles expresses with utter clarity the imperative under which such thinking had consistently placed itself. This formulation is found in Fragment B3, handed down by Sextus Empiricus. It consists of three distinguishable parts, though the divisions between them are not very explicitly marked, so that some scholars suspect that in citing the passage Sextus may have omitted some transitional lines.[2]

The first part of the Fragment is an invocation, opening receptively the space of the discourse to come, asking of the gods that "from

---

1. Diogenes Laertius mentions not only the work Περὶ Φύσεως but also οἱ Καθαρμοί (*The Purifications*), ὁ Ἰατρικὸς λόγος (the medical writings), and the tragedies (Diels-Kranz, A1; Diogenes Laertius, *Lives of Eminent Philosophers* 8:77).
2. See M. R. Wright, *Empedocles: The Extant Fragments* (Indianapolis: Hackett, 1995), 161.

hallowed lips . . . a pure stream [might] flow" and beseeching the Muse to send "that which it is right and fitting for mortals to hear." This opening makes it evident that the imperative of thinking that is about to be enunciated is not a pronouncement brought forth autonomously by the thinker; rather, it is to be evoked, its pure stream drawn forth, as the thinker hears what sounds from beyond, from the gods and the Muse, who, in letting the appeal to manifestness that constitutes the imperative be declared, remain themselves elusive.

In the second part of the Fragment, the thinker turns from the gods and the Muse to the mortal to whom the imperative is about to be declared. It is presumably Pausanias, Empedocles' young lover and pupil, who is now addressed in words intended to caution him against the danger of excessive pride. He is to beware of taking the garlands of honor that men will offer him and of coming thereby to sit on the high throne of wisdom.

Only with these preparations in place does Empedocles then, in the third part of the Fragment, state the imperative. He begins: "But come, consider by all means how each thing is manifest." Pausanias is thus enjoined *to consider* each thing in its manifestness. The word ἀθρέω, to consider, means to look closely at, to observe carefully, to ponder thoughtfully. The imperative is, then, to consider, in this sense, each thing in its way of being *manifest* (δῆλον), that is, as it is evident, visible, as it itself shows itself. Each thing in its manifestness is to be considered *by all means* (πάσῃ παλάμῃ), in a sense that does not exclude the use of artfulness, contrivance, even force or violence; παλάμη means *palm* or *hand* and thus connotes the force or skill that can be exercised by the hand; and, by extension, it alludes to any means by which a certain result can be achieved. Thus, what is enjoined does not necessarily take the form of a mere passive beholding; in some instances recourse must be had to means capable of enticing things into the open in order to catch a glimpse of them at their very moment of manifestness. Then the imperative would be to behold them precisely when, by such means as that of the hand, they are most striking, when they are at hand.

Following the initial statement of the imperative to consider by all means how each thing is manifest, the passage continues: "neither holding sight in greater trust as compared with hearing, or resounding hearing above piercings of the tongue." Note that Empedocles here refers to hearing as resounding (ἐπίδουπον). This designation is indicative of the doubling character that he takes hearing to have: to hear a sound requires that hearing redouble the sound, that it be echoed within.³ The piercings of the tongue are of course the pores through which the tongue senses taste. Thus, Empedocles is declaring that equal trust is to be given to sight, hearing, and taste. The passage continues by extending this trust still further: "and do not withhold trust at all from other parts of the body where there is a passage [πόρος] for thinking [νοῆσαι]." The injunction concludes by restating the imperative, now with utter directness: "but think [νοέω—that is, ponder, consider discernfully] each thing in the way in which it is manifest."⁴

The second of the two principal achievements by which Empedocles' thought brings early Greek thinking to a certain fulfillment concerns φύσις; it lies in the way in which he extends φύσις to its full expanse while also retaining, indeed intensifying, its vital character. Yet this achievement is not immediately evident from the Fragments. Very few of the passages cited by later authors include the word φύσις, and even in the non-citational reports concerning Empedocles' thought, the word occurs only rarely. When it does occur, either in citations or in reports, its usage seems to be, at best, only obliquely related to the decisive sense that it assumed in Empedocles' predecessors such as Heraclitus and the Milesians.

An example is Fragment B63, which comes from Aristotle's *Generation of Animals*.⁵ Here Empedocles is cited as follows: "But the φύσις of the limbs is separated, part in the man [ἐν ἀνδρός]." The context is one in which Aristotle is criticizing Empedocles' alleged theory of generation according to which part of the semen occurs in the male and part in the female, the preponderance of one or the other determining the sex of the embryo. Thus, in this context, filtered somewhat through Aristotelian lenses, φύσις refers simply to the semen from which is generated the limbs of living beings, that is, those beings themselves. While, in this context, the sense of the word is thus quite narrow, this very specificity

---

3. In the context of a discussion of Empedocles, Theophrastus reports: "Hearing comes about from sounds inside. For when [air] is set in motion by the voice, it echoes inside" (A86).

4. The connection that the imperative establishes between thinking and manifestness is expressed assertorically in B106, which reads: "For man's wisdom grows according to what is present." This Fragment comes from Aristotle (*Metaphysics* 1009b18–19), who, construing it quite differently, cites it in the course of criticizing Empedocles for failing to distinguish between thought and perception (φρόνησις and αἴσθησις).

5. Diels-Kranz, B63; Aristotle, *Generation of Animals* 764b17–18.

is such as to secure the bond that is decisive for φύσις in its broadest expanse. For in the passage, φύσις can be taken to refer to that from which living beings are generated, that is, to that from which, through conception and birth, through the natural process of reproduction, living things come forth. What becomes evident from this citation is that the sense of φύσις is determined in large part by its derivation from the verb φύω (to bring forth, to beget—or in the passive: to grow, to come forth, to be begotten or born). Whatever else may need to be said, φύσις does not, for Empedocles, refer to some remote or even abstract principle of natural things; rather, its sense is bound to the happenings in and through which things come forth, as plants, seeded in the earth, sprout and burst forth into the light, as animals are begotten and come to be born, as humans, granted life, come to behold the light of the sun.

Another among the few Fragments that include the word φύσις— the Fragment numbered B110—is again presumably addressed to the pupil Pausanias. Empedocles instructs him as to how he is to appropriate the thoughts expressed in his teacher's words and describes the consequence that will follow if they are thus appropriated. Here is how the appropriation is prescribed, in the form of a conditional: "If you push them firmly under your crowded thoughts and contemplate them favorably. . . ." Thus, the thoughts expressed in Empedocles' words are to be placed under (ὑπό) all the other, ordinary thoughts, including, as the passage goes on to say, "the countless trivialities that come among men and dull their meditations." If these underlaid thoughts are then favorably contemplated, they will remain, they "will be with you through life, and you will gain much else from them." What is it that is to be gained? What is the consequence of appropriating, contemplating, and thus retaining these thoughts laid under all others? The passage gives a succinct answer: "For they will make each thing grow into its ἦθος according to the φύσις of each." This says: if things are regarded by proceeding from the secure underlaid thoughts, then they come to appear in their ἦθος, that is, in their proper character but also (to retain the older sense of the word) in their proper place, in their abode. Furthermore, each comes to appear in its manifestness as regards its character and abode because each is bound to its ἦθος by its φύσις. The conclusion is evident: the underlaid thoughts, properly cultivated, can bring things to appear in their ἦθος, can let them be regarded in their manifestness, because what is thought thereby is nothing other than φύσις. The thoughts that are to be underlaid, the thoughts expressed in Empedocles' words, are thoughts directed precisely to φύσις, from which things grow into their character, into their abode, and, through the words and thoughts of the philosopher, into their manifestness.

There is a Fragment (B38), handed down by Clement of Alexandria, that purports to tell of that from which things become manifest. In its simplest form, omitting, for the moment, a much-disputed word, the Fragment reads: "Come, I shall tell you of the origin from which all the things we now look upon have become manifest, earth and billowing sea, damp air, and Titan aither who fastens his circle around all things." Here Empedocles uses the word ἀρχή (origin) rather than φύσις, though, judging from the Fragments already considered, it would seem that the sense of φύσις is convergent with that of origin. What is disputed in the passage is the word ἥλιον (*sun*—in the accusative singular), which in Clement's text occurs immediately before the word ἀρχήν, so that the passage would begin: "Come, I will tell you of the sun origin from which. . . ." Various proposals have been made for altering the passage. Freeman, for instance, considers ἥλιον corrupt and, marking it as such, retains it only in parentheses. Wright's view is that the word is wrongly positioned in the sentence, that ἥλιον should follow ἀρχήν, so as to yield the sequence: Come, I will tell you of the origin from which the sun and all things. . . .[6] Which of the various forms proposed is correct is probably not decidable on purely philological grounds, and preference for any particular form is likely to depend to an extent on the interpretation of the Fragment as a whole.

In this Fragment, Empedocles tells, in first person, of the ἀρχή (as he says) "from which all the things we now look upon have become manifest." In other words, the ἀρχή of which he will tell is that by which

---

6. Freeman thus renders the beginning of the sentence as: "Come now, I will tell you of (the sun) the beginning, . . . from which all the things . . ." (Kathleen Freeman, *Ancilla to the Pre-Socratic Philosophers* [Oxford: Blackwell, 1956], 57). Relocating the word ἥλιον and employing a hendiadys to render ἀρχήν, Wright translates this portion as: "Come now, I shall tell you from what sources, in the beginning, the sun and all those others . . ." (Wright, *Empedocles*, 196f.). Burnet alters ἥλιον to ἡλίου, though admitting that this is "a mere makeshift," and so translates: "Come, I shall now tell thee first of all the beginning of the sun, and the sources from which . . ." (John Burnet, *Early Greek Philosophy* [New York: Meridian Books, 1957], 212). Kirk and Raven, in their first edition, render the passage: "Come, I shall tell thee first of the sun, and whence became manifest all the things . . ."; this is altered in the second edition to: "Come now, I shall tell you first from what [origins] in the beginning the sun and all those others . . ." (G. S. Kirk and J. E. Raven, *The Presocratic Philosophers*, 1st ed. [Cambridge: Cambridge University Press, 1957], 332; Kirk, Raven, and Schofield, *The Presocratic Philosophers*, 301).

all the things that are to be seen, that lie visibly before us, received their visibility as well as their manifestness to the other senses. This ἀρχή is, then, the origin of the manifestness of things, that is, the origin that initiated and sustained their coming forth into manifestness; since the verb γίγνομαι means also *to be born*, the origin can equally well be described as that from which all things were born into manifestness. Most decidedly, it is not the origin of their being, for of being there can be no origin, can never have been any origin. Fragment B11 is explicit about this impossibility: it mocks the fools "who expect what was not before to come to be." There is no coming to be, hence no origin of being, but only coming to be manifest, coming forth there before our senses. Here already it is evident that what the disputed word ἥλιον designates pertains to the ἀρχή, regardless of how the word is to be positioned in the sentence. For the sun is what preeminently bestows visibility upon the things that we look upon; it is preeminently the origin, the source, of the visible manifestness of things, that which makes things visible and lets them be seen by those who possess the power of sight. Thus, the origin that is described in this Fragment cannot be taken as the origin of the sun, as some renderings of it would require, for the sun is itself preeminently an origin of the manifestness of all the things we now look upon.

In Fragment B23, Empedocles draws a parallel between the origination of visibility and that which painters accomplish when with their colors they form "shapes resembling all things, creating trees and men and women, animals and birds and water-nourished fish, and long-lived gods too, highest in honor." Empedocles insists on the strictness of the parallel. He stresses that just as these shapes on the painted surface are not brought there from elsewhere but become manifest there through the art of the painter, so likewise the ἀρχή simply lets things come forth in their manifestness, lets them take shape there in their proper abode. The Fragment concludes: "So do not let deception [ἀπάτη] convince you that mortal things are from somewhere else [ἄλλοθεν], all the things that become manifest." There is, then, no question of being. It is not as though things first came into being somewhere apart from the abode in which they come to be manifest. Things do not simply come to be, but only come to be manifest. Their character, their ἦθος, lies entirely in their being manifest in their abode—just like the forms that artists let take shape in their paintings.

Empedocles' exclusion of coming to be is stated even more directly in Fragment B12: "For from what in no way is, it is impossible to come to be." The parallel with Parmenides is conspicuous, most notably with the account given in the passage from his poem that is numbered Fragment 8: Parmenides explains that since coming into being could proceed only from what is not, and since what is not is unthinkable—and hence cannot be—there can be no coming into being. Thus: "Coming into being is extinguished." For Parmenides and for Empedocles, thinking begins—must begin—with being, even though, beginning thus, their paths could hardly be more divergent. This divergence results primarily from the manner in which each lets himself be directed by the philosophical imperative, in the one case primarily to being as such, in the other case primarily to φύσις.[7]

Empedocles' proposal, in B38, to tell of "the origin from which all the things we now look upon have become manifest" is carried out in the sequel, in which he proceeds to articulate the origin in its fourfold structure: "earth and billowing sea, damp air, and Titan aither who fastens his circle around all things." There is, then, as origin, first, earth. Empedocles uses the more poetic form γαῖα, which is found in Hesiod and most commonly in Homer, as well as in later writers. The word means land, as in a passage in the *Odyssey* that reads: "But when we had left Crete and no other land [γαῖα] appeared, but only sky and sea [οὐρανός, θάλασσα] . . ." (14:301f.). The word can also designate earth as something to be shaped as by a potter, or as loose earth to be piled up to form a grave mound, as in Homer's description of the burial of Patroklos (*Iliad* 23: 226–57). Perhaps most significantly, γαῖα can designate the earth in distinction from the heaven (οὐρανός) and in its expansiveness and depth, as in Xenophanes' Fragment 28: "This upper limit of earth is visible here at our feet touching air; the lower reaches down without limit." Second, there is the billowing sea, the sea swelling with many waves (πόντος πολυκύμων). By using the word πόντος rather than θάλασσα, Empedocles refers to the open sea, as in Homer's account of how Odysseus climbs to a high outlook on Circe's island and observes the boundless sea (πόντος ἄπειρος) that lies all around (*Odyssey* 10:194f.). The third

---

7. Later authors such as Diogenes Laertius and Simplicius, relying largely on Theophrastus, report that Empedocles was an admirer of Parmenides and that in his poetry he imitated Parmenides; both did in fact write in hexameter verse. Yet a degree of skepticism regarding these reports is required, especially considering that they vary, even to the point of conflict, from one author to another, and even within the writings of a single author. For instance, Diogenes Laertius reports that, according to Theophrastus, Empedocles was an enthusiast of Parmenides; but then immediately he goes on to report that according to Hermippus it was Xenophanes, not Parmenides, who sparked Empedocles' enthusiasm (*Lives of Eminent Philosophers* 8:55–56).

is damp air (ὑγρὸς ἀήρ). In Homer the word ἀήρ means vapor, haze, mist, cloud, especially as a means of rendering invisible, as in Homer's account of how, as Menelaus lunged at Paris determined to kill him with the bronze spear, Aphrodite saved Paris by wrapping him in a thick mist (ἀήρ) (*Iliad* 3:379–81). Later the word refers primarily to the air of the lower, denser atmosphere, which is often damp, misty, hazy. By attaching the adjective ὑγρὸς (damp), Empedocles stresses this character rather than the transparency (as with Anaximenes), transferring the latter character to the fourth of the origins, αἰθήρ. By αἰθήρ he designates the often bright, shining upper air or the sky (οὐρανός), which, thus encompassing all things, is aptly described as a Titan "who fastens his circle around all things." The word σφίγγω (to fasten) means specifically to bind tight or to bind together within; κύκλος, designating a circle or ring, could refer to the horizon or to the entire dome that arises from it, and indeed the word sometimes means simply the vault of the sky. It is also not uncommon for αἰθήρ to be identified or at least closely associated with πῦρ (fire), especially with the πῦρ Διός, the fire of Zeus, that is, lightning.[8] If the sun, designated by the seemingly misplaced word ἥλιος, is taken also to be named in this articulation of the ἀρχή, then it belongs with the fourth; and indeed it, too, though differently from the horizon, traces a circle that encompasses all things.

The fourfold ἀρχή consists, then, of broad earth, open sea, damp air, and bright, uranic aither. It is from these four that all the things we now look upon have become manifest. Yet these four, which constitute the ἀρχή of all things, are not themselves simply things; rather, they are elemental expanses within which or in the crossings or mutual limits of which things can become manifest—as when, illuminated by sunlight, an ancient temple set firmly on the promontory in the distance yet obscured by mist is glimpsed from out at sea. On the other hand, these expanses that make up the ἀρχή are not simply other than the things that can become manifest amidst them. They are not set apart from the things they let become manifest; they do not operate from afar, but rather things come to light in their very density and expanse, which, though in a different manner, also are manifest. The things that become manifest belong to these archaic moments. They are *of* these elemental expanses: the loose earth that is piled up to form a grave mound is nonetheless earth, comes from the earth, is *of* earth; the water that quenches

---

8. See Anaxagoras A84, from Aristotle, *Meteorology* 369b14–19; also Aristotle, *On the Heaven* 270b24.

the thirst of mortals comes from the sea, from an inland sea or river; the moisture that condenses on every cool surface comes from the surrounding damp air; and the fire by which mortals warm themselves replicates that of the heaven.

There are numerous other Fragments in which the four archaic moments are named, though, not insignificantly, they are in many cases named quite differently. In Fragment B98, Empedocles speaks first of the earth. But here the word is neither γαῖα nor the less poetic variant γῆ, but rather χθών. Though χθών can quite legitimately be rendered as earth, it refers especially to the surface of the earth—as in a passage in the *Odyssey* in which Homer describes how a dancer leaps up from the earth (ἀπὸ χθονός) (8:375). The phrase χθόνα δύμεναι (or δῦναι) means to go beneath the earth (beneath its surface), that is, to die—as in a passage in the *Iliad* in which Andromache, fearing that Hector will be killed in battle, tells her husband that if she loses him, it would be better if she too were to go beneath the earth, to die (χθόνα δύμεναι) (6:404–11). The expression οἱ ὑπὸ χθονός designates those beneath the earth, that is, those who are among the shades in the underworld. Clearly, then, χθών is not a mere interchangeable synonym of γαῖα: χθών, connoting surface, has a different directionality, tending toward what lies underneath, whereas γαῖα has much more the sense of opening upward (toward the sky) and outward (in its broad expansiveness). The difference could be marked as the distinction between the gaidic earth and the chthonic earth.

Here, then, is the first part of the Fragment (B98), in which the archaic moments are named: "Chthonic earth met with these in most equal measure, with Hephaistos, rain, and blazing aither, dropping anchor in the perfect harbors of Cypris." There is one very evident way in which the first two moments come together: it is from beneath the surface of the earth that the metals to be forged by the smithy god are taken. But why does Empedocles refer to Hephaistos at all? Why does he cite the name of a god when, on the contrary, his aim is to tell of the origin of natural things, an origin that presumably is itself natural rather than mythical and that should, accordingly, be told of by way of a natural explanation? Is it simply that Empedocles has not yet fully escaped from the shadows of mythology into the clear light of natural explanation? That he might fall short of giving a natural explanation would indeed be a curious failing on the part of a thinker whose every thought seems to be oriented precisely to what we call nature, that is, φύσις. Is it self-evident that citing the name of a god is contrary to the aim of giving a natural explanation, assuming that it is clear what constitutes a natural explanation? Yet can the requirements of a natural explanation be determined apart from, in advance of, the philosophical determination of nature itself, of φύσις? Would it not be necessary already to have given an account of nature as such in order to know what constitutes a natural account? It has of course been said that the name of the god is used merely to signify fire, of which Hephaistos is said to be the god. But why, then, the name Hephaistos and not simply the name fire (πῦρ)? What does the name Hephaistos say that goes unsaid by the word *fire*? What does it mean to say that Hephaistos is the god *of* fire? What does the *of* mean here? For there are other gods and demigods who have a distinctive relation to fire, most notably Zeus, who wields the thunderbolt, and Prometheus, who steals fire. Hephaistos' relation to fire is significantly different: as a smith, he uses fire in order to give shape to things, in order to forge metal into manifest, properly shaped things. In some cases what he produces is wonderful to see. Thus, in the *Iliad*, when Thetis comes to the house of Hephaistos, he finds him fashioning twenty tripods that are "a wonder to behold" (θαῦμα ἰδέσθαι) (18:377). Most marvelous of all is the shield that Hephaistos fashions for Achilles. On the shield he wrought, first of all, the earth, the sky, the sea, and the tireless sun (18:483f.). It is as if Hephaistos forged the shield in such a way that this wonderful thing to behold reflected, in the images that adorned it, the fourfold ἀρχή itself. Little wonder, then, that Empedocles lets the name of the god name a moment of this fourfold.

The other archaic moments are rain, not simply water, which can occur almost anywhere, but rain, which comes from the heaven that things might grow from the earth; and, finally, blazing aither, shining on high and beaming down upon the earth. The Fragment speaks of how these four, chthonic earth, Hephaistos, rain, and blazing aither, met, how they came together in a certain equilibrium, a certain accord. The Fragment locates this meeting in the perfect harbor of Cypris; Cypris (Κύπρις) is one of the names of Aphrodite, derived from the name of the island of Cyprus, where at the sanctuaries of Paphos and Amathus she was most venerated. In Homer she is the wife of Hephaistos. She is affiliated with the sea and with seafaring and is said to have been born from the sea; hence it is in her harbor that the four drop anchor and enter into accord. Above all, she is the advocate of generation and fertility, providing a place where, through crossings of the archaic moments, things might be born into their manifestness.

The Fragment (B98) concludes by identifying what, once anchor is dropped in the perfect harbor of Aphrodite, originates from the accord of the archaic moments. It is flesh and blood, that is, animate beings. Among these are humans, who, supported and nourished by the rain-soaked earth, not only are discernful but also possess the craft of forging images of that which their far-seeing vision beholds, even of the ἀρχή itself.

Fragment B6 again names—again differently—the four archaic moments. It reads: "The four roots of all things hear first: shining Zeus, life-giving Hera, Aidoneus, and Nestis, who by her tears moistens the mortal spring." What is perhaps most remarkable in this Fragment is that it offers another generic designation for the ἀρχή. The four are called roots (ῥιζώματα). The word refers primarily to the roots of trees, though there are various metaphorical extensions, for instance, to ancestry. Later sources such as Simplicius use the word στοιχεῖον (*elementum, element*) in their reports of Empedocles' "theories," in this connection following Aristotle and Theophrastus.[9] But the word does not occur in any of the Empedoclean Fragments, and with good reason: the four are not elements from which things are made. Originally the word στοιχεῖον referred to the "elements" of λόγος, that is, letters and syllables, and it is only with Plato—and not without expressed hesitation on his part—that the word is extended to φύσις. For Empedocles the four are not elements from which things are composed, but rather are roots from which things emerge and grow into the light.

When, in Book 1 of the *Metaphysics*, Aristotle reviews what his predecessors took to be the primary ἀρχαί, mentioning water, air, and fire, he credits Empedocles with "adding earth [γῆ] as a fourth to those already mentioned."[10] Yet what is remarkable is not only that he adds a fourth, one that in fact none had set down as the sole ἀρχή, but that he construes all four in reference to the earth, in which things take root. All four archaic moments, regardless of how they may be further characterized, have the character of roots and to that extent have their place in the earth, that is, in their way of reaching down into the earth.

This referral of the archaic moments back to the earth serves to underscore that Empedocles regards the ἀρχή entirely in relation to

---

9. "He makes the corporeal elements [σωματικὰ στοιχεῖα] four in number" (A28—from Simplicius, *Physics* 25:21–31). See also A52—from Aristotle, *Metaphysics* 1000b18–20).

10. A28, from Aristotle, *Metaphysics* 984a6–9.

generation, not generation of being, but the generation by which vegetative life germinates in the earth and emerges into the light and the open air, as well as that by which animate beings are born. What is perhaps most conspicuous by contrast with subsequent Greek philosophy is the total lack of reference to making or production (ποίησις, τέχνη). Beings are not to be regarded as if they—even those that belong to nature—were made through imposition of form on shapeless material. One could say that in this respect Empedocles' thought remains closer to nature, keeps it apart from the paradigm of human artifice, of τέχνη. There is here hardly a trace of the contention that will later erupt between these two sides, most conspicuously perhaps in Plato's *Timaeus*,[11] to say nothing of the dominance of τέχνη over nature that will subsequently set in.

In Fragment B6, each of the four roots is identified as a god. The first of these is the one who is foremost among the gods, shining Zeus. Zeus—one will readily say—is lord of the heaven (οὐρανός), ruling there like a king and wielding his deadly, yet light-giving, yet also blinding, thunderbolt. Yet there is at least one feature that renders Zeus quite different from ordinary kings: whereas mortal kings want nothing more than to be seen in all their glorious presence by those subject to them, Zeus is, like all gods, elusive. He is hardly to be seen at all, and when he does appear, it is often in disguise so that he goes unrecognized, as in his many amorous pursuits. Still, mortals, erecting temples for him, must somehow have caught sight of him, even if only in a fleeting glance, even if only in an evanescent presence. It is in the luminous heaven that traces of shining Zeus can be glimpsed. Whereas his brothers remain elusive by retreating from the light, Hades into the shadowy underworld, Poseidon into the depth of the sea, Zeus can go largely unseen amidst—and because of—the very excess of light. As one of the four roots, Zeus is not a mere mythical personification of sunlight or fire. Rather, in the figure of Zeus the very character of light, of the fire of heaven, is posed: that it reigns over and illuminates all things, while remaining itself largely unseen, even threatening us, by way of the lightning flash and of the intensity of direct sunlight, with temporary or even permanent blindness.

In the enumeration of the four roots, shining Zeus is followed by life-giving Hera. In the effort, launched already in late antiquity, to reduce this Fragment to pure allegory and so to demythologize it, commentators have debated as to which root Hera is meant to allegorize. On the one hand, Aetius proposes air, perhaps because of the assonance of

---

11. See my discussion in *Chorology*, chaps. 1–2.

the two words, also perhaps because in the form of breath, air is necessary for life. On the other hand, Hippolytus proposes to identify Hera with the earth; this proposal can be defended on the ground that in Hesiod and the Homeric Hymns, *life-giving* is an epithet of earth.[12] And yet, the word φερέσβιος has also the more specific sense of life-bearing, and indeed it is this sense that makes it a fitting epithet for earth, from which all vegetative life is born. If one resists the reductive approach, then it suffices to regard life-bearing Hera as the archaic moment from which things are born into their manifestness. In this case, Hera would not be simply one moment alongside others but rather would bear the character of ἀρχή as such. From the life-bearing origin, all things would be born into the light, the reign of which lies with her consort Zeus.

There has been similar debate regarding the identification of Aidoneus. The name (Ἀιδωνεύς) is a lengthened, poetic form of ἀϊδής (unseen). Hippolytus thus argues that Aidoneus allegorizes air (ἀήρ) on the ground that "although we see all things through it, it is the only thing we do not see" (A33). On the other hand, this is the same word as Ἅιδης (Hades), and on this basis Aetius proposes that the name stands for earth (γῆ). Yet it would be more fitting to affiliate this root with χθών rather than γῆ, with the chthonic earth rather than the gaidic earth. But, still resisting reductionism, it would be even more fitting to let it be informed by the connection with the words for Hades and for the unseen. For these are ways of saying the retreat, the withdrawnness, that belongs to life—after it ends, of course, but also especially before it begins, the withdrawnness that must be endured by all living things in order that they might then grow into the light. Before they emerge so that we may look upon them and they may behold the light of the sun, living things must persist within the closure of the earth or the darkness of the womb.

How the name of the fourth root, Nestis, is to be heard borders on the undecidable. She barely appears in classical literature and is identified only as a Sicilian goddess. Hippolytus takes her as an allegorical figure for water, since the name means fasting, not eating; his argument is that water is the vehicle of—but does not provide—nourishment. It has been suggested that Nestis is a Sicilian name for Persephone; Empedocles' description that "by her tears [she] moistens the mortal spring" could, then, be taken to locate her with the underground

---

12. Hesiod, *Theogony* 693; *Homeric Hymn to Apollo* 341; see also the discussion in Wright, *Empedocles*, 164–66.

streams capable of providing moisture to the nourishing chthonic earth. But here there is scant evidence.

The passage that makes up Fragment B21 Empedocles offers as a witness meant to compensate for any lack in his previous account.[13] In the first part of the passage, he again names—again differently—the four roots: "sun, brilliant to sight and everywhere hot, and immortal things soaked in heat and bright sunlight, and rain, dark and chilling in everything, and from the earth come forth things rooted and solid." Two points need to be stressed in this part of the Fragment. First, the immortal things soaked in heat and bright sunlight may be taken as the heavenly bodies (as Wright actually translates the phrase)[14] or, more broadly, as the aither in a sense that expands to include the sky (οὐρανός). Second, Empedocles makes explicit that the earth is here to be regarded as that from which solid vegetative forms, sustained by their rootedness in the earth, emerge and grow into the light.

Yet what is most remarkable about this Fragment (B21) is the subsequent description it gives of the manner in which all the things we now look upon have become manifest. Empedocles declares, first of all, that in rancor (κότος) the roots remain divided and separated, but in friendship (φιλότης) they come together. Several other passages reiterate in various terms this double speaking, as Empedocles calls it: the roots are said to be "gathered together by love [φιλία] and separated one from another by strife [νεῖκος]" (A28); it is said that "at one time they grew to be one alone from many, at another time they grew apart to be many from one" (B17). In this connection nothing requires that love and strife (or rancor) be construed as independent, perhaps even substantial, forces or agents—no more so than in the case of love and strife among

---

13. In the source text, Simplicius' *Physics*, Fragment B21 is cited almost immediately after B17, and on this basis it would appear that B17 is the account that B21 sets out to supplement. On the other hand, there is no guarantee that passages cited sequentially by Simplicius were necessarily sequential in Empedocles' text. The issue has now been further complicated by the publication of the Strasbourg Papyrus, which contains what appears to be a continuation of B17 that extends far beyond the citation given by Simplicius (see Daniel W. Graham, *Texts of Early Greek Philosophy* [Cambridge: Cambridge University Press, 2010], 350–54).

14. Wright, *Empedocles*, 177. In Kirk, Raven, and Schofield, the suggestion is that what is probably intended are "breezes and expanses of air"; also perhaps, considering the assonance between ἄμβοτος (immortal) and αμβροσία (ambrosia), the food of the gods regarded as vapors steeped in heat and light by the sun (*The Presocratic Philosophers*, 294).

humans. It is much more in accord with the tone of Empedocles' verses to regard these as one way of naming the manner in which the roots gather together and are separated one from another. As such, they mark the motility that belongs to the fourfold configuration of the ἀρχή, to the σχῆμα of φύσις, the figure of nature.

In any case, what makes Fragment B21 stand out among all these passages is the way in which, as it continues, it tells how, through the coming together of the roots, through this radical gathering, the things we now look upon come to lie there before our senses. Empedocles writes: "From them [i.e., from the roots] all things that were, that are, and that will be sprang [βλαστάνω—to bud, sprout, burst forth, grow]—trees, men and women, beasts and birds and water-nourished fish, and long-lived gods foremost in honors. For there are just these [namely, the roots], which, running through each other, assume different appearances; so much does the mixing change them." There is perhaps no other Fragment that is so explicit about the manner in which all things come to grow into their appearance from the four roots. What determines things in their manifest appearances is the way in which the roots run through one another like the intertwining roots of a tree. Everything depends on their intertwining, on their coming together, on their mixing to the point of entanglement. Everything depends on how—in the idiom of this Fragment—the sunlight shining in the aither comes together with the rain-soaked earth. That even the gods are mentioned among these things, even though some are also identified as roots, is again indicative that the ἀρχή is not something set apart from the things brought forth.

In this regard, the beginning of Fragment B22 is especially pertinent. It reads: "For all these—shining sun and earth [χθών] and sky and sea—are one with their own parts that by nature [πέφυκεν] wander off [ἀποπλαχθέντα] among mortal things." The god who is a root—Zeus, for instance—is one with the god who appears—if always elusively—from the mixing of the roots. The mixing occurs as the roots go wandering out, go astray amidst the very things that they let come forth. The mixing and the wandering out occur *by nature*. As Empedocles writes in the concluding lines of Fragment B8: "There is only mixing and separating of what has been mixed, and to these men give the name φύσις."

In the end, it is imperative to declare that in Empedocles the ἀρχή is said in many ways. The many names given to the four moments, even the generic name *root*, are not to be dismissed as mere poetic metaphor or as mythological personifications of natural phenomena. Rather, these names are the names by which Empedocles undertakes to think the manifold workings of the ἀρχή. Since these workings, the mixing and wandering out of the roots, are the very workings of what is called *nature*, it follows that these names, as they themselves mix and wander off semantically toward one another, provide the means for writing, in the most fitting way, on nature.

5 MONSTROUS WONDER. THE ADVANCE OF NATURE

Monsters abound in the *Theaetetus*. They stride across its surface, not only when the word actually occurs but throughout, disturbing the otherwise smooth surface, setting it in motion as if a quake had commenced, opening deep chasms in it while also drawing it up to the heights, stretching it toward the heaven; then it is as though a chain of high mountains had erupted from—and disrupted—what was once—or had seemed to be—a level plane. Nature would thus be brought to exceed itself, and figures of excess would take shape, assuming various guises. Indeed, monstrosity consists precisely in an exceeding of nature that nonetheless—and in the utmost tension—belongs to nature. Such monstrosity is released both by the words of the *Theaetetus* and by the deeds enacted through and along with these words. It is preeminently when words of a certain order are set in deed together in the staging of a certain kind of scene that monstrosity comes—almost paradoxically—to ally itself with truth. Then there occurs a showing of τὸ πρᾶγμα αὐτό, in the phrase from the *Seventh Letter* (341c), which extends across the entire history of philosophy, repeatedly enjoining thought to attend to the things themselves.[1] Thus it is that philosophy, far from shunning monstrosity, ventures to engage it, even when appearances are quite otherwise.

---

1. For a sketch of some of the major junctures in the history of this injunction with special reference to the way it becomes explicit and a theme of critical reflection in phenomenology, see my *Delimitations*, chap. 16.

(A) OPENINGS, CHRONOLOGY, TOPOLOGY

The chronology of a Platonic dialogue locates it with respect to other dialogues and events, while its topology determines its internal structure. Yet neither the chronology nor the topology is merely a formal determination bearing only externally on what would be shown in and through the dialogue. Rather, both serve to orient the dialogue to the manifestation that is to be accomplished through its words and deeds.

The chronology of a dialogue is that of the words and deeds themselves. In some cases these are presented directly; in other instances, as in the *Theaetetus*, their presentation is enclosed in a frame consisting of words and deeds distant in place and time from the primary conversation. In either case the chronology is conveyed by means of indications within the dialogue that display its temporal connection to other dialogues and to events that have significant bearing on the conversation; in many instances this display is effected by means of correspondences between indications internal to the dialogue itself and indications in the other dialogues to which it is temporally connected. Though the chronology has the effect of extending the compass of the dialogue beyond its direct words and deeds, it is established and thus displayed within the dialogue itself and in many instances through correspondence with indications internal to the other pertinent dialogues. In this sense it is an internal chronology even though its function is to refer the dialogue outside itself, beyond itself, establishing thereby a set of relations between the dramatic time of a dialogue and those of certain other dialogues or events.

The topology of a dialogue, which gives it its internal structure, involves three distinct moments. The first consists in the articulation or partitioning of the dialogue. By this means the dialogue is divided in a way suited to its specific mode of disclosure and to what is to be shown through its words and deeds. The second moment consists of the directionalities operative in the dialogue. A paradigm of such directionality is presented in the *Republic*, in the depiction of an upward, ascensional directionality offered by the account of the divided line and by the image of escape from the cave. In the *Theaetetus*, too, an ascensional directionality is displayed in the figure of the philosopher with his gaze fixed precariously on the starry heaven above. The third moment lies in the texture of the dialogue; that is, it is constituted by the way in which different textual dimensions such as words and deeds as well as the various modes of discourse (irreducible to mere assertoric statements) are layered or woven together. As including all three moments in their interplay, the topology of a dialogue has the character of a spacing. This spacing is no external framework imposed on the dialogue but rather is determined in and through the dialogue itself as it unfolds its distinctive manifestation. It is, in this sense, a self-spacing.

The very first word of the *Theaetetus* inscribes the present, announces the present moment. The scene is set in Megara, and Euclides is speaking to Terpsion. Euclides asks him tersely, almost elliptically, about his return to the city: "Just now, Terpsion, or long ago from the country?" (142a). The first word, ἄρτι, can be translated as *just now*—as I am just now translating it, namely, as *just now*—as *right now, right at the present moment, in the present moment*. The word is uniquely reflexive: to say it is to instantiate precisely what is said; it is to mark the very moment in which it is said, the moment when the sounding word is uttered by Euclides and heard by Terpsion. Even if it goes unmarked, unsaid, even if some other sound is heard instead, this sound will always be heard in the present moment, in the moment of presence. It is no different with sights, for instance, with the sight of Euclides at the moment when Terpsion, who has looked for him in vain, suddenly meets him. Neither is it any different with the other kinds of what we call perception, translating—or rather, taking over the translation of—the Greek word αἴσθησις. Yet as the unity of the alleged modes of perception is affirmed—and it has long since come to seem self-evident in philosophy—it should be noted that it was not always so readily affirmed, that it was precisely such texts as the *Theaetetus* that brought about the ready affirmation of this unity. Thus, at the most advanced stage of the discussion, Socrates queries Theaetetus as to whether, despite the many differences between seeing, hearing, smelling, feeling cold, and feeling hot, he calls them all by the same name. Theaetetus answers that he does and that the name he uses is αἴσθησις (186d–e).

Perception has, then, a unique bond to the present moment; it is bound into, bound up in, the present moment, and whatever it reveals, whatever it makes present, it presents in the present, which is thus always the moment of presence. But then, the moment one goes beyond the present moment, some other power will have come into play, some power other than perception. If, in particular, the move is into the past, even if only to bring the past back into the present, then memory will have become instrumental.[2]

---

2. Here the question developed by Derrida is left open, the question whether the bringing of the past into the present (into what with respect to the past is future) must

Such is precisely the span set out disjunctively in the opening sentence of the *Theaetetus* when Euclides asks Terpsion whether he is just now (ἄρτι) arriving from the country or whether he returned long ago (πάλαι). Terpsion's answer, that he returned fairly long ago (ἐπιεικῶς πάλαι), stretches the discourse beyond the present moment, opening the interval in which, as Terpsion explains, he was given over to a double engagement, searching and wondering, that is, searching for Euclides in the agora and wondering that Euclides was not to be found there. These allied engagements virtually define philosophy, which is thus, from the beginning, set within the opening beyond the present moment, within the interval bounded by perception and memory.

As the country spreads, stretches out, from the city in which, just now, the two Megarians are conversing, so there would be a stretching beyond perception and its present moment. This stretch is set out in the dialogue as a problem in the Greek geometrical sense; it is to be laid out, constructed, as Theaetetus, in one of his two principal contributions to the history of Greek mathematics, worked out the construction of the five regular solids.

That which is perceptually present in the present moment (ἄρτι) can be called an image (εἰκών). This connection is reflected in the first word of Terpsion's reply, which is his first word in the dialogue. The word, ἐπιεικῶς, is conventionally translated as *fairly* or *moderately*. Yet, if the root word, εἰκών, is emphasized, a possible—if perhaps all too literal—rendering would be: in addition to, or over and above, the image. Hence, in this single word, taken in this manner, the same issue is broached: that of the opening, the extension, the stretching, beyond the *just now*, beyond the image present—presented in perception—just now.

The extension beyond the *just now* can take various forms. The most conspicuous is the extension into the past by which the past returns in the form of remembrance. Also there can occur an extension into the future through various kinds of anticipation. Still another form is exemplified in the construction of a geometrical proof. Though the

---

always already have been carried out. Were such the case, then the very constitution of the present would involve the presence of the past within it; the past would be constitutively implicated in the present. But then, there would be no pure perception independent of a certain kind of memory (akin to what Husserl calls retention or primary memory). See Jacques Derrida, *La Voix et le phénomène* (Paris: Presses Universitaires de France, 1967), 67–77. There are points where the analyses of perception in the *Theaetetus* as well as in the *Phaedo* intersect with Derrida's development of this question, though, as goes without saying, it cannot be a matter of congruence.

constructing and the actual figure that is drawn are linked to a series of present moments, what is intended in the demonstration is quite beyond any sequence of moments and any particular figure that can be drawn and perceived. Such a demonstration goes beyond the perceptual and the present moments to which perception is bound; indeed, it seems to do so even more decisively than do memory and anticipation. It is not insignificant that in the main conversation of the *Theaetetus* two of the three principal characters are mathematicians, one of them already renowned, the other, though still young, already beginning to surpass his renowned master.

Thus, in the *Theaetetus* the question that is preeminently addressed is that of the extension beyond perception and its *just now*. Yet the addressing of this question is undertaken in response to a threat, a danger; the course of the dialogue shows just how precarious the opening beyond perception is, how easily this interval can collapse into mere stigmatic presence, and how utterly dissolute the consequences of such a collapse would be.

In the opening sentence Plato writes in such a way as to allude playfully to this constantly impending collapse. Over against the initial ἄρτι, *just now*, he sets the word πάλαι, connecting them disjunctively: Ἄρτι, ὦ Τερψίων, ἢ πάλαι.... Most often πάλαι means *long ago*; thus in such cases it is opposed to ἄρτι, as well as to νῦν, the near-synonym of ἄρτι. However, the semantic spread of πάλαι is such that it can also signify *just past, not long ago*, and even *just now*, almost even just *now*, coming to have virtually the same meaning as ἄρτι, letting the difference otherwise opened in the initial sentence collapse. Even if πάλαι falls slightly short of meaning precisely *now*, the gap is readily bridged from the other side: for ἄρτι, too, has its spread of meaning, stretching back a short way toward the past. This spread is expressed if the ambiguity of the phrase *just now* is activated such that it can mean *at the present moment* but also *just a moment ago*.[3]

---

3. Aristotle uses πάλαι both in the sense of *long ago* as opposed to *now* (νῦν) (*Metaphysics* 1069a29) and in the sense of *just past* or *just now* (*Politics* 1282a15). The explicit use of ἄρτι with the imperfect tense of the accompanying verb to designate an action in the recent past is found in Plato's *Gorgias* at 454b. A similar slight spread from the present moment to the recent past is displayed by νῦν (*Republic* 341e; *Statesman* 258a; *Iliad* 3:439), which also is taken up in a gesture to the future when, at the end of the *Theaetetus*, Socrates declares that he must go to the portico of the King to hear the indictment brought against him (210d).

The last line of the *Theaetetus* indicates quite transparently the most proximate chronology of the main conversation, for it forges a link to a future conversation. Socrates says: "But in the morning [or: tomorrow morning at dawn—ἕωθεν], Theodorus, let us come back here to meet" (210d). The conversation that begins early the next day is that of the *Sophist*, as indicated by its opening line. Theodorus is speaking: "According to yesterday's agreement, Socrates, we ourselves have come in due order" (216a). The connection could not be more evident: the conversation in the *Sophist* takes place on the day after that in—or rather, reported in—the *Theaetetus*. The participants in the conversation in the *Sophist* are the same as in the *Theaetetus*, except for one new character whom Theodorus introduces at the beginning of the *Sophist* as a stranger from Elea. It is significant that this character, who as a representative brings Parmenides onto the scene, is absent from the conversation in the *Theaetetus* and arrives on the scene only on the following day; for he would have been entirely out of place in that conversation, a stranger to it, not only because its principal theme is foreign to Eleatic thought but also because engagement with Parmenides is explicitly deferred in the conversation.

Near the beginning of the *Statesman*, Socrates refers unmistakably to both previous conversations: "Now I myself associated with Theaetetus yesterday through speeches [διὰ λόγων], and I have just now [νῦν] heard him answering" (258a). Thus, the three dialogues form a series spread over two days. On the first day, the conversation in—reported in—the *Theaetetus* takes place. Then, beginning early on the second day, the conversation in the *Sophist* occurs. It is then followed (seemingly without a break) by the conversation in the *Statesman*.

Both ἄρτι and νῦν display a very different kind of semantics from that of ἐξαίφνης. As an adverb, ἐξαίφνης means *at the present moment*, so *now*, but without the least spread from the punctual instant, hence *suddenly* (see *Theaetetus* 162c, 203e). In the *Parmenides* it occurs as the noun τὸ ἐξαίφνης, the moment, the instant. Posing to Socrates the question: "Of what sort is it?," Parmenides explains: "The instant, this strange nature [φύσις ἄτοπος], is something inserted between motion and rest and is in no time at all" (156d-e). Thus, having no spread at all, being absolutely stigmatic, the instant is a strange φύσις, a nature that is out of place (ἄ-τοπος) in nature. Strangest of all, it is an instant that is not in time at all; it is a moment of time that, because it lacks all connection, all communication, with other moments past and future (when there would have been motion and will be rest), falls entirely out of time. This is, then, the most extreme danger: the collapse into sheer stigmatic presence would result in the disruption of time itself.

64 THE FIGURE OF NATURE

The *Theaetetus*, along with its two sequels, is also linked to several other dialogues by way of internal chronology. Though there are numerous indirect references or allusions in the three dialogues, a direct indication occurs in the penultimate sentence of the *Theaetetus*, just prior to Socrates' proposal that they meet again on the following day. Socrates declares: "Now, however, I must go to the portico of the King to answer to the indictment that Miletus has drawn up against me" (210d). In complying with this imperative, Socrates is following the prescribed legal process. In order that a charge be brought against someone, Athenian process required that the prosecutor first issue an indictment, and that he and the defendant then appear before the appropriate magistrate for a hearing. At this time the charge was read and questions were put to the defendant by the magistrate; the prosecutor and the defendant could also question each other. If, at the end of the hearing, the magistrate decided that the case would go to trial, he would set a date for the trial. Since Miletus' charge against Socrates was impiety, the hearing took place before the King Archon (βασιλεύς), who dealt with all legal processes pertaining to such matters.[4]

The *Theaetetus* thus concludes with Socrates setting out for the hearing. By the time of the opening line of the *Euthyphro*, he has arrived at the portico of the King Archon, where Euthyphro, who is waiting to file an indictment, expresses surprise at seeing him at such a place: "What strange thing has happened, Socrates, that you have left your usual haunts in the Lyceum and are now spending your time at the portico of the King Archon?" (2a). Thus, it is indicated that the conversation in the *Euthyphro* takes place as Socrates awaits the hearing, hence very shortly after the end of the conversation in the *Theaetetus*.

Another indication is given in the *Cratylus*. It occurs in a passage in which Socrates is speaking with Hermogenes. They have been discussing the fitness of names and producing etymologies that are supposed to demonstrate such fitness. The entire passage constitutes one of the most masterful comedies to be found anywhere in the dialogues.[5] As Socrates is spinning out his ludicrous etymologies, Hermogenes characterizes him as an "inspired utterer of oracles." Socrates' response

---

4. See Douglas M. MacDowell, *The Law in Classical Athens* (Ithaca, NY: Cornell University Press, 1978), 237–42.

5. See my *Being and Logos*, 215–62.

is not without irony: "Yes, Hermogenes, and I am convinced that the inspiration came to me from Euthyphro the Prospaltian. For I was with him and listening to him a long time early this morning. So he must have been inspired, and he not only filled my ears but took possession of my soul with his superhuman wisdom" (396d-e). There is every reason to believe that the reference is to the conversation in the *Euthyphro*. In this case there would be a series of five dialogues linked by their internal chronologies and spread over two days. On the first day there would have taken place, in order, the conversations in the *Theaetetus*, in the *Euthyphro*, and in the *Cratylus*. On the second day the conversation in the *Sophist* and then in the *Statesman* would have occurred.

But, in turn, the hearing before the King Archon sets into motion the chain of events that lead to Socrates' trial (depicted in the *Apology*), his imprisonment (the setting and theme of the *Crito*), and his death (as presented in the *Phaedo*). Though the exact length of time between the hearing and the trial cannot be determined, it is clear that a short time after the two days when the series of five conversations occur, the trial takes place. The *Crito* is set twenty-eight or twenty-nine days later, and the *Phaedo* thirty days after the trial. Thus, the *Theaetetus* is the first in the series of dialogues that lead up to Socrates' trial and execution, that is, the series that concludes with the *Phaedo*.

The topology of the *Theaetetus* is more complex than its chronology and more resistant to linear presentation; its delineation—necessarily along various lines—cannot but engage the content of the dialogue. Yet, in the dialogues form and content are so inseparable that the very distinction tends to lose its pertinence. Thus, the topology of a dialogue is thoroughly bound up with its words and deeds and, hence, with the manifestation to which the dialogue in its entirety is oriented.

In the *Theaetetus* there is much that is theatrical, much that belongs to theatre, scenes that one could well imagine seeing onstage. Think of how Socrates dons the disguise of a midwife and sets about aiding, as midwives do, the natural process of birth, bringing τέχνη to the aid of nature, philosophy to the aid of φύσις. Or think of the scene where Theaetetus with his gymnast friends has just been exercising and, having just finished oiling himself, his body gleaming in the full bloom of youth, suddenly appears before Socrates and Theodorus, as if his presence had been invoked by the words of praise that had just been uttered by Theodorus. Or think of the scene pictured by Socrates in which the

66 THE FIGURE OF NATURE

head of the deceased Protagoras pops up out of the ground in order to castigate Socrates for talking nonsense.

What is striking is not just that the *Theaetetus* is dramatic, not just that its temporal and topical settings—both doubled in this case—shape the sense of its discourses, not just that the identity and deeds of the various characters, including the deeds carried out through λόγος itself, contribute essentially to the dialogue's disclosive capacity, to its power to make something manifest. What is striking is that it stages the drama, that it stages certain scenes corresponding to what is said and shown, certain scenes that contribute to the showing of what is said. What is striking in this dialogue is that it translates its philosophical openings, themes, and questions into concrete scenes, into spectacles that one can imagine seeing.

Though there are a number of highly impressive vignettes such as that of the sudden appearance of Theaetetus, there are also scenes that evolve and that are of somewhat larger compass, encompassing and setting in relation the various vignettes. It is in and through these overarching, developing scenes that the primary manifestations achieved by the dialogue occur. The first part of the dialogue is determined by two such evolving scenes. One is the scene of φύσις, the scene into which is translated a certain thesis regarding φύσις. It could be called even a thesis about—producing thus a scene of—what φύσις is, were it not precisely such that in its inception it dissolves all whatness and indeed all being. The other scene is that of the appearance of the philosopher; it is the scene of the philosopher's coming upon the scene. These two scenes run throughout the first part of the dialogue until finally, in the concluding section of this part, they coalesce. In their fusion something comes to be made manifest about φύσις and about the philosopher's relation to φύσις.

It will be necessary to trace the contours of these two extended scenes as they evolve and intersect in the first part of the dialogue and to mark especially the discourses and enactments by which are achieved decisive showings of φύσις and of the appearance of the philosopher. Most decisive will be the concluding fusion in and through which is made manifest the inception of philosophy, its beginning, in relation to φύσις.

To say that the evolution of these two scenes spans the first part of the *Theaetetus* is to refer of course to the usual, conventional partition of the dialogue (excepting the introductory sections) into three parts corresponding to the three different answers that Theaetetus appears to give to Socrates' question as to what knowledge is, answers that prove incapable of withstanding the interrogation that Socrates brings to bear on them. If regarded solely in this way, the dialogue appears to end aporetically, and the question of the significance of this aporetic ending would, then, need to be confronted. And yet, while this way of partitioning the dialogue has, no doubt, a certain legitimacy, it is by no means the only way in which the shape and structure of the dialogue can with justification be construed. To this extent there is some warrant, then, for mutually superimposing various spacings, various ways of configuring the dialogue, and for opening thereby a certain exchange between them.

One configuration that may be superimposed on the tripartite division can be drawn by marking the center and the extremes of the dialogue. For the topology of the *Theaetetus* is such that precisely at its center there occurs a discourse on the philosopher. Indeed, it is not simply a discourse, not simply a defining of the philosopher; rather, it is a discourse that stages a scene in which, by which, it is allegedly shown what a philosopher is. The name of the philosopher who appears in this scene is Thales. Here is the well-known passage in which Socrates describes the scene: "While Thales was studying the stars and looking up, he fell into a well, and a graceful and elegant Thracian servant girl is said to have jeered at him, that in his eagerness to know the things in the heaven he was unaware of the things in front of him and at his feet" (174a). So, casting his vision upward, gazing fixedly at the heaven above, the philosopher Thales is oblivious to the everyday world in which the Thracian servant girl makes her way elegantly, gracefully, with ease. Because her everyday comportment is uninterrupted by any engagement beyond, she enjoys a certain superiority and mocks the philosopher Thales, whose everyday comportment is so thoroughly disrupted by his higher vision that he is incapable of coping with what is at his feet.

Socrates says of this comic scene: "The same jest suffices for all those who engage in philosophy" (174a–b). In this scene the philosopher appears as casting his vision above while stumbling about in the world around him, inviting the derision that common sense with its servant girls heaps upon him. As he appears in this scene, the philosopher is determined primarily by his ascensional orientation, by the upward directionality of his vision. It is as if the cost of maintaining this upwardness were that he must unwittingly play a role in a comedy.

This little story with the seemingly comic scene it presents has been told again and again so as to show, in behalf of—and from the viewpoint of—common sense, that the philosopher is so set on higher things that he is oblivious to the everyday and thus cannot avoid falling into wells and being laughed at by servant girls. Yet the story need not be understood only in such a straightforward way. Falling into the well could be regarded not merely as a result of Thales' inattention to mundane things, but rather as a descensional movement counterposed to his ascendancy. It has been suggested that Thales, as presented in the story, did not fall into the well at all but rather climbed down into it in order to view the stars without the interference of peripheral light. In this case it would be the servant girl, indeed all who serve the cause of common sense, and not Thales who would be portrayed in the story as ignorant.[6] Furthermore, the story could then be regarded as presenting the descensional movement as a condition of—or at least bound up with—the ascensional vision. In addition, on the assumption that there would have been water in the well, the story would serve to make a thematic link to Thales' alleged account of the ἀρχή as water; in the well, everything except the enclosing well itself would in fact be water.

It is around the scene of the philosopher's ascendancy that the larger, evolving scene of the appearance of the philosopher is deployed. The opening and closing scenes of the dialogue belong to this larger scene. Consider the opening scene, set in Megara. The two Megarians, Euclides and Terpsion, between whom the initial conversation takes place, are known to have been closely associated with Socrates. In the *Phaedo* (59c) they are mentioned as being among those who were present on the day of Socrates' death, though in the discussion presented in that dialogue they do not speak, and nothing is said about them except that they were from Megara. Most of what can be said about them has to be pieced together from later authors and doxographers. In most instances what is stressed is their engagement with λόγος. Diogenes Laertius, for example, cites the words of a hostile critic: "I dislike these babblers and all others besides..., and wrangling Euclides, who inspired the Megarians

---

6. P. Christopher Smith includes the following note in his translation of Hans-Georg Gadamer's *The Idea of the Good in Platonic-Aristotelian Philosophy* (New Haven: Yale University Press, 1986), 39n6: "In his lectures at Boston College, Gadamer pointed out that in fact Thales would not have fallen into the well, as the maidservant presumed (174b), but would have climbed down in order to view the stars without the interference of peripheral light. A contemporary reader of Plato would have understood just whom Plato is portraying as ignorant here—not Thales, but self-proclaimed 'practical' people."

with a mad passion for contention [disputation—ἐρισμός = ἔρις]."[7] The Megarian school, founded by Euclides, is reputed to have had recourse to contentious words in dealing with all problems and all phenomena.

The opening scene in Megara occurs many years after the death of Socrates. As the scene opens, stretching from just now to long ago, Terpsion affirms the long-ago, declaring that he returned from the country fairly long ago. He reports having wondered that he could not find Euclides, who responds that he was not in the city. Euclides then proceeds to stretch the discourse again back beyond—that is, before—the just-now of their conversation. He stretches it in deed, performatively, stretches it across the span opened by memory. He carries out a kind of double remembrance, both remembering and narrating, saying what he is remembering, translating it into λόγος. He says: "On going down to the harbor, I met Theaetetus being carried from the army camp in Corinth to Athens" (142a). *Going down*: the word is καταβαίνω. This is the same as the very first word of the *Republic*, where also it denotes going down to the harbor, Socrates saying: "I went down [κατέβην] yesterday to Piraeus" (*Rep.* 327a). Both passages may be read as citations of the passage in the *Odyssey* where Odysseus tells Penelope of the day when, as he says, "I went down [κατέβην] to Hades to inquire about the return of myself and my friends" (*Odyssey* 23.252–53). In the *Republic* the descent is counterposed to the philosophical ascent described and enacted in the images of line and cave in the center of the *Republic*, just as, in the *Theaetetus*, it is counterposed to Thales' ascensional vision. And in all three texts, the going-down is intrinsically linked to death. Just as Odysseus went down to Hades to speak with the dead, and as Socrates, in the *Republic*, enacted at the beginning what finally is told in the myth of Er's descent into the place to which the dead pass, so likewise Euclides went down to the harbor of Megara, where he met Theaetetus on the verge of death. He tells Terpsion that Theaetetus was "barely alive," suffering indeed from wounds inflicted in battle but still more from the dysentery that has broken out in the army. Euclides reports that he begged Theaetetus to stop in Megara but that Theaetetus refused. So Euclides simply accompanied him as far as the town of Erineos, situated between Eleusis and Athens. Though he makes no mention of the μῦθος associated with Erineos, it should be noted that it was said to be the place

---

7. Diogenes Laertius, *Lives of Eminent Philosophers* 2:107. The Megarians are also the target of Aristotle's criticism, which is aimed at their identification of δύναμις and ἐνέργεια (*Metaphysics* 1046b29–1047b2).

where the god Hades abducted Persephone so as to take her down to the underworld.

Euclides reports that as he then returned to Megara, he remembered and wondered at how prophetically Socrates had spoken about Theaetetus. For shortly before Socrates' death, he had met Theaetetus, then just a lad, and had had a conversation with him. It turns out—remarkably—that Socrates had subsequently narrated the speeches of this conversation to Euclides, who then, at his leisure, had written down the conversation, conferring further with Socrates regarding points he failed to remember. Once Euclides has mentioned writing this book, as he calls it, the stage is set for a boy to read it to Euclides and Terpsion. What is then read constitutes the entire remainder of the dialogue. Hence, except for the opening conversation, the dialogue is doubly authored, written both by Plato and by the Megarian Euclides, or, more precisely, written by Plato as—or as if—written also by Euclides. The *Theaetetus* is a book containing a book, a book that introduces and then, beyond this brief introduction, presents directly another book, presents it so directly that, except for the brief introduction set in Megara, the two books appear identical.

This double book is a narrative of the conversation that Socrates, just before his death, had with Theaetetus, who at that time was in the full bloom of youth. In the middle of that conversation, Socrates told Theaetetus of the philosophical ascent, and on the basis of their conversation, Socrates—as Euclides puts it—"expressed great admiration for his nature [φύσις]" (142c).

Thus the dialogue incorporates a layering of discourses. There is the original conversation between Socrates, Theodorus, and Theaetetus. Then there is Socrates' report of the conversation to Euclides, supplemented by subsequent consultations with Socrates. On the basis of Socrates' report, Euclides then composed his book, in which the original conversation (as reported by Socrates) was recorded. Now, in the just-now of the dialogue, this book is read to Euclides and Terpsion, this reading constituting the entirety of the *Theaetetus* beyond the opening scene. This layering thus exemplifies the opening from the just-now to the long-ago, that is, the operations by which, at successive levels, memory brings the past back into the present, the long-ago back into the just-now.

Euclides explains in detail how, on the basis of what Socrates had told him about the conversation with Theaetetus, he went about composing his book. He says: "In order that the statements between the speeches might not cause trouble in the writing, whenever either Socrates spoke about himself, for example, 'And I said' or 'And I spoke,' or in turn about whoever answered, 'He consented' or 'He refused to agree,' it's for these reasons that I removed things of this sort and wrote it as if he himself were conversing with them" (143c–d). What Euclides does not mention is that his way of writing the book not only will have deleted the troublesome repetition of such phrases as "And I said," but also will have eliminated anything else that Socrates reported about the conversation other than the actual speeches. If, for example, Socrates had reported that at a certain point in the conversation Theaetetus hesitated, blushed, or shook his head in dismay, or that his face lit up in wonder, all these expressions would have been lost in Euclides' transcription except for those that happened to be actually mentioned in one of the speeches. All that Euclides transcribed into his book were the λόγοι themselves; this would have been entirely in character if, as attested, the Megarians occupied themselves primarily with disputation and thus with words more than with things. Euclides' way of composing the book—the book that coincides with the *Theaetetus* itself except for the opening scene—has the effect of reducing φύσις to λόγος, or, at best, of translating φύσις into λόγος. At the same time, by transposing both the actual conversation and Socrates' oral report of it into a written λόγος, Euclides lifts the scene out of the incessant flow of the just-now and so preserves what otherwise would long ago have vanished in that flow. By transposing it into a λόγος, Euclides not only reduces φύσις but also effects its return from the oblivion of the past. By translating it into speech, he prompts a return of the perpetually vanishing things of nature. By inscribing this λόγος, he secures it even against the loss of remembrance, a loss that becomes absolute with death, in this case with the deaths of Theaetetus and Socrates.

The opening conversation in Megara thus already identifies the passage to λόγος as another way of passing beyond the just-now of perception, as a way other than that provided by memory. And yet, this way, the passage to λόγος, is presented precisely as a way of securing remembrance. Thus, in these initial dramatic allusions, the passage to λόγος is portrayed not so much as an alternative way over against that effected by memory of the long-ago, but rather—to say the least—as a compounding of the way opened by memory as such.

Already it has been noted that at the end of the conversation with Theaetetus, which is also the end of the dialogue *Theaetetus*, Socrates makes a remark that serves to link the dialogue to the chain of events that will lead to his death. For he says: "Now, however, I must go to the portico of the King to answer to the indictment that Miletus has drawn up against me" (210d). The larger scene of the appearance of the philosopher thus begins to take shape through the juxtaposition of the central image of philosophical ascendancy with the κατάβασις invoked at both the beginning and the end of the dialogue. This juxtaposition, this spread, is indicative that Thales is not the only philosopher in the dialogue, that he is not even the only one whose appearance is to be staged. One suspects already, from the case of Socrates, that ascendancy alone does not suffice to make one a philosopher. And yet, the other philosopher whose appearance as such is staged in the dialogue is not so much Socrates as it is rather Theaetetus.

What is especially remarkable is the way in which the initial scene of Theaetetus' appearance broaches the other extended scene, that of φύσις. Indeed, even prior to this scene, already in the opening conversation between the Megarians, there is—as mentioned—a reference to φύσις; in this very first occurrence of the word in the dialogue, the reference is—significantly—to Theaetetus, to his φύσις. Euclides reports that Socrates, on the basis of his conversation with Theaetetus, "expressed great admiration for his φύσις." This reference recurs almost immediately as the boy proceeds to read from Euclides' book, in which Socrates' conversation with Theaetetus is recorded. As the scene of the conversation opens, Theaetetus is not yet present but only Socrates and Theodorus, who speak about the youth of Athens. Without yet naming him, Theodorus tells Socrates about Theaetetus, about his resemblance to Socrates, and about his "wonderfully fine nature [θαυμαστῶς εὖ πεφυκότα]" (144a). Then Theodorus concludes his praise of Theaetetus with a very remarkable figure: "But he goes so smoothly, so unfalteringly, and so effectively to learning and investigation, and all with so much gentleness, just as a flow of olive oil flows without a sound, as for it to be a cause of wonder that someone of his age behaves in this way" (144b). This figure of wonderful Theaetetus silently flowing like olive oil is decisive for the entire first part of the dialogue: once the scene becomes that of φύσις, once it is the figure of nature that is staged, it will turn out that virtually everything flows. There will be the flow of youth and vigor, to be sure, but also the flow of decay and death.

Although the figure of Theaetetus as flowing like a flow of olive oil is the most striking, there are, from the beginning, other figures that associate Theaetetus with flowing. When Euclides met Theaetetus being carried back to Athens, he reportedly had "some wounds," from which blood would, earlier and perhaps still, have been flowing. Also, he was suffering most severely from dysentery. Then, just after Theodorus draws the figure of the flow of olive oil, he mentions that Theaetetus' inherited property has been wasted, drained away, by guardians, but that he is "most wonderfully free" (144d) with his money, liberal, generous, in giving it away. Socrates' observation that Theaetetus' family comes from Sounian is also perhaps not insignificant. For Cape Sounian, just south of Athens, juts out into the sea, and at its very tip is a great temple of Poseidon. This magnificent site was well known in antiquity (see *Odyssey* 3:276–85), and by the mid-fifth century the temple had been erected there, replacing the colossal marble κοῦροι that had once stood there.

(B) APPEARINGS

As the opening conversation comes to an end, Euclides says to the boy: "Well, boy, take the book and read" (143c). The book that the boy reads is a narrative of the conversation between Socrates and Theaetetus, as later reported by Socrates, and as then written down with such care by Euclides that, as he says, "Nearly the entire λόγος has been written down by me" (143a). This narrative as read by the boy constitutes the entire remainder of the dialogue.[8]

Initially the conversation is between Socrates and Theodorus; Theaetetus is not yet present. Theodorus hails from Cyrene, a prosperous Greek colony in Libya. Originally he was a pupil of Protagoras, who in various imaginary guises will be lent a voice by Socrates so as to make his appearance in the dialogue. Theodorus did not, however, continue under the tutelage of Protagoras but instead eventually concentrated on mathematics. Shortly after the conversation gets under way, Socrates observes that Theodorus is also skilled in astronomy, calculation, music, and everything connected with education (παιδεία). Still further into

8. Since the *Sophist* and then the *Statesman* explicitly continue the conversation begun at this point in the *Theaetetus* but begin straightaway with the conversation and not with introductions that would frame the conversations, the question arises as to whether all three conversations are to be taken as being read from Euclides' book. The fact that Euclides' description of his book mentions only that it records the conversation between Socrates and Theaetetus—whereas the conversations in the other two dialogues are between different pairs of characters—dictates against the supposition that all three are framed by the introductory conversation in the *Theaetetus*. In addition, there are no explicit indications in the *Sophist* or the *Statesman* that they are framed in this manner, but only that they continue the main conversation in the *Theaetetus*.

the conversation, Theaetetus will describe some of Theodorus' mathematical research.

Socrates' opening remark sounds a political note, resonating in this respect with his announcement at the end of the dialogue that he must set out to confront the indictment that has been brought against him. Confessing to Theodorus that he cares less about the youth of Cyrene than about those in Athens, he inquires whether there are any worthy of mention among the young Athenians who associate with Theodorus because of his prowess in geometry. In orienting the conversation toward the youth of Athens to the exclusion of the Cyrenian youth who might have been associated with Theodorus, Socrates attests to a certain bond with the πόλις. It is a bond that does not exclude opposition, that does not prevent him from assuming the role of a gadfly, as he will soon declare in his defense. It is a bond by which, as he will also declare, he is a gift to the πόλις rather than, as the would-be judges will charge, a corrupter of the Athenian youth. It is this bond and all that it entails that has now come under indictment and that will soon be put on trial but to which Socrates will continue to attest to the end. Thus, the beginning of the conversation opens, from afar, onto the entire course of what is to come; it gestures toward the entire chronology in which the *Theaetetus* is inscribed.

Without yet calling him by name, Theodorus proceeds to praise Theaetetus; it is at this point that he describes Theaetetus' φύσις as wonderfully fine and offers the image of him as flowing like a flow of olive oil. Theodorus stresses the youth's resemblance to Socrates, his snub nose and bulging eyes. Theaetetus looks very much like Socrates; he is, in his appearance, a double of Socrates. Shortly after Theaetetus appears on the scene, he will refer to another double of Socrates, one who will remain silently present throughout the conversation but who, on the following day in the conversation presented in the *Statesman*, will replace Theaetetus as the interlocutor of the main speaker. He is a companion of Theaetetus and is named Socrates. Theaetetus calls him Socrates' ὁμωνύμος (147d), his homonymous double, his double in λόγος. Thus, there are two doubles of Socrates in the dialogue: his double in appearance and his double in λόγος.

As if his presence were evoked by Theodorus' praise of him, Theaetetus at that very moment appears on the scene. One assumes—though it is not said and hence not indicated—that at this moment Theodorus gestures toward the youths who are approaching, as he reports to Socrates that the remarkable young man he has just described is the one "in the middle" (144c). Thus, Theaetetus—his name still not mentioned—is accompanied by at least two fellow gymnasts, one of them Socrates' homonymous double.[9] As Theaetetus approaches, Socrates recognizes him and identifies him as the son of Euphronius; but Socrates does not know his name, which Theodorus has still not mentioned. Thus, the scene is one in which appearance is privileged and λόγος is deferred. This scene mirrors the course that the conversation will follow, from an interrogation of appearances alone to one in which λόγος, too, is finally brought under consideration.

Theaetetus and his companions have been exercising. Thus, the scene of the ensuing conversation can be identified as located near a gymnasium. They have been oiling themselves, as was the practice after vigorous exercise. Having finished, they walk toward Socrates and Theodorus, gliding smoothly—one assumes—their bodies well-oiled. As they approach, Theodorus finally calls the name of the youth on whom he has heaped such praise. Addressing Theaetetus directly, he asks the youth to come over and sit by Socrates.

It should be noted that none of this action, none of these deeds, is directly reported as such in Euclides' book. It is reported only by being described in what Theodorus says, only in his λόγος.

The point of departure for the conversation between Socrates and Theaetetus is provided by Theodorus' remarks about Theaetetus' resemblance to Socrates and about his virtue and wisdom. Socrates proposes an interrogation in this regard, and though Theaetetus suggests that perhaps Theodorus was speaking in jest, Socrates assures him that this is not Theodorus' way. Socrates formulates his proposal in these words: "Well then, it is time, my dear Theaetetus, for you to display and for me to examine" (145b). The word Socrates uses to designate what Theaetetus is to do is a form of ἐπιδείκνυμι: display, exhibit, demonstrate, show forth. So, Theaetetus is to show himself forth, and Socrates is to look at, to behold, to examine (σκοπέω) what gets shown forth.

As the showing is set to begin, Socrates mentions that there is one small point about which he is in a state of perplexity, that is, in an ἀπορία,

9. Nothing that is said precludes there being more than two youths accompanying Theaetetus. If there were more, it is necessary only that there was an even number of them, since Theaetetus is said to be in the middle. If it is supposed that there were only two, one of whom was the young Socrates, then there remains an unnamed and indeed otherwise unmentioned youth who presumably listened silently to the conversation. There could of course have been other such youths in attendance along with Theaetetus and the young Socrates, any odd number of them.

a place without passage, where it is hard to see one's way through, where one is at a loss as to how to get through. Linking wisdom (σοφία) and knowledge (ἐπιστήμη), Socrates then formulates the question expressing that about which he is perplexed. It is the question: What is knowledge (ἐπιστήμη)? The comparison that Socrates draws between taking up this question and playing a certain child's game[10] signals that, though it is not Theodorus' manner to jest, the conversation between Socrates and Theaetetus is likely to include a bit—perhaps more than a bit—of playfulness. Soon it will appear that the conversation incorporates even the kind of playfulness in which a person (an actor, for example) plays at being another, enacting a role in the theatre.

Theodorus implores Socrates to urge one of the youths to answer the question, declaring that he is "unused to conversations of this sort" (146b) and appealing also to his age. Theodorus' reluctance to engage in such conversations will continue throughout, and he will repeatedly resist Socrates' efforts to draw him into the questioning. Socrates thus turns to Theaetetus and poses the question directly: τί σοι δοκεῖ εἶναι επιστήμη? (146c). In a conventional translation, this says: What in your opinion is knowledge? More literally it says: What does knowledge seem to you to be? In the question everything depends on the verb δοκεῖ/δοκέω. It can mean *to suppose, to think*, and the question could be translated accordingly as: What do you suppose knowledge to be? Or: What do you think knowledge is? The corresponding noun is δόξα, which means *supposition*, what one thinks about something, what one supposes or thinks something to be—hence the conventional translation as *opinion*. Yet, the verb δοκέω means not only to suppose or think but also *to appear, to seem,* even *to appear to be something*. What the double meaning indicates is that, for the Greeks, a supposition or opinion is not merely a subjective state maintained independently of the way things appear or seem. Rather, the connection is such that one comes to have a supposition or opinion on the basis of the way in which things appear, in accordance with how they seem. It is imperative that this connection between opinion and appearing be constantly borne in mind in order to understand what the Greeks take to be at issue in their discussion of δόξα, in discussions such as that which occurs later in the *Theaetetus*.

---

10. The game involves throwing a ball against a wall and counting the number of bounces before it is caught. As Socrates mentions, the one who makes a mistake must sit down and be donkey, whereas the one who is correct is declared king.

To Socrates' question, Theaetetus responds by offering several knowledges: whatever one might learn from Theodorus—geometry and the others mentioned earlier, as well as shoemaking and all other τέχναι. Socrates' response to this lavish offer is decisive: "Yes, but the question, Theaetetus, was not this, of what there is knowledge, nor how many of these there are; for we did not ask because we wanted to count them [ἀριθμῆσαι] but in order to come to know knowledge [γνῶναι ἐπιστήμην] whatever it itself is" (146e). Socrates' words introduce, without calling attention to it, the enormous complexity and difficulty that will necessarily haunt any attempt to answer the question "What is knowledge?" Indeed, Socrates' formulation leaves this complexity and the resulting difficulty somewhat under cover by employing two different (though hardly distinguishable) words for knowledge. Yet this usage only veils the complexity; it does not by any means entirely conceal it. To answer the question "What is knowledge?" would amount to coming—as Socrates says—to know knowledge. And yet, it is evident—and the *Meno*, for instance, makes it even more so—that to come to know anything requires that one already know it in advance. For if one knew nothing about that which one aimed to know, one could not aim at it, that is, one would not know how to go about seeking to know it; nor, having come to know it, could one know that it was precisely this that one had set out to know. In the unique instance of knowing knowledge, the difficulty is still further compounded: unless one already knows what knowledge is, one will not even know what it means, what is required, to set about coming to know. Once one enters the orbit of such questioning, one is inevitably exposed to the risk that, as Socrates says, "one goes around on an endless road" (147c).

Stymied by Socrates' refusal of the bounty he has offered, Theaetetus appeals to what he knows best. Surmising that Socrates is asking the same kind of question that he and his companion, the young Socrates, recently asked, Theaetetus launches an account of the mathematical research that, under the tutelage of Theodorus, he and his companion had undertaken. His account concerns specifically the research on incommensurables that he and his companion had carried on beyond what they had been taught by Theodorus. Theaetetus refers to some drawing shown them by Theodorus concerning δυνάμεις, literally *powers*, but in modern mathematical terminology *roots*; the sense is that to say that 3 is the power of 9 means that 3 has the power, if multiplied by itself, to produce 9. In the present passage the word δύναμις is used initially to mean roots (Greek: powers) in general, but then is restricted to those kinds

78 THE FIGURE OF NATURE

of roots on which the research has been focused. Theaetetus reports that with the drawing Theodorus had shown them that the three-foot (i.e., the side of a square of area 3—so what we call √3) and the five-foot (so, √5) are incommensurable with the unit; he had gone on through the other incommensurables up to the seventeen-foot. What Theaetetus and young Socrates attempted was to extend this without limit, to gather into one (συλλαβεῖν εἰς ἕν) all the roots, since their multitude seemed unlimited, to gather them into one, by which all these roots can be named (147e). Yet—curiously—they began not by gathering into one but by dividing into two, indeed by dividing into two ones. Specifically, they divided all numbers into square numbers (i.e., those that can be formed by multiplying two equals) and oblong numbers (i.e., those that cannot be formed in this way but only by multiplication of two unequal numbers). The line that forms a side of the square of a square number they determined as—gathered under the one name—a length (μῆκος). The line that forms a side of the square of an oblong number they determined as a root (δύναμις in the more restricted sense). These two kinds, lengths and roots, correspond to what later will be termed rational and irrational numbers.

THEAETETUS' MATHEMATICAL RESEARCH

I. Divide all numbers into two groups
   1) Square numbers (product of equal factors)

       e.g., 4:

   2) Oblong numbers (product of unequal factors)

       e.g., 3:   8:

II. Then divide into:
   1) Lines that form square of square number = length (μῆκος)

                                    2 is a length

2) Lines that form square of oblong number = root (δύναμις)

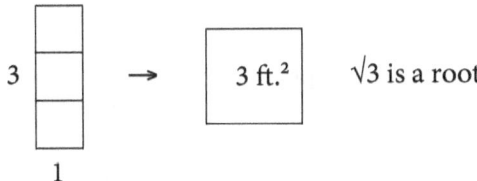

The ostensible point of this mathematical paradigm is that just as Theaetetus and his comrade gathered the roots into a one corresponding to the name, determining the bounds or limits of what the name δύναμις names, so now—Theaetetus understands—he is to gather knowledges into a one corresponding to the name *knowledge*, delimiting what the name names. And yet, this example has turned out to be rather curious. In order to gather a certain multitude of numbers (the roots) into one, Theaetetus and his comrade have had to gather *all* numbers, the entire multitude, into two ones. More precisely, they have gathered all numbers into two ones two times, into two pairs of ones, first into square and oblong numbers and then into lengths and roots. Furthermore, one of these ones, the one designated by the name *root* (δύναμις), is such that each of the many gathered under it is incommensurable with the unit, incommensurable with the one; here there is, then, a gathering-into-one of a many none of which is one or even has a common measure with one. Once these features are noted, one cannot but suspect that the gathering of knowledge into one will likewise turn out to be something like a gathering into two ones, even a double gathering into two ones. Still further, one will anticipate that in the gathering of knowledge, the many to be gathered into one of the two ones will be such that each of that many will be incommensurable with the one. In other words, one will expect that the multitude gathered into one of the two ones would contain no ones whatsoever nor anything even commensurable with one. This is, then, the anticipation, a kind of still open forestructure, that is evoked by the mathematical paradigm, a kind of schema for the gathering of knowledges that the dialogue will venture.

Theaetetus has thus begun the self-display enjoined by Socrates. In fact, by the time he has finished describing his research on the incommensurables, he has shown himself three times. There is, first of all, his appearance on the scene as he, in the middle of the band of youths, all with well-oiled bodies, walks toward Socrates and Theodorus. Then, secondly, he shows himself as a mathematician in his way of responding initially to Socrates' question about knowledge: he *counts off* a number of knowledges rather than offering the one that would be knowledge itself. Then, thirdly, he again shows himself as the mathematician he is, but much more elaborately through his account of his research on the incommensurables. Interwoven with these appearings of Theaetetus, there is a playful debate between Socrates and Theaetetus about the appearance of Theodorus. Theodorus has praised Theaetetus, but if Theaetetus fails to live up to that praise, then—as Theaetetus says—Theodorus appears false (φαίνεται ψευδής) (148b).

This series of intersecting appearings and suspicions of appearings enacts in anticipation what will be taken up in the subsequent discourse of the dialogue, the deeds (ἔργα) thus mirroring in advance the λόγοι. More specifically, this play of appearings foreshadows the interrogation of φύσις in which everything will center around the question of how natural things appear. But more immediately this little drama of appearings leads up to a very remarkable statement in which Socrates exhorts Theaetetus to address the question about knowledge just as he dealt with the question of the incommensurables. Socrates says to him: "Come then—you just now [ἄρτι] showed the way beautifully—try to imitate your answer about powers; just as you comprehended them, though they were many, in one εἶδος, so too try to address the many knowledges in one λόγος" (148d).

In this passage the word *just-now* (ἄρτι) recurs. But now, inconspicuously, it marks a small interval opened from the now. For it refers not to the moment in which Socrates is speaking, but to the very recent moment when Theaetetus presented his mathematical research. Now Socrates is asking him to open a broader interval, an interval of imitation, a mimetic interval: in the time just about to come, Theaetetus is—is exhorted—to imitate what he did in—and in reiterating—his mathematical research. Thus it appears still more clearly that the mathematical research that resulted in a double gathering into two ones will provide the model, the schema, for addressing the question of knowledge. It is from mathematics that the paradigm will be taken for the attempt to understand what knowledge is.[11]

---

11. *Paradigm* is to be understood here in the full sense developed in the *Statesman* (277a–278e). Most importantly, the word designates both a model or archetype in reference to which something is to be understood *and* an example from which something is, by comparison, to be understood. The word is to be taken literally: a παράδειγμα (from παραδείκνυμι) is something to be placed alongside (παρά) in such a way as to show, to demonstrate (δείκνυμι), something about something else. In the *Statesman* the Stranger offers a paradigm of paradigm: boys learn to recognize letters in longer, more

In his way of formulating the exhortation to Theaetetus, Socrates interrupts the natural flow of the discourse in order to refer to beauty, to Theaetetus' having just now shown the way beautifully (καλῶς). The word says precisely what Theaetetus has accomplished and what he is being exhorted to undertake. To show the way—through and beyond an ἀπορία, for instance—means to light it up, to make it shine forth brightly so that one can make one's way along or through it. It is precisely such engendering of luminosity that is said in the word: to show the way beautifully is to make it shine forth and appear luminously. Indeed, in the Platonic dialogues beauty has always to do with shining, as the sun and the moon shine; it has to do with something coming forth—or being brought—into the light so that it shines forth and shows itself.[12]

In the exhortation to Theaetetus, Socrates specifies the precise sense of the imitation that he urges the youth to carry out: as he comprehended the many powers in one εἶδος, so now he is to address the many knowledges in one λόγος. The word εἶδος, which here makes its first appearance in the dialogue, is derived from εἴδω, a verb that in classical Greek was obsolete in the present active, this form being supplied by ὁράω. The verb means *to see*, and εἶδος designates *that which is seen*, that is, the look that something has—that it shows—when one looks at it. The sense of the word extends, however, beyond the look of a particular thing. For not everything has an entirely unique look; many things look alike, many share a look. Thus, εἶδος also comes to designate the common look that things share, that things of the same kind share; extended along this line, it acquires the sense of *kind*, converging—if not quite coinciding—with γένος. To comprehend as one a manifold of things that have a common look or that constitute a kind (such as the incommensurable powers) is precisely to grasp them in their εἶδος. Even when what is seen stretches beyond momentary perception, as in arithmetic operations or demonstrations, the connection with seeing and the seen remains decisive, and the translation of εἶδος as *look* is to this extent justified.

Yet in the wake of the exhortation to Theaetetus, the question remains: How is it that addressing a manifold in one λόγος would

---

complex syllables by placing syllables in which they already know the letters alongside the longer, more complex syllables in which they do not yet recognize the letters.

12. In the *Phaedrus* (250d–e) one of the words that Socrates uses to describe the beautiful (τὸ καλόν) is ἐκφανέστατον, the most shining forth, that which from itself appears most luminously. See my discussion in *Being and Logos*, 153–59.

constitute an imitation of the operation of comprehending a manifold in one εἶδος? What is the relation between λόγος and εἶδος, between word and look, such that addressing a manifold in speech amounts to imitating the gathering of a manifold into one εἶδος? At this point in the dialogue, the question goes unanswered, not even posed as such.

Now it is Socrates' turn to put in a special appearance, or rather, to put on appearances, to play at being something other than merely Socrates. The playfulness of what is to follow is indicated by the word *laughable*, by which at the outset of the play Socrates addresses Theaetetus ("you laughable fellow"—ὦ καταγέλαστε [149a]). In his play-acting, Socrates transforms himself into a midwife, yet in such a way that this figure reflects disclosively on his actual practice. The reflection is especially evident in the way that his description of his maieutic practice parallels in many respects the description of his practice that he gives in his defense as presented in the *Apology*.

Indeed, Socrates' initial remarks concerning his maieutic practice serve to link this τέχνη (as he calls it) to the charges that will soon be brought against him. While imploring Theaetetus not to reveal his practice of this τέχνη, he confides to him that others are unaware of his practice and say that he is most strange and that he makes people perplexed. Socrates is well aware of the antipathy that he has aroused and that has led to the charges soon to be officially brought against him by Miletus. His portrait of himself as a midwife can be regarded as an apology given even before—though not long before—the hearing at which he will be formally charged.

Another point of contact with the defense speech that Socrates will soon deliver at his trial is broached by his expressed lack of pretension to wisdom. Just as midwifery is assigned to those who because of age can no longer bear children, so likewise, Socrates attests, he is "barren [ἄγονος] of wisdom," is "hardly wise at all" (150c–d). It is precisely in this connection that he invokes the name of Artemis: just as midwives, incapable of bearing children, attend to those in childbirth, so Artemis, the virgin goddess, "has childbirth allotted for her protection" (149b–c). Like ordinary midwives, Socrates merely assists others to give birth, applying his maieutic practice to men rather than women and to the soul rather than the body. Inasmuch as the practice of ordinary midwives imitates that of Artemis and, in turn, Socrates' practice is analogous to that of midwives, his practice is also carried out in imitation of the goddess. Artemis provides a mythic paradigm both for ordinary midwifery and for Socratic maieutics.

The invocation of this mythic paradigm resonates with the account of his practice that Socrates will present at his trial, the account in which he links his practice to a pronouncement of Apollo delivered through the Delphic Oracle. Receiving this pronouncement, that there was not one wiser than he, yet realizing his own lack of wisdom, he put the pronouncement in question by interrogating others, searching thereby for someone wiser than himself. It was precisely such interrogations that led his fellow Athenians to regard him as most strange and as guilty of making people perplexed. And yet, as he also explains, his practice eventually became a kind of service to the god.[13] In his account of his maieutic practice, he refers repeatedly to the god (ὁ θεός). He attests that "the god compels" him to act as a midwife (150c); thus, he declares—as he will again at his trial—that his practice is in service to, at the command of, the god. He declares also that among those who associate with him, it is those "whom the god allows" who make "wonderful progress" (150d). The midwifery, he says, is the responsibility of "the god and me" (150d). The god—or, rather, goddess—with whom Socrates thus links his maieutic practice would seem to be Artemis, since it is she whom he explicitly mentions. Indeed, the masculine form θεός can be used in place of θεά to designate a goddess,[14] though the latter could have been used in order to make the reference unambiguous. That the ambiguity remains can perhaps be taken as an allusion to Apollo, the twin brother of Artemis.

One other link to the *Apology* is forged by Socrates' account of what happens with the young men who come to him and seek his service as midwife. Some of them, he says, have gone away from him too soon and have lost the child; he mentions, in particular, Aristides.[15] Others who have left later return and beg to join him again. Then, says Socrates, his

---

13. See my discussion in *Being and Logos*, chap. 1, sec. 3.

14. In the *Timaeus* (21a) Plato uses θεός (rather than θεά) to refer to Athena. Such usage is also found in Homer; for example, in the *Iliad* (8:7) he refers to female gods using the form θήλεια θεός in distinction from the male (ἄρσην).

15. At the outset of the *Laches*, Lysimachus expresses his concern for the education of his son Aristides. He seeks a teacher who will know what kind of educational undertakings will instill excellence in his son and make him worthy of the name he bears, that of his distinguished grandfather, a famous general who commanded the Athenians at Marathon and at Salamis (179b–180a). At the end of the dialogue it is decided that Socrates will undertake the task of educating Aristides (200e–201c). Beyond what Socrates says when mentioning Aristides in the *Theaetetus*, there is no reliable report on the youth's failure as a student. (See Debra Nails, *The People of Plato: A Prosopography of Plato and Other Socratics* [Indianapolis: Hackett, 2002], 49–50.)

δαιμόνιον comes and checks him from associating with some, while allowing him to associate with others. The reference to the δαιμόνιον links the present discourse to the *Apology*, in which Socrates evokes this figure as a voice (φωνή) that sometimes holds him back from certain undertakings, while at other times it poses no hindrance, presumably by remaining silent, certainly not by urging him on (*Apol.* 31d). In the account given at his trial, he says that it is from engaging in politics that he is held back, whereas in the *Theaetetus* he speaks of being held back from exercising his maieutic practice on certain of those youths who want to return to him. Yet these two spheres in which the δαιμόνιον voices its prohibition are closely allied: it is primarily Socrates' allegedly corruptive influence on the youths—along with his talk of such strange divinities as his δαιμόνιον—that has led to his entanglement with the current political factions in Athens.

Yet, what is Socratic midwifery? What is this maieutic practice? In a sense it is imitative of ordinary midwifery, which quite conspicuously serves as a paradigm set alongside Socratic practice in such a way as to demonstrate the character of this midwifery of the soul. Yet, in turn, both Socratic and ordinary maieutics fall under the reign of Artemis, which is thus a paradigm for both, a paradigm primarily in the sense of an archetype. But granted the mimetic and paradigmatic interweavings, what actually constitutes Socratic maieutics?

A midwife must be skilled at recognizing who is pregnant. Such recognition occurs precisely at the juncture where, in response to Socrates' exhortation, Theaetetus reiterates that he cannot answer the question about knowledge (as he did those about lengths and powers) and yet adds, most significantly: "I am incapable . . . of getting rid of my concern with it" (148e). Theaetetus thus attests that he is caught in an ἀπορία, as in a narrow passage where he is unable to see the way through yet equally unable to retreat. Appearing in this condition, it is as if he cannot bring forth that which, at once, it is his concern to bring forth. Socrates the midwife declares: "Dear Theaetetus, it is not because you are empty that you are suffering labor pains but because you are pregnant" (148e).

It belongs to the midwife's practice to administer drugs and incantations in order to induce labor and make the delivery easier. In Socratic midwifery the drugs and incantations consist of questions—of just such questions as "What is knowledge?"—and of interrogation such as that by which Socrates has exposed the weakness of Theaetetus' answer to this question. The semantics of the word φάρμακον (medicine/poison) serves to emphasize that drugs are dangerous, that they can bring relief but also can inflict harm, that they can heal or kill. In administering such drugs along with the words of incantation that go with them, Socratic maieutics is dangerous not only for the one for whom they are prescribed but also, perhaps even above all, for the one who administers them. Precisely such danger looms over the series of conversations that begins with the *Theaetetus*.

Socrates advances the claim that midwives are the most capable matchmakers, that they know just what kind of men and women should be brought together to produce the best children. When Theaetetus expresses doubt about this claim ("I do not know that at all" [149d]), Socrates insists that midwives in fact take great pride in this capacity but that they tend to avoid the practice lest they seem to be engaged in pandering. Yet what kind of matchmaking does Socrates practice? He says that some he recognizes as not being pregnant, and that in such cases he sends them off—gives them in marriage—to Prodicus or some other wise person.[16] The question that remains is whether this is the only kind of matchmaking that Socrates practices, namely, matching a young student with a teacher. Or is there something else—a certain λόγος, for instance—that might make one pregnant with knowledge? Can one be impregnated by words?

Finally, with his account of his maieutic practice virtually completed, Socrates assumes the role of midwife. Already recognizing that Theaetetus is pregnant and is suffering from labor pains, Socrates now prepares to engage what he describes as the greatest capacity of his τέχνη, that of "testing whether the thought [διάνοια] of the young man is giving birth to a phantom and falsehood [εἴδωλον καὶ ψεῦδος] or to something genuine and true [γόνιμόν τε καὶ ἀληθές]" (150c). Socrates encourages Theaetetus to submit to his midwifery, asking that the youth not be angry if, once this greatest capacity is exercised, it turns out that Theaetetus' offspring is only a phantom and is to be thrown away.

---

16. It is unclear whether the reference to Prodicus is entirely ironic. He was highly respected in Plato's time as a teacher of rhetoric, and he is mentioned in several dialogues. In the *Laches* Socrates says that he is the best of the sophists at drawing exact distinctions between words (197d; cf. *Meno* 75e). In the *Protagoras* where Prodicus appears as a speaker, Socrates calls himself "a pupil of Prodicus" (341a—but see also *Meno* 96d).

Both the discourse on midwifery and the playful enactment that accompanies it belong to the two evolving scenes that run through the entire first part of the *Theaetetus*, the scene of the appearance of the philosopher and the scene of φύσις. Here the philosopher appears—both in word and in deed—in the guise of the midwife. As such the philosopher is displayed through the paradigm of ordinary midwifery, while both are set against the archetypal paradigm of the reign of Artemis. Yet the reign of the goddess extended beyond childbirth to encompass the bestowal of fruitfulness on trees and of fertility on man and beast. Everything having to do with the birth and flourishing of living things came under her dominion. All that gathers around the semantics of the word φύω (beget, generate, bring forth) and its middle-passive form φύομαι (to be born or begotten, to come forth) falls under the reign of Artemis, even, most remarkably, the privative counterpart, the death that she has the power to inflict on women (in childbirth primarily) and on the beasts that she pursues in wild nature. Her domain is φύσις, nature as inseparable from birth, from coming forth into the light.

The image of the philosopher thus converges with the scene of nature. In aiding the process of giving birth, the philosopher imitates the maieutic practice that Artemis carries out in reigning over nature as such. Like the goddess, the philosopher aids in the birth of something pertaining to nature; he brings to light something about nature that otherwise goes unheeded, indeed something—a kind of supplement—that must be grasped, that must be brought to light, if nature in its perpetual flow is to be heeded in truth.

(C) VENTRILOQUY, THE PROTAGOREAN ΛΟΓΟΣ, AND THE SCENE OF ΦΥΣΙΣ

Encouraged by Socrates, Theaetetus ventures to say what knowledge is: "It seems to me, then [δοκεῖ οὖν μοι], that whoever knows something perceives that which he knows, and as it now appears [φαίνεται], knowledge is nothing else than perception" (151e). Though now saying it as a one rather than many, Theaetetus actually says twice what he takes knowledge to be. Though they may appear to be merely appositional, the two statements are not at all identical. In saying that "whoever knows something perceives that which he knows," Theaetetus leaves open the possibility that, though knowledge involves perception, it may also involve something else, something beyond perception. This excess, only hinted at here, will come decisively into play later in the dialogue. However, the other statement, that "knowledge is nothing else than perception," completely excludes this possibility. According to it, knowledge in no way goes beyond perception. Much of the discussion to follow is geared to the second statement, up to the point where, near the end of the entire first part of the dialogue, an exceeding of perception finally comes into view. Only then will it be possible to discern how, in the response to Socrates' question that finally takes shape, Theaetetus will have proceeded in a way analogous to that pursued in his mathematical research. Also, in anticipation of what is to come, it should be noted that both statements are couched in the idiom of seeming and appearing, which will be precisely the theme once the interrogation of Theaetetus' answer commences.

Socrates proposes right away that they examine in common the answer that Theaetetus has given: in this proposal Socrates slyly slips in the word *common* (κοινόν), though without as yet giving the slightest hint that this word will eventually name the excess to which Theaetetus' first statement alludes. Donning the guise of the midwife, Socrates specifies that the goal of their common examination is to determine whether the progeny to which Theaetetus has given birth is genuine or full of wind.[17]

Socrates begins by immediately identifying Theaetetus' answer with something said—and written—by Protagoras, though "in a somewhat different way" (152a). Socrates quotes from Protagoras' book entitled *Truth*: "Man is the measure of all things, of the things that are, that they are, and of the things that are not, that they are not" (152a). That this Protagorean λόγος has some connection with Theaetetus' answer is suggested by Theaetetus' ready admission that he has read it often. Yet it is by no means immediately apparent that the Protagorean λόγος says the same as what Theaetetus has said in saying that knowledge is perception.

Thus Socrates proceeds to interpret the Protagorean λόγος. His interpretation is cast as a series of equations. He begins by explaining exactly what he takes Protagoras to have meant: that as each thing appears (φαίνεται) to me, it is such to me. He mentions the example of the same wind that appears cold to one person and not cold to another. In such a

---

17. The word here is ἀνεμιαῖον, which is derived from ἄνεμος, meaning *wind*. Literally translated, ἀνεμιαῖον means *windy* or *full of wind*, but commentators and translators have typically taken it to mean *wind-egg*, that is, an egg fertilized only by the wind, that is, an unfertilized egg.

case it will be said that the wind is cold to one and not cold to the other. This is, then, the first equation: of being with appearing. But, in turn, to say that the wind appears cold is to say that we perceive it as cold. Hence, the second equation identifies appearing with perception. The third equation follows from the first two: in Socrates' precise formulation, "perception is always of being [or: of what is—τοῦ ὄντος]" (152c). Socrates then draws the conclusion: perception is knowledge—just as Theaetetus said (at least in his second statement). And yet, the conclusion does not quite follow, or rather, it follows only if a tacit assumption is granted, namely, that knowledge is of being, or, more precisely, that whatever is of being, whatever is directed at being, is knowledge. Once this assumption is granted, then from the third equation (perception is always of being) it follows that perception is knowledge. This series of moves serves to draw Protagoras and all that is associated with him into the conversation, and indeed, though he is deceased at the time of the conversation, he will appear in it in various guises. Still more significant thematically, Socrates has shown indirectly that the equation of perception with knowledge depends on their common reference to being; granted this result, the stage is set for differentiating them by showing that perception is not *of being* but only *of becoming*.

To Socrates' declaration linking perception, being, and knowledge, Theaetetus answers: "It appears so [φαίνεται]." This response hints at one of the primary tensions in the entire discourse on knowledge as perception: the appearing in which the identity of knowledge and perception appears cannot have been a matter merely of perception, despite the identification made between appearing and perception. Theaetetus cannot have perceived that perception is knowledge, as one perceives that the wind is cold.

At this point something very remarkable happens. This ugly man Socrates, whose ugliness—precisely, his not being beautiful—was mentioned earlier by Theodorus in comparing Theaetetus to him, suddenly *swears*: πρὸς χαρίτων—By the Graces! Thus he invokes the goddesses, all daughters of Zeus, who represent charm, beauty, grace. The Graces were associated with flowers, especially those of spring. They were bringers of Olympian joy. When they danced enchantingly to Apollo's lyre, the gods delighted in them. They bestowed beauty and charm on every scene to which they came. The invocation of the Graces gestures toward what Socrates is about to venture, namely, to translate the Protagorean λόγος into a scene, to carry out a *mise-en-scène* of his statement that man is the measure of all things. As Socrates invokes the Graces—not in a charming fashion but by swearing—one wonders whether he does so because this scene is to be beautiful and graceful or because it lacks— and so is in need of—beauty and grace. As he goes on to depict the Protagorean scene, it will become ever more manifest that this scene is indeed so devoid of beauty and grace that nothing less than the Graces, nothing less than a gift from above, would be required for its restoration. Yet the scene must first be displayed, as it is and even more with respect to what it is not, before there can be any hope of enticing the Graces to descend upon it.

Even before the swearing, at the point where he finally establishes the link between the Protagorean λόγος and Theaetetus' thesis that knowledge is perception, Socrates says that perception as knowledge is not false (ἀψευδές). The evident point is that there is no such thing as false knowledge, that knowledge as such is true. And yet, it is significant that he avoids—conspicuously avoids—the word *true*, substituting instead *not false*. This avoidance has to do with a particular rhetorical feature that he is about to introduce and that remains in play throughout the remainder of this passage. What his swearing actually introduces is the curious supposition that Protagoras put forth an enigma for the many (namely, the saying that man is the measure of all things) while, on the other hand, telling the truth as a secret to his pupils. In this supposition Socrates' irony is unmistakable. And yet, irony is not simply a matter of lying, of declaring something that one knows is false. It is, rather, a way of saying that also reveals something, perhaps even something that cannot be said directly. It is a way of saying something that does not, as with a simple, straightforward declaration, allow one to place before what is said the words: it is true that . . . So, as Socrates proceeds to speak about the truth that Protagoras would have told his pupils in secret, he is not simply representing as true something that in fact he takes to be false. Rather, his relation to what he goes on to say is more subtle and complex. This can be seen in the rhetorical structure that his speech will display and in the shifts this structure undergoes: sometimes, as at the beginning, he lends his voice to the Protagorean λόγος; sometimes he turns critically against it, only then to assume the voice of Protagoras, speaking for him as if he were present.

Such rhetorical structure is evident as Socrates begins to say the Protagorean truth: as he begins to say it, he defers saying it in order first to take a certain distance from what he is about to say. Before saying it, he declares: "I will speak a very non-trivial λόγος, that . . ."—then going on to say the Protagorean λόγος. Thus, instead of simply saying that λόγος, he says first that he is going to say it—that is, he lends his voice to it, almost as in ventriloquy.

Socrates proceeds to ventriloquize the esoteric Protagorean truth by drawing out the consequences of the exoteric maxim, which equates appearing with being. There are three consequences. The first he states immediately: "Nothing is itself one alone by itself [or: in relation to itself (αὐτὸ καθ' αὑτό)]" (152d). The example of the wind has already broached this consequence. Since the wind appears cold to me and not cold to you, it *is* both cold and not cold. But this means that it is not one in relation to itself, not one with itself, not one and the same as itself. For, being one thing, for instance, cold, it can also be something other than what it is, something different, not cold—hence, not one but two, cold *and* not cold.

From this dissolution of oneness the second consequence follows directly: "You could not name correctly anything of whatever sort, but if you address it as large, it will also appear small, and if heavy, light . . ." (152d). Thus, the dissolution of the oneness of things, of their self-sameness, makes it impossible to speak of them correctly. If something is called by one name, for instance, large, it can—and, presumably, will—appear as something other, as calling for a different name, for instance, small; hence, in calling it large, one will have spoken incorrectly. The dissolution of oneness thus engenders a disruption of the capacity of speech to address things correctly; it produces a disempowering of λόγος.

As Socrates broaches the third consequence, his speech begins to evoke the scene that results from the dissolution of oneness. In other words, he lends his voice to the Protagorean λόγος in such a way as to translate that λόγος into a scene in which the consequences deployed by that λόγος are depicted. His description is of a scene of genesis: "From locomotion and movement and mixing with one another, there come to be all the things that we say *are*, addressing them incorrectly; for nothing ever is, but [everything] always becomes" (152d). The scene is one of unceasing genesis, of perpetual becoming. It is not that things come *to be*, that they undergo becoming and then *are*. Rather, they become without ever having come *to be*, without ever being. The scene is aptly described when, a bit later, Socrates speaks of "becoming in becoming" (153e). Or, as Protagoras presumably would have told his pupils in secret, it is a matter of the dissolution of being. This is the third consequence.

Little wonder, then, that Theaetetus, whose thesis Socrates has equated with the Protagorean λόγος and thus linked to this scene, was described, even before he appeared, as flowing just as a flow of olive oil flows without a sound. For this provided at the outset a mobile image of the scene that has now been displayed, a scene in which being as such is dissolved into sheer flow and in which, with the disempowering of λόγος, there can be only silence, a flowing without a sound.

From the third consequence another follows directly. If being is utterly dissolved into perpetual becoming, then it can no longer be maintained—in accordance with the third of the equations—that perception is of being. But if perception is not of being, then it cannot be identified with knowledge. Hence, at this point in the dialogue, as the discussion of Theaetetus' thesis has just begun, this thesis—that knowledge is perception—is already refuted. This development alone suffices to suggest that in the first part of the dialogue much more is at stake than merely Theaetetus' thesis.

Already, at the moment when he first declares the dissolution of being, Socrates—ventriloquizing—invokes all the wise (except Parmenides) who are said to attest to this dissolution: not only Protagoras but also Heraclitus and Empedocles, and indeed poets too, Epicharmus of comedy and Homer of tragedy.

The references to Heraclitus and Empedocles cannot but appear problematic, and this appearance can perhaps never be entirely dispelled, if for no other reason than that the extant textual basis is very limited in comparison with that to which Plato could—though here too there is uncertainty—have had access. To be sure, there are Fragments cited from Heraclitus that can be construed as declaring the dissolution of being into becoming, perhaps most notably those that invoke flowing, as with rivers: not only the oft-cited dictum "It is not possible to step twice into the same river" (B91) but also, perhaps more pertinent, Fragment B49a, which reads, "Into the same river we step and do not step, we are and are not." Also, in the declaration that nature loves to hide itself, Heraclitus can be taken as referring to the withdrawal of nature from the capacity of λόγος to grasp it. On the other hand, there are Fragments in which Heraclitus appears to be declaring a limit to the dissolution of things into sheer flow. For instance, the statement from Fragment B1, "I distinguish each thing according to φύσις and declare how it is," seems not only to declare a certain distinctness of things but also to accord being to them.

In the case of Empedocles, there are indeed Fragments that describe the separating and coming together of the roots from which all things come forth. Furthermore, Empedocles emphatically denies the possibility of an origination of being. Yet the sense of this denial is that the things that are cannot have come from nothing; it is not a denial of things that are, not a declaration of the dissolution of being. That there are things having a certain distinctness seems to be explicitly proclaimed when in Fragment B21 Empedocles writes that from the roots "all things that were, that are, and that will be sprang."

Perhaps in the final analysis—if there can be a final analysis—what is most appropriate is to take the reference to the two earlier philosophers as invoking only a single aspect of their thought, an aspect that borders on—though it is not identical with—the dissolution of being. Thereby the reference abstracts entirely from those moments by which both Heraclitus and Empedocles rigorously limited the dissolution into mere flow.

Socrates cites neither Heraclitus nor Empedocles, nor the comic poet Epicharmus. It is only the poet of poets who is actually cited: "Homer with the line 'Oceanos and mother Tethys, the origin [or: progenitor—γένεσις] of the gods' has said that everything is the offspring of flowing and motion" (152e). Since Oceanos is the river that encircles the entire world, and Tethys, his sister and consort, is the mother who gave birth to all other rivers, to link the genesis of the gods to this couple is tantamount to saying that they—and, by implication, all things—are the offspring of flowing and motion. The word *flowing* (ῥοή) is the same word that Theodorus used earlier in the figure of Theaetetus as flowing like a flow of olive oil. But now the scene is one where all things flow forth from flowing, even the gods themselves. In the scene into which Socrates has translated Theaetetus' thesis (or at least the allegedly equivalent Protagorean maxim), the youth is presented with an image that, though carried to the extreme, nonetheless resembles him. In ventriloquizing Protagoras, Socrates has furthered Theaetetus' display of himself, now in the guise of a scene where all is determined as flowing like a flow of olive oil.

The line cited from Homer occurs twice in the *Iliad* (14.201, 302).[18] Both times the line is spoken by Hera, and both times the speech in which

---

18. The line is also cited in the *Cratylus* (402b) and, as in the *Theaetetus*, is linked to Heraclitus. The line is also repeated later in the *Theaetetus* (180d). Oceanos is also mentioned by Homer in other connections; conceived as the river encircling the whole world, Oceanos is, according to Homer, represented on the rim of the shield of Achilles (*Iliad* 18:607; see also 20:4). In the great myth of the earth at the end of the *Phaedo* (112e), Socrates refers to Oceanos as the greatest and outermost of rivers.

it occurs is introduced with the words "Then, with false lying purpose, the lady Hera said . . ." In the first instance she is speaking to Aphrodite, to whom she addresses the following request: "Give me loveliness and desirability, graces with which you overwhelm mortal men and all the immortals." Then she continues: "Since I go now to the ends of the generous earth, on a visit to Oceanos and mother Tethys, the origin of the gods." In the second instance she is speaking to Zeus and begins with this same line about going to visit Oceanos and Tethys. In both cases she is being deceptive. She says that she is going off to reconcile Oceanos and Tethys, who raised her and who have now become estranged from one another. However, she puts forth this pretense only as part of her scheming to entice Zeus into making love to her; and it is in order to be able to seduce him that she asks Aphrodite to bestow loveliness and desirability on her. Yet, not only are these words spoken in the cause of a deceptive, seductive act, not only are they uttered in a situation marked by lying and deception, but also what they say is false: though Oceanos and Tethys were responsible for the generation of the Oceanids and river gods (*Theogony* 364), the gods—at least the Olympians—are descended, not from them, but from Cronus and Rhea (*Theogony* 453–58), who were siblings, not progeny, of Oceanos and Tethys (*Theogony* 132–37).[19] Thus, within this λόγος, itself disempowered by the very disempowerment of λόγος that it says, even the words of Homer—like all others—turn out to be false and deceptive, a lie even about the gods.

Socrates has shown how the dissolution of oneness is entailed by the Protagorean maxim: if the wind, appearing cold to one person and not cold to another, can thus be both cold and not cold, then it is not one but two. However, the further consequence, the dissolution of being, does not simply follow from that of oneness. For it would seem that even something that is not one with itself could still *be*. In fact, as the conversation continues, it becomes clear that the dissolution of being can be legitimately declared only on the basis of an analysis of perception.

19. In the passage in the *Timaeus* (40d–41a) where the genealogy of the gods is reported, Chronos and Rhea are listed as children of Oceanos and Tethys, in open conflict with the familiar genealogy given by Hesiod. This falsification could be regarded as allied with the irony with which the entire discussion of the traditional gods—in distinction from the δημιουργός and those associated with him—is introduced. We must, says Timaeus, believe what those in earlier times reported about the gods; for they claimed to be offspring of the gods and so must have had reliable knowledge about their ancestors, even though—here the irony is unmistakable—what they say has scant likelihood and no demonstration.

Shortly after Socrates assembles all those philosophers and poets who are said to be in agreement about the dissolution of being, he launches such an analysis. According to this analysis, vision involves the interaction between the eyes and what strikes the eyes. In any given case, the actual seeing and the color seen are products of this interaction. If something different had struck one's eyes, if another's eyes had been struck, or if one's eyes had been struck at another time (when their condition would have been different), the products, that is, what would have been seen, would have been different. Born from the interaction, color is relative and momentary, constantly changing as other eyes or one's own in another condition are struck by something different. Thus, Socrates says to Theaetetus: Do not suppose the color white "to be itself as something other outside your eyes" (153e). Rather, he says, it is "something in between that has become private [ἴδιον] for each" (154a). One sees only private singularities or occurrences as they are generated in the flow of radical becoming.

In the midst of the analysis of perception, Socrates inserts a remark that serves to refer this entire discussion back to the beginning of the dialogue. He says: "Let us pursue the speech of the moment [or, more literally: the just-now speech—τῷ ἄρτι λόγῳ] and set down nothing as being one itself by itself" (153e). The word ἄρτι, the first word of the dialogue, refers the discussion back to the beginning. Yet, what is most significant about the repetition of this word at this point is that it says precisely the scene that has come to be displayed at this juncture of the dialogue: it is a scene of utterly stigmatic, idiotic singularities that in no way extend beyond themselves, not even to the extent of being themselves. Thus, as Socrates says when, a little later, he reiterates the analysis: "Nothing is itself by itself [αὐτὸ μὲν καθ' αὑτὸ μηδὲν εἶναι]" (156e–157a).

As he is discussing the color white as something momentarily generated in between the eyes and that which strikes the eyes, Socrates says: "Do not even assign any place [χώρα] to it" (153e). Here Socrates brings to bear on the analysis the word that, in several dialogues and especially in the *Timaeus*, assumes a sense so enigmatic and radical that it, at once, undermines and reconfigures the very sense of sense. Χώρα does not simply mean place (τόπος). It would be more appropriate to regard it as the very condition of there being place at all, thus as a kind of place before place. In the *Timaeus* the χώρα is spoken of as "granting an abode [ἕδρα] to all things having generation" (52b). It is by being generated in the χώρα that phantom-like things are able in some degree to cling to being and so to be.[20] Yet, on the Protagorean scene, what is generated cannot even be assigned to the χώρα; for with the utter dissolution of being, these idiotic singularities do not even cling in the least to being.

Once Socrates has invoked the grand assembly of philosophers and poets as though they formed a great army marching by with General Homer at their head, he offers a series of signs (σημεῖα) in the sense of marks or indications by which something can be recognized. He begins by identifying that of which the signs to be offered are signs, that which they serve to indicate: they are signs "of the λόγος that says that motion produces what seems to be and what becomes, while rest produces non-being and perishing" (153a). They are signs, then, that make it possible to recognize in fact what this λόγος says; they are signs that make manifest the connections declared by this λόγος. And yet, the entire discourse on these signs is rife with comedic moments, through which what is in deed made manifest are the laughable consequences to which the Protagorean λόγος and its *mise-en-scène* can be made to lead. For example, Socrates mentions that windlessness and calm seas are instances of the kind of motionlessness that is destructive. Yet he forgoes mentioning something else, this omission constituting the comedic moment: while windlessness and calm seas might make sailing a bit slow and even require that one take to the oars, this is of little consequence compared to the destructiveness of high winds and storms at sea. As another such sign, Socrates mentions that it is by locomotion and rubbing that heat and fire are generated, and that these, in turn, generate everything else; yet what he forgoes mentioning is the destructiveness of which fire is also capable. Thus, what the comedy serves to expose is the utter ambiguity of these allegedly adequate (ἱκανά) signs.

Socrates adds that it is also from motions of this kind that "the genus of animals gets born" (153b). The reference to being born (φύεται) broaches a connection to φύσις. It thus offers a first hint at what will gradually come more and more to light: that this scene of becoming, of sheer becoming where nothing ever is, this scene from which being is entirely removed, is, in a sense, just φύσις. That this scene is the scene of φύσις becomes unmistakable at the point where, having declared the dissolution of being, Socrates—still ventriloquizing—brings this consequence to bear explicitly on λόγος itself. The voice of—that is

---

20. See my account in *Chorology*, chap. 3.

lent by—Socrates declares what is required in the wake of this dissolution: "being [τὸ εἶναι] must be removed from everywhere" (157b), that is, the word *to be* must be removed from λόγος, deleted entirely from discourse. Yet he adds, with evident irony: "not that we have not been often compelled even now by habituation and lack of knowledge to use it." But, he continues, in place of a discourse of being, "one must make utterances in accord with φύσις [κατὰ φύσιν]—becomings and makings and perishings and alterings" (157b). Here the identification is explicit: the scene into which the Protagorean λόγος has been translated, the scene on which oneness and being are dissolved in favor of sheer becoming, is a scene of φύσις, and to speak of it requires that one's utterances be in accord with φύσις. But, if φύσις is a scene of incessant flow, if it is a perpetual becoming in which the dissolution of oneness and being disempowers λόγος itself, how is it possible to speak κατὰ φύσιν? Is it perhaps because this requirement is aporetic that Socrates avoids the usual words that denote speaking (such as λέγω, φημί), substituting for them the word φθέγγεσθαι? The word can mean *to make utterances* in the sense of speaking; but it can also be used to designate the manner in which an animal makes sounds (as a horse neighs) or even the production of sound by an inanimate object (as a door creaks).[21] It is also the word that Heraclitus uses in Fragment B92 to describe the raving, prophetic voice of the Sibyl: "The Sibyl with raving mouth, uttering mirthless, unadorned, unperfumed sayings, reaches a thousand years with her voice because of the god."[22] How, then, is it possible to speak κατὰ φύσιν? How is it possible to speak appropriately of φύσις? Must one resort to a raving, prophetic voice like that of the Sibyl? What sounds could possibly resonate with φύσις? Or with the flow of olive oil flowing without a sound?

---

21. Forms of the word φθέγγομαι (φθέγγεσθαι is the middle-passive infinitive) occur several times later in the *Theaetetus*. It is used in reference to Protagoras' book *Truth*; Socrates suggests that in making his utterances, Protagoras was merely jesting (162a). The word is used also to refer to the speech of foreigners, which can only be heard but not understood (163b). Much later in the dialogue it is used to designate the sounding or ringing by which one can test whether something that is tapped on rings solid or hollow (179d).

22. In the *Phaedrus* Socrates mentions the Sibyl, along with the prophetess at Delphi and the priestess at Dodona, as an example showing that madness (μανία) is not simply an evil but rather that the greatest blessings come to us through madness when it is sent as a gift of the gods (244a–b).

Yet, even before he fully unveils the scene of φύσις and—with the detachment of the ventriloquist—poses the danger that λόγος could degenerate into the ravings of the Sibyl, Socrates already begins to resist being utterly carried away by the incessant flow of becoming. He declares, in effect, that even in the flow of φύσις there is a certain determinacy or continuity. Or, more precisely, he poses the following conditional: "Then if that against which we measure ourselves or with which we come in touch were large or white or hot, it would never become anything different when it ran into something else, if, that is, it itself did not alter at all" (154b). Socrates' declaration thus says that something could not come to be something else if it did not itself undergo alteration.

On the other hand, Socrates refers to the wonderful and laughable things (θαυμαστά τε καὶ γελοῖα), which seem to be counter to what he has just said: "Since as it is now, my friend, we are being compelled somehow or other to say without qualms wonderful and laughable things, as Protagoras would say and everyone who tries to say the same as he does" (154b). Socrates explains by referring to, as he calls it, a small paradigm: "we say surely that six dice, if you apply four to them, are more than the four and one and a half times as much, and if you apply twelve, they are less and half as much, and it is unsupportable to speak in a different way" (154c). He then formulates the wonderful and laughable things as a question put by Protagoras to Theaetetus: "If Protagoras or someone else asks you, 'Theaetetus, is it possible for anything to become larger or more otherwise than by increase?' what will you answer?" (154c). In view of the small paradigm, Theaetetus must answer *yes*, that it is possible. Protagoras' declaration thus proclaims indeterminacy and discontinuity, proclaims that it is possible for something to become larger or more otherwise than by increase.

Socrates stresses the opposition between the two declarations, referring to a battle between the two being waged within their souls. He mentions still another example: he is now taller but a year later will be shorter than Theaetetus, even though his size will not have altered. Then he exclaims: "And there are moreover myriads upon myriads of these" (155c). The opposition is between two ways of construing the scene of becoming. According to the first, something can become larger (for instance) only by itself gradually increasing; it will have been a determinate size, and there will be continuity as it increases to a larger size. According to the other construal, change can be utterly discontinuous and indeterminate.

In setting up the opposition as he does, Socrates is in effect posing the question: How can the flow of φύσις be granted and yet a certain moment of determinacy be maintained? How, within the flow of φύσις, can a certain determinacy come to hold sway and to limit the flow? How can oneness and being be dissolved without determinacy also vanishing? If there is no determinacy within the flow of φύσις, then λόγος will be virtually silenced, at least in its capacity to say things as they are, to speak κατὰ φύσιν. And yet, what could limit φύσις without simply violating it? For, if determinacy were to come to φύσις from elsewhere, it would not be a determinacy that truly belonged to φύσις. A λόγος geared to such alien determinacy would still remain incapable of speaking κατὰ φύσιν. It would not really touch φύσις but would be more like the raving, prophetic, mad voice of the Sibyl sounded from beyond φύσις.

It is curious—indeed remarkable—that Socrates says these wonderful and laughable things precisely at the threshold of what may be the most decisive dramatic moment of the dialogue: the moment when Theaetetus confesses his wonder and Socrates declares wonder to be the beginning of philosophy. How is it that wonder breaks out precisely at this moment when Socrates has just said these wonderful and laughable things? One cannot but wonder whether something is at stake here that is less than apparent on the surface.

A hint is provided when Socrates refers to the opposites battling within their souls, when he refers to them as φάσματα (155a). The word φάσμα is related to φαίνω (bring to light) and so to the middle voice form φαίνεται (appear). It can designate an *apparition* or *phantom*, that is, a strange appearance, as of something not present. Φάσμα can also mean a *sign from heaven*, a *portent*, something exceeding, yet given to, human vision. Or, if there is stress on the moment of strangeness, of deviation from the natural course of things, the word can mean *monster*.

What is at stake here is the peculiar logic outlined by the wonderful and laughable things. It is a logic of excess or of monstrosity. If the wonderful and laughable declaration is reformulated as a statement, it reads as follows: something can become larger or more otherwise than by increase, that is, in some way other than by itself altering, increasing. What must this involve? In such a case a certain excess will be added to the thing so that it becomes larger; that is, something else exceeding the thing will be added to it, so that it becomes larger yet without itself increasing. And yet, it will *itself* become larger through this excess only if the excess *also belongs* to it. Otherwise it would simply be conjoined with something else (the excess), that is, would not *itself* become larger. Thus, the excess that comes to be added proves already to belong. *And yet* it must also *exceed*, must also remain other than the thing; for otherwise, if it were simply homogeneous with the thing, there would be mere increase rather than a becoming larger *otherwise* than by increase.

It is only by way of such a logic that φύσις can gain a certain determinacy. On the one hand, the determinacy must come upon φύσις from beyond; it must as such exceed φύσις. Yet, on the other hand, in order to be the determinacy *of* φύσις and not merely something externally imposed, it must also somehow belong to φύσις. Thus, the determinacy must be such that it both supervenes upon φύσις and yet also belongs to it; the determinacy must exceed φύσις and yet be integral to it. If there is such determinacy of φύσις as would make it possible to speak κατὰ φύσιν, then it must be governed by such a logic of excess. In different terms, what is to be added to nature in order that it actually be nature rather than mere Protagorean flow must be something other than nature, something that exceeds nature but that belongs nonetheless to nature. This figure is one of inverted monstrosity: it is a divergence from nature within nature that comes not from within nature but from beyond it.

This figure corresponds to that into which the three kinds are assembled in the *Timaeus*. According to that discourse, everything that is generated—which itself (if it could be itself) is a mere phantom, a mere image that is not yet even an image of anything, that utterly lacks determinacy (like the incessant flow on the Protagorean scene)—is generated in the χώρα in order that it might cling "to being at least in a certain way on pain of being nothing at all" (*Timaeus* 52c). Only in this way, by being generated in the χώρα, do generated things acquire a modicum of the determinacy that belongs to and hence is derived from the entirely selfsame first kind.[23]

Both in the *Theaetetus* and in the *Timaeus*, the figure of φύσις is that of sheerly or largely indeterminate things (that are therefore not yet things) on which a determinacy from beyond these (non-)things supervenes, so that, clinging thus to being (to determinacy), they become natural things rather than remaining mere phantoms engulfed in the Protagorean flow. To be sure, there is no mention of the χώρα at the point in the *Theaetetus* where this logic of excess takes shape. Yet

23. See my *Chorology*, 118–24.

the earlier injunction regarding such a (non-)thing as color, not to "assign any χώρα to it" (153e), expresses in a privative mode the manner in which the χώρα could be properly inserted in the figure of nature drawn in the *Theaetetus*.

It is, then, at the moment when this strange logic of excess has just been broached that Theaetetus—not without swearing—declares: "And by the gods, Socrates, I wonder exceedingly as to what these things are, and sometimes when I look into them I truly feel dizzy" (155c). As Theaetetus voices this performative exclamation, one can imagine the look of wonder on his Socratic-like face. One can even imagine that in the account of this moment that Euclides heard from Socrates there may have been a description of the appearance of wonder in Theaetetus' bulging eyes. Yet, one could *only imagine* the appearance of wonder, since Euclides' book presents only the λόγοι of the conversation. Theaetetus in the flesh, even just remembered in the flesh, Theaetetus' φύσις, which Socrates came to admire, is reduced to Theaetetus' λόγος. The event of Theaetetus' wonder thus offers a glimpse of the larger battle, that between φύσις and λόγος. Just as φύσις, equated at this point with radical becoming, disempowers λόγος, drives it out, reduces it to silence, so that there remains only the inarticulable flow, as with the flow of olive oil flowing without a sound; so, on the other side, the λόγος, Euclides' λόγος, drives out φύσις, reduces it to λόγος. As the boy reads from Euclides' book, both Terpsion and we who, in turn, read what the boy reads become aware of Theaetetus' wonder only because in Euclides' book he declares that he wonders, only by way of his performative statement.

Theaetetus declares not just that he wonders but that, in view of the wonderful and laughable things, he wonders *exceedingly*. If construed literally, the word ὑπερφυῶς means: in a manner that goes beyond (ὕπερ), that exceeds, nature (φύσις). Thus, Theaetetus is saying that, in view of the excess or exceeding of nature to which the wonderful and laughable things point (by their contrast with things subject to determinate change), he wonders in a way that exceeds nature. Indeed, his words attest that he wonders in a way that exceeds *his* nature, so that he loses his natural sense of balance and grows truly dizzy. Thus, in and through his wonder, there occurs a discordance: Theaetetus remains who he is, retains the nature to which Theodorus referred and to which Socrates will immediately refer again, and yet he wonders in a way that exceeds his nature, in a way that draws him beyond the limits of his nature, outside the natural course that he otherwise would follow. A living creature that, while within nature, also exceeds nature so as to be, in some manner, beyond or outside the natural course of such creatures is nothing less than a monster (τέρας). Theaetetus' wonder as he attests to it through what he says is monstrous.

Socrates responds: "For Theodorus appears, my friend, to have guessed not badly about your φύσις. For this pathos is very much that of a philosopher, that of wondering [θαυμάζειν]. For nothing else than this is the origin [ἀρχή] of philosophy, and it seems that whoever said that Iris was the offspring of Thaumas made a not bad genealogy" (155d). This response, together with Theaetetus' attestation, constitutes a pivotal moment in the dialogue, and especially in the first part. It is the moment when the appearance of the philosopher first fully takes place. In Theaetetus' wonder, as it appeared to Socrates and as it is attested in Euclides' book, the very origin of philosophy comes to light. Through his wonder there shines forth the ἀρχή from which the practice of the philosopher originates and by which it continually is governed. This is the moment when philosophy, making its appearance in Theaetetus, is also turned back upon itself so as to disclose its origin. Furthermore, the appearance of the philosopher occurs at the very moment when φύσις is exceeded and monstrosity comes into play. In this way it is attested that the origination of philosophy is integrally connected to the exceeding of nature.

To his identification of wonder as the origin of philosophy, Socrates conjoins the observation that whoever said that Iris was the offspring of Thaumas made a not bad genealogy. The conjunction conveys a parallel: just as Thaumas (whose name means wonder) produced Iris as his offspring, so wonder is the origin of philosophy. Iris is the goddess of the rainbow and indeed is hardly differentiated from the rainbow itself.[24] What, then, is the sense of the parallel between philosophy and Iris? What does philosophy have to do with the rainbow, to such an extent that they have a common origin?

In this regard two features of the rainbow need to be considered. The first is its character as joining heaven and earth, as binding together the upper region and the region in which humans have their abode, namely, the earthly region or nature. In the course of the *Theaetetus*, signs have begun to appear that philosophy, too, is charged with bringing something of the upper region, of what lies beyond nature, to bear

24. See Aristotle, *Meteorology* 375a1.

upon nature. It is significant also that Iris was regarded as a messenger of the gods, at least according to a passage in the *Cratylus* that reads: "Iris also seems to have received her name from εἴρειν [to speak], because she is a messenger" (408b).²⁵ A messenger of gods not only may convey something from beyond to the natural, human region but also, precisely in and through speaking, will articulate something, will reveal something in its articulation, in its determinacy. Hence the second feature consists in the rainbow's articulating the light of heaven.²⁶ The rainbow is a spectacle in which light is articulated and the various colors are distinguished, the colors to which humans give names and so take up into λόγος. Thus, it could be said that the rainbow is a paradigm within φύσις for the bringing of determinacy into φύσις. It is precisely the demand for such determinacy, provoked by the contrary case of the wonderful and laughable things, that has evoked Theaetetus' wonder.

The genealogy, which, according to Socrates, is a not bad one, comes in fact from *the* genealogist Hesiod. According to the *Theogony* (265), Iris was the offspring of Thaumas and Electra. In turn, Electra is identified as the offspring of Oceanos and Tethys, the true offspring in contrast to the lie told by Hera and quoted earlier in the dialogue in feigned support of the Protagorean λόγος. The name Ἠλέκτρα corresponds to the word ἠλέκτωρ, which means *beaming* or *shining sun*.²⁷ Thus, her name connotes shining such as that in which things come to appear. Thus, if Iris is regarded as a mythic name and image of philosophy, then Socrates' genealogical remark leads to the conclusion that both Iris and thus also philosophy arise from shining and wonder; they arise when a shining breaks forth that evokes wonder and thereby prompts articulation, which is brought to bear on the shining spectacle of what appears.

---

25. The *Iliad* tells of how Zeus sends Iris as a messenger to turn back the chariot of Hera and Athena (*Iliad* 8:398; cf. Hesiod, *Theogony* 780).

26. This phenomenon is already described by Anaximenes according to the reports numbered A7 and A18 (discussed in chap. 2).

27. The word occurs in Homer. For example: "So Paris, son of Priam, came down from high Pergamon, gleaming [παμφαίνων] in his armor like the shining sun [ὥ τ' ἠλέκτωρ]" (*Iliad* 6:513). Or again: "Achilles . . . gleaming [παμφαίνων] in his armor like shining Hyperion [ὥς τ' ἠλέκτωρ Ὑπερίων] (*Iliad* 19:398). The word also occurs in Empedocles' Fragment B22 (discussed in chap. 4), which names four roots and describes their operation: "For all these—shining sun [ἠλέκτωρ] and earth and sky and sea—are one with their own parts that by nature [πέφυκεν] wander off among mortal things."

Just as Iris bestows articulation on the beaming sunlight, so the philosopher brings the articulation of speech to bear on the shining within φύσις, matching, indeed marking, the determinacy that renders φύσις otherwise than the Protagorean scene of perpetual flow. Both Iris and the philosopher prove, then, to be messengers to the abode that is called φύσις.

Since wonder has been identified as the ἀρχή of philosophy, it is to be expected that once Theaetetus comes to wonder exceedingly, there will be a shift in the character of the discourse. Whereas previously Socrates has spoken largely in behalf of Protagoras, though with ironic distance, practicing a kind of ventriloquy, he will now begin to assume other—indeed various—stances toward Protagoras, not only speaking in his defense but also sometimes turning against him in criticism, at other times speaking even in his voice.

Such a shift indeed occurs shortly after the discourse on wonder. Socrates proposes that, rather than simply presenting the Protagorean λόγος, they now undertake to expose the truth that lies hidden in it, that is, "to seek out the truth hidden in the thought of a famous man" (155d-e). In this proposal Socrates is playing on the title of Protagoras' book: they are to expose the truth that, in Protagoras' book *Truth*, remains hidden. As Socrates is about to begin this further quest, he alerts Theaetetus to be sure that none of the uninitiated are listening. The uninitiated he identifies as those who believe that nothing *is* except what they can grasp with their hands. Lacking the Muses, they are too crude to apprehend the truth beneath tangible things. Socrates extends his playful simulation of the mystery rites, now informing Theaetetus that he will tell him about the mysteries from which the uninitiated are excluded. It turns out that the very first mystery that Socrates reveals, namely, that all is motion (τὸ πᾶν κίνησις ἦν) (156a), is such that the uninitiated would be conspicuously incapable of grasping it. As long as they persisted in their belief that what *is* is identical with what can be grasped with the hands, they would only be stymied by the mystery, which thus would remain for them an inaccessible mystery. For, if everything is motion, then nothing can be grasped, neither with the hands nor by any other means; as soon as one tries to grasp something, it will—in one or more respects—have changed into something else, will have elusively slipped away. It is in order to establish this hidden truth, to reveal it in its truth, that Socrates extends the analysis of perception to the point where being is dissolved and is entirely excluded from λόγος.

Following the analysis there is an indication of another change of stance on the part of Socrates. Theaetetus exclaims: "I am not even capable of understanding how it is with you, whether you are speaking your own opinions or you are testing me" (157c). In response, Socrates reiterates that his role is that of midwife, thereby insisting that the consequences to which the analysis led are not his own opinions; thus Socrates stresses his distance from the discourse to which he has been lending his voice. In this manner he introduces a series of critical discourses aimed at the Protagorean λόγος. His first critical assault appeals to the cases of dreams and of illness, including madness, and of every other condition that is said to bring about misperceiving. In all such cases there are "false perceptions," so that it is not true that what appears to each person *is* for him. Rather: "None of the things that appears is [so]" (158a).

On the one hand, Socrates' appeal to such cases constitutes a refutation of the Protagorean maxim and the consequences to which it has been shown to lead. Socrates thus asks: in view of such cases, what λόγος now remains for one who says that perception is knowledge and that what appears *is* to the one to whom it appears? Already, in fact, Socrates has shown that for those who hold these opinions, virtually no λόγος remains, not even enough to allow them to state these opinions, since such a statement is compelled to use the word *is*. On the other hand, the statement "None of the things that appears is [so]" says not only the opposite but also the same thing as the Protagorean discourse, namely, that nothing (not even what appears) *is*, but all is sheer becoming. The opposite thus turns into that to which it is opposed—a reversion that is entirely appropriate on the Protagorean scene.

Socrates again changes his discursive stance. He proceeds to tell how those who espouse the Protagorean λόγος would answer the apparent refutation that he has just given by his appeal to cases of misperception. More precisely, Socrates now speaks in the name of these Protagoreans as if they were conversing with Theaetetus. Thereby he installs an imaginary dialogue within the actual dialogue between himself and Theaetetus. The response that the Protagoreans (imagined as present) give through the voice of Socrates simply appeals to the analysis of perception already developed: when wine tastes sweet to Socrates in health and bitter to him in illness, the perception of wine as bitter is not a false perception but rather is just the offspring of a different interaction, of an interaction of wine with the ill Socrates rather than with the healthy Socrates. Socrates generalizes—speaking still as the

Protagoreans in conversation with Theaetetus—and leads the entire discourse back to the assertion that all things are in motion, that there are only flowings (ῥεύματα). This assertion, along with Theaetetus' identification of knowledge with perception, is then cast as Theaetetus' newborn child—Socrates now dropping his role and addressing Theaetetus directly. The stage is thus set for the amphidromia, the "run-around." The reference is to the custom whereby a week after birth, a child was carried around the hearth, introduced to the family, and named; at this time a decision was made whether to raise the child or abandon it. So it is, then, with Theaetetus' newborn: it must be decided whether it is worthy of being raised or is a mere wind-egg to be abandoned.

As the run-around is about to begin, Theodorus suddenly interrupts. He swears ("By the gods") and demands that Socrates speak, that he explain just what he considers wrong with the view of the Protagoreans. Socrates is, no doubt, aware that the interruption is prompted by Theodorus' earlier association with Protagoras as his teacher, and as the discussion with him gets under way, Socrates refers to Protagoras as Theodorus' comrade (ἑταῖρος).

Socrates does not immediately give the speech that Theodorus demands he give. Though very shortly he will present such a speech, he first of all refers, once again, to his own lack of knowledge and to his role as midwife. Yet, in the way in which he now construes these, there is a slight difference, one that will prove to make all the difference. He says: "I know nothing superior, *except a little bit*, as much as to take a λόγος from another who is wise and accept it in a measured way" (161b; emphasis added). One wonders what this "little bit" is, whether it is really just a little bit. One wonders, too, whether in making this statement he is simply disclaiming in advance the speech that he is about to make, the speech demanded by Theodorus, to whom it will be addressed, or whether he is assuming some responsibility for it, at least for applying to it some measure.

The speech begins, as does philosophy itself, with wonder, with wonder about the beginning: "I wonder about the beginning [ἀρχή] of the λόγος [the reference could be to the Protagorean λόγος or to Protagoras' book *Truth* or to both], that in beginning his truth he did not say 'Pig is the measure of all things or dog-faced baboon" (161c). Socrates' question is simply: Why could one not say of any animal that has perception that it is the measure of all things? Furthermore, as he goes on to explain, if whatever view one holds—based on what appears—is true, so that one is the measure of one's own wisdom, then no one is wiser than anyone else, nor even wiser than any other perceptive animal such as a tadpole. Thus, Protagoras in particular has no claim to such wisdom as would entitle him to be the teacher of others and to demand great wages for his service. If the truth (the book *Truth* perhaps) of Protagoras is true, then his tacit claim is ludicrous, as, Socrates slyly suggests, are his own maieutic conversations. Socrates even suggests, in a playfully ironic tone, that Protagoras' declarations may have been made in jest, as mere play.[28]

Theodorus' response is a blunt reminder that Protagoras was his friend. He disavows all responsibility for his friend's being refuted and urges Socrates to resume conversing with Theaetetus as his respondent. There follows a brief exchange about wrestling, about stripping and wrestling with the young men. The exchange serves as a reminder that the entire conversation takes place near a gymnasium where the young men—Theaetetus and his companions—have been exercising, and perhaps wrestling. For the time being, Socrates releases Theodorus from the contention and resumes his conversation with Theaetetus—with *wondering* Theaetetus: "Do you not share my wonder at being no worse in wisdom than any human being, nor perhaps even than the gods?" (162c). Theaetetus swears: "By Zeus," and replies that he does indeed share this wonder. At this point Socrates again shifts his stance, now speaking for Protagoras himself or for someone else who would speak for Protagoras. Speaking as if he were Protagoras, he reprimands all three of them—Theaetetus, Theodorus, and himself—for not providing any demonstration (ἀπόδειξις) but rather proceeding solely by way of semblances or images (εἰκών).

Socrates abruptly drops his impersonation of Protagoras and now, assuming his own voice, launches into criticism of the thesis that knowledge is perception. He cites the case of a foreign language and asks Theaetetus whether, when we hear someone speaking a foreign language,[29] we know what the person is saying. If this were the case, then it could be said that in this instance hearing, which is a kind of perception, is knowing. Theaetetus' response displays his acute sense: he says that in such a case we know just so much as we hear, namely, "the sharpness

---

28. Socrates uses here the aorist form (ἐφθέγξατο) of the word φθέγγομαι (see note 21 above), thus suggesting that Protagoras' "declarations" may have been utterances hardly at the level of coherent speech.

29. Here again Socrates uses a form of the word φθέγγομαι. See note 21 above.

and flatness of the sounds" (163b–c), though what interpreters make of them we neither hear nor know. Socrates compliments Theaetetus, calling his answer "the best." That Socrates then immediately abandons disputing further with Theaetetus on these points indicates, not so much that the youth's response has rendered further dispute unlikely to produce results, but rather that his response has served to bring into focus precisely the difference that the further dispute will eventually address, the difference between merely hearing sounds and knowing what they signify. Theaetetus' response has in fact touched on the most decisive result: that to know what the sounds signify requires more than merely hearing (that is, perceiving) the sounds; it requires passage beyond mere perception, requires that perception be exceeded. No doubt it is because Theaetetus' response broaches this difference that Socrates calls it the best.

As Socrates shifts to the question of memory, broaching thereby another such difference, something monstrous begins to make its appearance. Socrates begins with a counter-statement in the form of a question: Is it possible that someone who has learned something and then remembers it could not know it when he remembers it? Theaetetus' reply exposes the monster lurking in this statement: "But how could that be, Socrates? What you are saying would be a monster [τέρας]" (163d). Passing over his own question whether he is being foolish, Socrates calls up a memory of something said in the recent past that concerns the present: "According to the speech just now [or: the just-now speech, the speech of the just-now—κατὰ τὸν ἄρτι λόγον], whoever saw something has become a knower of that which he saw" (163d–e). Implicit in Socrates' words is the thesis that an alleged knowing confined to the just-now would be simply perception, whereas, as he will proceed to show, memory—and hence knowledge as such—exceeds perception and its just-now. Socrates poses the situation in which someone, with his eyes shut, remembers something. Since he does not see it, it follows that he does not know it; but since he remembers it, he does know it. Now it is Socrates who declares this result to be a monster. The monstrosity lies in the fact that here there are two moments that do not naturally go together: knowing as seeing and knowing as remembering. The result is monstrous in a way not unlike that of a creature with the head of a human and the body of a lion.

In view of this monstrous—or, as Socrates also says, impossible (ἀδύνατον)—result, it cannot any longer be maintained that knowledge and perception are the same. But if knowledge cannot be identified with perception, then the initial question as to what it is must be undertaken anew. They must "speak again from the beginning" (164c).

And yet, the return to the beginning has only just been proposed when suddenly, abruptly, it is interrupted. Rather than taking up the question of knowledge anew, Socrates proceeds to sketch an image of himself and Theaetetus as gamecocks who have begun crowing before winning the victory. But—he declares—it would have been different if the father of the λόγος—or rather, as he now terms it, the μῦθος—were still alive. Since not even Protagoras' guardians—among whom is Theodorus, who is ready with excuses—will come to the rescue, Socrates insists that they must do so for the sake of justice. Socrates sketches still another image, a scene of someone stuck in a well—somewhat like Thales—who has one eye covered while seeing a cloak with his other eye. Such a person both sees and does not see, and if perceiving is knowing, he both knows and does not know.

Just before Socrates poses explicitly the question that is posed in deed by this scene, the question whether it is possible to know and not know, he calls it "the most dreadful question [τὸ δεινότατον ἐρώτημα]" (165b). The word δεινόν, used here in the superlative, means not only *dreadful* but also *powerful* as well as *wondrous*. The question not only is dreadful in the sense that the answer is lacking or unintelligible; it also is wondrous in the sense that it evokes wonder, that it is most evocative of wonder. It is also in this respect most powerful, but also in the sense that it is most capable of opening up the question of knowledge as such. For it will turn out that a conjunction of seeing and not seeing—and hence, on the assumption that perceiving is knowing, of knowing and not knowing—is possible; just as, later, knowledge will prove to involve a conjunction of perceiving with not perceiving, that is, with a moment that is not a matter of perceiving.

Now the feigned rescue of Protagoras begins. Socrates assumes the role of Protagoras, who is pictured as coming to engage in close combat. Socrates speaks simply as if he were Protagoras, even to the point of voicing Protagoras' charge that he, Socrates, has confused the youthful Theaetetus in such a way as to make Protagoras' views appear laughable. He charges also that in talking about pigs and dog-faced baboons, Socrates has himself acted like a pig. However, what Socrates presents—speaking as Protagoras to Socrates and Theaetetus—is not a conversation but rather, as is typical of the sophists, a long speech, a monologue, indeed one that is wordy and repetitive. Thus, Socrates is not only speaking for Protagoras but also is engaging in a kind of parody of sophistic rhetoric.

In the lengthy speech that Socrates voices in the name of Protagoras, there are two developments to be stressed. First of all, Socrates/Protagoras formulates in a precise manner the difference that earlier was said to generate a monster. It is the difference between the memory of something and the perception of it, that is, in the precise formulation, the difference between the now-present memory of something by which one was once affected but is no longer and the original affection. The second development concerns the paradoxical result that if each is the measure for himself, then all will be equal in wisdom, from the gods down to tadpoles. Socrates/Protagoras addresses the paradox by distinguishing between true and good: whatever appears to someone is true for him, but what appears to one may be better than what appears to another. The wise man is, then, the one who can make good things appear (and so be true to someone). He is the one who can bring about a change of condition so that what appears is better, as a physician can bring about improvement in one's condition so that food appears (tastes) good rather than bitter. It is likewise with a πόλις. Whatever appears to be right is so to that πόλις. The wise man is the one who can bring it about that the good, instead of evil, appears and so is right for the πόλις.

Marking the conclusion of his impersonation and defense of Protagoras, Socrates finally finds a ploy by which to draw reluctant Theodorus into the conversation. He recalls Protagoras' charge that he had confused the youthful Theaetetus in order to make Protagoras' views look ridiculous. Then, Socrates observes that all the others who are present, except for Theodorus, are boys. Consequently—says Socrates—the only way they can respond to Protagoras is to launch a critical discourse in which Theodorus serves as respondent; his age will prevent the earlier charge from being sustained. Socrates coaxes him by mentioning his mathematical expertise, which, if Protagoras' view were accepted, would come to nothing, since all would be just as competent in such subjects as he.

Theodorus responds by bringing up again the reference to wrestling and stripping; he refers even to battle, yet now not so much to resist Socrates' insistence that he enter the conversation but to underline the force of this insistence. Whereas the earlier reference was to the Spartans, now Theodorus declares that Socrates is less like the Spartans than he is like Sciron: the Spartans give one the option of going away rather than stripping, whereas Socrates—so says Theodorus—lets no one go until they have stripped and wrestled with him in λόγοι. The mention of Sciron offers a mythic image of Socrates in his capacity as insisting on combat in λόγοι; for Sciron was a mythical bandit who occupied the Scironian Cliffs near Megara and who, requiring passersby to wash his feet, kicked them over the cliff as they did so. Theodorus also compares Socrates to the mythical figure Antaeus, son of Poseidon and Gaia, a giant who lived in Libya and who compelled all comers to wrestle with him until, when they were overcome, he killed them. The mythic tales of both figures go on to relate how they were killed. Sciron met his end when Theseus, on his way to Athens, threw him into the sea. Antaeus was defeated and killed by Heracles. One account is that since Antaeus, whose mother was Gaia, derived his strength from the earth, Heracles lifted him into the air and then could crush him.

The two mythic references serve to indicate that wrestling in λόγος can expose one to extraordinary danger, that it may indeed be a matter of life or death. Again one is reminded that Socrates will soon go off to the portico of the King to face the indictment brought against him by Miletus. To these comparisons Socrates responds by declaring that they are excellent semblances of his disease (illness, affliction—νόσος). His point is that the mythic images depict him as involved in a struggle where the stakes are life or death, just as a disease or illness may expose one to the threat of death, just as Socrates, going off to the porch of the King, will be exposed to the threat of death. Socrates goes on to extend the mythic references to include a mention of the figures responsible for the deaths of Sciron and Antaeus. Insisting that he is more stubborn than Sciron and Antaeus, he declares that he has wrestled with myriads of Theseuses and Heracleses and, though he was thrashed, has not withdrawn, since, as he attests, a "dreadful love [ἔρως δεινός] of such gymnastics has slipped into me" (169c). So Socrates is, so it seems—or is he now beginning to play another role?—overtaken, afflicted by this dreadful love, this dreadful, powerful, wondrous love, by an erotic engagement in contesting λόγοι. It is curious that, as the contest is set to proceed, Socrates remarks that they should be careful not to "produce a playful kind of λόγος" (169c-d)—curious because what could be more playful than all this talk about wrestling?

Adopting a critical stance, speaking now in his own voice with Theodorus, who will be able to offer little resistance, Socrates brings the entire engagement with Protagoras to a conclusion. He offers three basic criticisms of the Protagorean λόγος.

He begins by citing Protagoras: "That which appears to each *is* to him to whom it appears" (170a). This declaration entails that all opinions are true. And yet—Socrates observes—especially in times of greatest danger (when there is war or pestilence or storms at sea), all believe that some are wiser than others, that some exercise true thinking, while others have false opinions. Socrates asks: "Are we to assert that humans always opine what is true, or at times true and at times false?" (170c). Socrates himself immediately gives the answer: "For it surely turns out on the basis of both that they do not always opine what is true but both" (170c). His point is: if one assumes the first alternative (that humans always opine what is true), then since humans (many, at least, in times of danger) opine that there are false opinions and since (by the assumption) this opinion must be true, it follows that there are false—as well as true—opinions.

Socrates' second criticism lets this result recoil on Protagoras himself. He refers to the many myriads who in any particular instance will regard one's opinion as false. He continues: if neither Protagoras nor the many (the many myriads, now called οἱ πολλοί) held the opinion that man is the measure, then the truth that Protagoras wrote (in his book *Truth*) would be true to no one. But if he believed it, as the many do not, then it is just so much more false as the number of those who do not hold the opinion. Thus, the many myriads rob Protagoras of his truth, just as the suitors robbed Odysseus.

Finally, Socrates lets the result recoil even further. Since Protagoras holds that all opinions are true, he concedes the truth of the opinion of those who think his opinion is false. Hence, he concedes that his own opinion is false.

Theodorus exclaims that they are running down his friend too much. Socrates responds with a comic image of Protagoras as run down into the ground (as, being dead, he would have been), but now as emerging from the ground but only as far as the neck. Protagoras' head—the bearer of λόγος, just ousted by the λόγοι of Socrates—would charge Socrates with talking nonsense, but then would sink back down again out of sight and be off running again, ever in motion.

As the extended engagement with the Protagorean λόγος comes to a conclusion—or rather, as it is about to be interrupted—Socrates finally makes it explicit that what is primarily at stake in this engagement—what has been at stake all along—is nature itself. The specific context is political: Socrates reiterates in a slightly different guise the distinction that, earlier, Protagoras was pictured as drawing between the true and the good. Now Socrates refers to the just and unjust and the holy and unholy; yet, rather than setting these over against the true, as Protagoras set the good over against the true, Socrates now closes the gap by directing his remark to the truth of precisely these things, the just and unjust, the holy and unholy. The advocates of the Protagorean λόγος are thus denied the only possible avenue of escape from the consequences that have now been demonstrated. As Socrates understates it, "they are willing to insist"—in fact, they have no choice but to say—"that none of these"—the just and unjust, the holy and the unholy—"is by nature [φύσει] with a being of its own [οὐσίαν ἑαυτοῦ]" (172b). Rather, as he adds, the common opinion about them becomes the truth.

Thus, not even these things, much less any others, are by nature. Rather, they appear now in one guise and then in another, their truth determined solely by the common opinions correlative to these appearings and shifting continually with them. In other words, not even these things remain the same as themselves; not even they retain the same determination. It is precisely this lack of selfsameness that marks them as things that are not by nature. They are not natural, because they have no being of their own but merely appear in ever varying guises. This, at any rate, is what the friends of Protagoras—including Theodorus, who indeed now assents—cannot but agree to.

What is most remarkable in this statement is the connection that it forges between nature and being. What belongs to nature and so is natural (φύσει) lies not in the flow of ever varying appearances but rather in what has a being of its own, in what remains itself, in what retains its determination even amidst the flow of appearances.

Thus it is that Socrates declares: "A greater λόγος, Theodorus, from a lesser λόγος is overtaking us" (172b–c). The stage is set for the advent of the philosopher and for the return of nature.

(D) THE SCENE OF PHILOSOPHY

The greater λόγος that now commences is the λόγος on the philosopher. Socrates adds almost immediately that they "are now taking a third λόγος in exchange for [or: from out of] a λόγος" (172d). Though the two previous λόγοι are not identified, their defining character and limits can with some degree of assurance be indicated. The first λόγος would have been the Protagorean λόγος as Socrates, in his ventriloquy and impersonations, lent it his voice (151e–157d). The second would have been the λόγος in which Socrates, reclaiming his own voice, turned against the Protagorean λόγος and carried out his criticism of it (157d–172d). The third is the λόγος, just now beginning, on the philosopher; as the second proceeded by turning against the first, so presumably the third will turn somehow on or from the second. On the other hand, at the end of this third λόγος (177b), Socrates will describe it as a πάρεργον: something beside the main work, something subordinate, secondary, even digressive. This description serves to indicate that there is a certain discontinuity with the previous λόγος. Especially pertinent in this regard is the contrast between the Protagorean and the counter-Protagorean orientation to the flow of φύσις, to φύσις construed as sheer becoming, and Thales' ascensional orientation, which is directed beyond φύσις so regarded, opening philosophy to a "beyond" that, in turn, bears on φύσις and breaks with the Protagorean figure. It goes almost without saying that there is playful irony in treating as a digression the λόγος that constitutes the center of the *Theaetetus*. The treatment is, in this regard, not unlike that accorded the extended account of philosophy that forms the center of the *Republic*.

Socrates begins the new—the third, the greater—λόγος by remarking on "how likely it is that those who have passed much time in the practice of philosophy appear as laughable speakers when they enter the courts" (172c). Precisely such an appearance will be made by Socrates himself. Soon on his way to receive the indictment, he will, shortly thereafter, appear in court and there will emphasize that his speech is quite contrary to—and perhaps laughable in comparison with—what is normally heard in a court of law. This remark, autobiographical in advance, is indicative of the reflexivity of the λόγος just now commencing: it is a λόγος not only about Thales but also about Socrates himself, and it has the effect of setting out, also in advance, the difference between Thales in his laughable ascendancy and Socrates in the κατάβασις that will lead to his death. This difference structures the λόγος as fundamentally ambivalent: the philosopher as he will be described is ambivalently both Thales and Socrates, indeed in their very difference. Thus, in presenting the λόγος, Socrates speaks in a double voice. The more prominent voice speaks of the ascendant Thales; it is chiefly to this voice that Theodorus' responses are addressed. But in the other, reflexive voice, Socrates speaks of himself as a philosopher who, falling short of such sheer ascendancy, will soon be off to face his death. In this double-voiced λόγος, interruption and the prospect of interruption play a major role, whether it is the comic interruption of falling in a well or the absolute interruption of death.

But first, before the double talk sets in, Socrates draws a contrast between those who frequent the courts and those who have been brought up in philosophy. He observes that those in the courts are always hurried in their speech, because "water in its flow is bearing down on them" (172d). The reference is to the water clock used in court to limit the length of time one could speak. Here again the figure of flowing is introduced, though now in a kind of pairing with λόγος; the flow of the water limits the extent of speech, just as previously the flow of φύσις proved to limit—indeed to render impossible—the articulation of λόγος. But now the flow is not even like the smooth flow of olive oil but is, rather, the more rapid flow of water. On the other side, those brought up in philosophy have leisure and conduct their talks at their leisure. The word *leisure* (σχολή), which Socrates immediately repeats, marks the opposite of the hurried speech governed by the water clock; more generally, it marks opposition to the incessant motion that defines the Protagorean scene. Thus, the philosopher is to be differentiated not only from those who frequent the courts but also from those whose λόγος remains immersed in the Protagorean flow of φύσις.

Socrates compares their own conversation to those who converse at their leisure and who do not hesitate to digress from the λόγος that lies immediately before them, as he and Theodorus have now done in launching this third λόγος. Remarking then on how bent and stunted the souls of those in court are, he continues: "Do you want us to tell completely about those of our chorus or to let it go and turn back to the λόγος [that is, the previous, second λόγος], in order that we may not abuse too much the freedom and possibility of exchanging λόγοι that we were now speaking of?" (173b). Socrates' question poses the possibility—even perhaps the need—of interruption, indeed even as the description of the philosopher has barely begun. Those who are to be described—if the discourse is not interrupted (and Theodorus, echoing the dominant voice, insists it not be interrupted)—are called "those of our chorus." The word χορός designates a dance in honor of the gods or a band of dancers and singers or eventually the chorus in a drama. It is as if Socrates and Theodorus were being joined by—or were joining in with—a band of dancers, dancing and singing in honor of the gods; or as if they were now assuming the role of actors performing a drama for which those brought up in philosophy would provide a suitable chorus. It is as if the very voice that raises the question of interruption were also alluding to a dance, a drama, a play about to begin.

A divergence, a difference, now begins to appear, no longer between philosophers and those in court, but within the philosophical band. It appears initially as a difference in the respective relations to λόγος that are broached. On the one hand, Theodorus declares "that we who are choristers in this sort of thing are not servants of the λόγοι, but the λόγοι are, as it were, our domestics" (173c). On the other hand, though Socrates has just spoken of their leisure to carry on as long as they like—unlike those ruled by the water clock—he has also spoken of a greater λόγος overtaking them. The word καταλαμβάνω means *to catch, to overtake*, but also *to take possession of*, even *to bind*, as by an oath (a certain kind of λόγος). A λόγος that can overtake, take possession of, and bind can hardly be regarded as a domestic in service to those who voice it.

Yet Socrates leaves the difference unmarked and proceeds to speak about the leaders of the chorus, about those who head the chorus. Almost parenthetically he asks and leaves unanswered the question: "For why should one speak of those who spend their time [διατρίβοντος—participle of διατρίβω] in philosophy so poorly?" (173c). The verb διατρίβω has also a pejorative meaning, and hence the question can also be rendered as referring to "those who waste their time in philosophy." Socrates has now begun to speak in such a way as to let his words turn back toward himself; for he was indeed notorious for spending—or wasting—his time conversing with all sorts of people.

He proceeds to describe the leaders of the chorus, speaking now in the double voice for which the foregoing ambivalences have opened a space. He characterizes these people as not even knowing the way to the agora, to the courts, or to any other common places of assembly. In addition, they are oblivious to the laws and to all that goes on in politics. Furthermore, such a person "does not even know that he does not know all these things." Socrates continues: "His body alone is situated in the πόλις and resides there, whereas his thought . . . flies, as Pindar puts it, 'deep down under the earth' and geometrizes the planes, 'and above the heaven,' star-gazing and exploring everywhere every nature [φύσις] of each whole of the things that are [or: of the beings—τῶν ὄντων] and letting itself down to not one of the things nearby" (173e–174a). It is at this juncture, where φύσις—even in its farthest extensions deep down under the earth and above the heaven—has been taken up completely into the ascent, that Socrates then tells the story of Thales, of utterly ascendant Thales falling into a well.[30]

And yet, in all that Socrates says here about those who engage in philosophy—indeed, about those who are foremost among the choristers—there is to be heard a discordance between what he *says* and what he *is*. There is to be heard another, reflexive voice not in accord with what is being said by the dominant voice, which is also associated with Theodorus, as suggested by the mention of "geometricizing." What goes unsaid in the silence of this other voice is that each of these descriptions, if preceded by negation, fits Socrates quite exactly. Precisely contrary to what he says of the philosopher, Socrates himself knew very well the way to the agora, where in fact he had spent—or wasted—much of his time talking with whomever he chanced to meet there (see *Apology* 17c). Likewise, he knows the way to the court, knows at least the way to the portico of the King, to which he must go immediately after the conversation in the *Theaetetus*; and it is the indictment he will receive there that will require that later he make his way to the court where he will stand trial. That he is not oblivious to the laws is attested most forcefully when in the scene presented in the *Crito* he refuses to flee from prison and so to save his life solely out of respect for the laws of the πόλις. Nothing could be more contrary to the character of Socrates than the supposition that he does not even know that he does not know all these things. Rather, it is precisely in this regard that he is preeminent and is, as the Delphic Oracle proclaimed, one than whom no one is wiser. His self-portrayal in the *Theaetetus* as a midwife attests, perhaps most directly, to his knowing that he does not know. In the trial scene presented in the *Apology*, he not only tells of his response to the Oracle's proclamation but also speaks directly against the accusation that he investigates things under the earth and in the heaven. He declares: "But I, men of Athens, have nothing to do with these things" (19c). Dissociating himself from the ridiculously elevated and loquacious personage portrayed in Aristophanes' comedy, he challenges the "men of Athens" to speak up and "tell if anyone has ever heard [him] talking much or little about

---

30. Some questions have already been posed above as to whether Thales, as portrayed in the story, must be regarded as an entirely ascensional figure. If he were taken, on the contrary, to embody a descensional moment, then his characterization would be brought closer to that of Socrates, and the apparently univocal divergence would prove to be, at once, also a convergence.

such things" (*Apology* 19d).[31] In the dialogues themselves, there is only one occasion when Socrates does speak of such things, in the conversation with his friends on his last day, though even on that occasion he speaks of such things in a way that also turns back toward the abode and dispositions (ἦθος) of humans.

The entire description of the Thales-like philosopher has the effect of marking a divergence, even a certain opposition, between the philosopher as Socrates describes him and Socrates himself. What then follows serves only to amplify this divergence up to the point where Socrates abruptly interrupts the λόγος.

Once he has related the story of Thales, Socrates continues largely in the dominant voice, emphasizing the aloofness of those brought up in philosophy and their difference from those whose souls as well as their bodies remain in the πόλις. He observes that such philosophers as Thales are laughed at for falling into wells and into "all kinds of perplexity [ἀπορία] because of inexperience [ἀπειρία]" (174c). The pun may be taken to call attention to the double meaning of ἀπειρία: as the privative of πεῖρα (experience), it means *inexperience*, as with one who has not ventured into anything, who lacks enterprise; but as the privative of πέρας (limit, bound), it means *boundless, without limit, limitless*. Thus, while observing once again that those brought up in philosophy do not know their way around amidst everyday things, Socrates is also saying—more decisively—that they fall into perplexity because they lack limits. In more precise and specific terms, they find themselves in difficult straits from which there seems no way out, because, in their inexperience, they are without limits, boundless in what, if anything, they venture.

The further portrayal of the philosopher accentuates his ascendancy virtually without limit. Socrates' own voice is drawn into the flight as he declares that because of the evils that "necessarily haunt mortal nature [θνητὴν φύσιν] and this region here, . . . one ought to try to flee from here to there as soon as possible" (176a). Thus, the ascendancy of the philosopher would be carried out as a flight from φύσις to the beyond, a flight that—as all limits fall away—Socrates describes as "becoming like [ὁμοίωσις] a god as far as possible" (176a–b). The flight would ascend not only beyond φύσις but—as far as possible—beyond mortality, toward likeness to the immortals, passing beyond the limit of all limits, death.

---

31. See my discussion in *Being and Logos*, 31–38.

Extending the discourse, while also continuing under its guise to enact the very flight spoken of, Socrates describes it as becoming "just and holy with thoughtfulness" (176b)—even though, contrariwise, he has just declared that evils necessarily haunt mortal nature and the region mortals occupy. But then, following the injunction "Let us say the truth as follows," he says: "A god is in no way unjust in any respect" (176c). To become just, fully just, would be to cancel, to overcome, the difference separating mortal from immortal. Even if, as he goes on to say (adding the qualification), it is a matter only of becoming as just as possible, such becoming would still be directed toward reducing the difference between the human and the gods.

He then adds, most decisively: "In this is truly the δεινότης of man" (176c). The word δεινότης can mean simply *cleverness*; but its more originary meaning, especially if the word is taken in relation to the corresponding adjective δεινός, is *terribleness, wondrousness, strangeness*.³² Only the slightest shift would be required in order to broach in this connection a discourse on monstrosity and to regard the movement across the difference separating the human from the gods as something truly monstrous. It would be to this monstrous movement toward assimilation that Socrates could be taken to refer as he concludes: "For the knowledge of this is wisdom and true virtue" (176c).

Amidst Socrates' subsequent descriptions of the godless, of those who lack such knowledge, there is a decisive indication that portends the transformation that the motif of ascendancy will soon undergo. Instead of speaking of the gods and the godly, Socrates reorients the discourse to paradigms of the godly: "Paradigms stand in being [ἐν τῷ ὄντι], my friend, of the godly, which is most happy, and of the godless, which is most miserable" (176e). Now the discourse as well as the course of the philosopher extends not to the immortal gods themselves, but rather from φύσις to the paradigms that, beyond the flow of φύσις, stand in being.

---

32. Benardete translates δεινότης as the hendiadys "dreadful uncanniness" (*Plato's Theaetetus*: Part I of *The Being of the Beautiful*, trans. Seth Benardete [Chicago: University of Chicago Press, 1986], 43). The corresponding adjective δεινός occurs often in Homer: for example, "terrible [δεινός] Charybdis and Scylla" (*Odyssey* 12:260); "terrible [δεινός] was the clash that rose from the bow of silver" (*Iliad* 1:49). The word occurs twice at the beginning of the first choral ode in Sophocles' *Antigone*: "Manifold is the uncanny [τὰ δεινά], yet nothing uncannier [δεινότερον] than man bestirs itself, rising up beyond him" (332; cf. Sophocles, *Electra* 770).

Quite abruptly Socrates interrupts the discourse, the entire third discourse, which he declares a mere πάρεργον: "Let us turn back away from these things—they were in fact said as πάρεργα—for if we do not, more will keep on flowing in and will cover up [or: bury—καταχώσει] the λόγος with which we began" (177b–c). Socrates' deed here, interrupting the λόγος, carries out in deed the interruption of the flow of φύσις that has just been broached in λόγος, first, by the reference beyond to the immortals, and, more decisively, through the positing of the paradigms in being. There is irony, then, in Socrates' reference here to the flowing that will cover up the λόγος, for what the λόγος—the third, allegedly parergonal λόγος—has produced is precisely a surpassing of the flow. Yet in the irony there is also a hint that the scene of unlimited ascendancy is perhaps not so entirely separated from the Protagorean scene as might otherwise be supposed.

Interruption continues, now more in λόγος than in deed, an interruptive λόγος that indeed has the effect of interrupting a certain kind of λόγος akin to that of Protagoras. Socrates ventures to say that no one would maintain (would be so manly as to fight it out) that what a πόλις lays down as beneficial would remain beneficial as long as it remained laid down. Then he adds the exception: no one would maintain this unless he gave it the name, that is, called it advantageous regardless of how it actually turned out. Yet this would be—says Socrates—to turn what they are saying into a joke. For, says Socrates, "he is not to say the name but to observe the matter [τὸ πρᾶγμα] that is named" (177e). The injunction could hardly be more definitively stated—the demand that one attend, not merely to words, but to the things themselves to which words refer. This injunction is sounded again, in a very different context, in the *Seventh Letter* (341c). It will be sounded again and again at those historical junctures where philosophy undertakes to launch a new beginning, escaping the mere lure of words and attending anew to the things themselves. When Husserl issues the requirement to attend *zu den Sachen selbst*, he simply renews—if more rigorously, indeed as the very sense of rigor—this demand that animated Greek thought from its beginning.[33]

In the injunction it is a question of measure, of whether the measure of what is lies in what is said, in what is declared, in what is laid down as being, or whether the measure can be provided only by one

---

33. Already operative in the earlier Greek thinkers, this injunction is explicitly stated in Empedocles' Fragment B3 (discussed above in chap. 4).

capable of actually apprehending what is. In order to pursue the question—in opposition to Protagoras, for whom each person is himself the measure, the tribunal, of what is—Socrates shifts from the present to the future. Then it is manifest that the physician, not the layman, is the measure of what will be, that it is he who has in himself the tribunal by which it can be determined whether the layman is likely to get a fever. So it is also with those who practice other τέχναι, the farmer, the musician, the cook. Thus, having himself provided measure by appeal to the things themselves, Socrates concludes: "So it will be stated by us in a measured way [μετρίως] before your teacher that it is necessary for him to agree that someone is wiser than someone else and that whoever is of that sort is the measure [μέτρον]" (179a–b).

The conversation returns to the question of the flow in which being would be dissolved and the reference to being that Socrates has just enjoined would thus be vitiated. When Socrates mentions that there has been a battle about this, Theodorus identifies those who wage the battle as the comrades of Heraclitus. That the reference is to the comrades and not to Heraclitus himself may be taken as an indication that what is to come under scrutiny is, at most, only an aspect of Heraclitus' thought, the sole aspect that these Ionic comrades have taken up.

Theodorus declares that it is hardly, if at all, possible to converse with these Heracliteans. For not only do they dissolve everything into flow, but also, in accord with what they declare, they sweep along in their discourse without ever staying with a λόγος and permitting it to be stable. Socrates is a bit skeptical about their sustaining such mobility. He suspects that to their pupils they point out things not carried away by the flow, that they do so at their leisure (ἐπὶ σχολῆς), that is, when—contrary to Theodorus' depiction of them—they and their words are not carried away in the flow.

Yet, Theodorus refuses to grant Socrates' proposal that these Heraclitean λόγοι might be stabilized if some things were pointed out that escape the sheer flow. Over against the suggestion that this is how they proceed with their pupils, Theodorus insists that they are such that it is impossible for them to have pupils. On the contrary, he maintains, "they sprout up spontaneously [αὐτόματοι]" whenever they are filled with enthusiasm (180c). The word αὐτόματος means primarily *of one's own accord, on one's own, of oneself*; because they are on their own, they are, as

Theodorus indicates, oblivious to others and thus incapable of having pupils.³⁴

Socrates now mentions those who declare the opposite of what the Heracliteans maintain. Referring by name to Melissus and Parmenides, he cites their declaration: "As it is immovable, the name of the all is being" (180e).³⁵ He elaborates: they maintain "that all is one and that it is at rest in itself without a place [χώρα] in which it moves" (180e). The one being, which is all, is thus taken to be stationary in a compounded way: it is not just that it is at rest in a space in which it could—but does not—move; rather, there is no space in which it stands at rest but could conceivably move. There is no space, nor anything else, outside the one being—indeed, in such an absolute manner that even the designation *outside* must be cancelled.³⁶

The particular context in which Parmenides is mentioned, and especially the opposition within which his thought is placed, precludes

---

34. Both the word αὐτόματος and the discussion of measure (μέτρον) resonate with segments of one of the discussions that take place on the day after the conversation in the *Theaetetus*, namely, the discussion presented in the *Statesman*. The word αὐτόματος occurs near the beginning of the myth when the Stranger tells how the god who had conducted the revolution of the cosmos lets go so that the cosmos then "turns around on its own [αὐτόματος] in the contrary direction" (269c-d). The discussion of measure (283b-287a) is centered on the distinction between relative measure and measure that is carried out by reference to a measure or standard (μέτριον).

35. οἷον ἀκίνητον τελέθει τῷ παντὶ ὄνομ᾽ εἶναι. Though this passage is quoted twice by Simplicius, it is not found in the extant Fragments. There have been various attempts to account for the citation. On the basis of a modification of the passage, Cornford proposes that it is an independent fragment, which can be placed at the end of Fragment 19 (Francis M. Cornford, *Plato's Theory of Knowledge* [New York: Liberal Arts Press, 1957], 94n1). Taran, on the other hand, suggests two possible explanations: either "the text of Plato is corrupt in this place," or "he misquoted the fragment or purposely parodied line 38 [in Fragment B8] in order to make it fit his context (Leonardo Taran, *Parmenides* [Princeton, NJ: Princeton University Press, 1965], 135).

36. In this connection it is evident that the *Timaeus*, and not only the *Sophist* (and in an entirely different way the *Parmenides*), constitutes an implicit response to Parmenides. Taking over the pluralizing of being carried out in the *Sophist*, the *Timaeus* demonstrates that the very possibility of the operation of being requires the χώρα, even though being is not, as such, in the χώρα. See my discussion in *Chorology*, chap. 3.

discussion of his account of sensible appearances. Thus, in the *Theaetetus* his account of φύσις is not taken up at all; only the ontological account is mentioned, though even its treatment is brief and is soon broken off entirely. When in the *Sophist* there is a return to the thought of Parmenides, it is again only the ontological account that is taken up.[37] Sensible appearance—that is, φύσις—does not become a theme at all.

Yet, this is precisely the theme of the second of the two parts into which Parmenides' poem is divided. Following the testimony of Diogenes Laertius, the two parts are commonly entitled *On Truth* (κατὰ ἀλήθειαν) and *On Opinion* (κατὰ δόξαν).[38] These titles express the themes to which the two parts are devoted. Indeed, Parmenides marks clearly the point where the division occurs. Having laid out the truth of being, he then writes: "Here I end my reliable account [πιστὸν λόγον] and thought concerning truth. From now on learn the opinions of mortals" (B8). Ancient sources attest that he "traveled both roads" (A7). These are the two ways to be taken; for what might seem still another way, that of not-being, is "unthinkable and unnamable" (B8).

The poem begins mythically. The one who relates the mythical beginning tells how he was set traveling on the "road of the goddess, which carries through all places the man who knows." Conveyed in a chariot with maidens leading the way, he traveled "toward the light" and eventually reached the gate separating the ways of day and night. He tells how the maidens accompanying him persuaded Dike, who holds the keys, to open the gate that he might enter, and how then he was graciously welcomed by the goddess (A1). It is the goddess who will instruct him about truth and opinion, and it is this instruction that will constitute the entire remainder of the poem. The mythical form with which

---

37. A bit later in the *Theaetetus*, though in the same context, Socrates mentions having once gotten together with Parmenides when he was very young and Parmenides very old (183e). In the conversation in the dialogue *Parmenides* to which Socrates is referring, it is primarily Parmenides who speaks and who indeed instructs Socrates. It is in the *Sophist* (241d–245e), closely linked dramatically to the *Theaetetus*, that the task of critically addressing Parmenides, deferred in the *Theaetetus*, is undertaken—not, however, by Socrates but by the Stranger, who, coming from Elea, is associated with Parmenides. See my discussion in "Plato's *Sophist*: A Different Look," *New Yearbook of Phenomenology and Phenomenological Philosophy* 13 (2014): 283–91, and *Being and Logos*, 487–94.

38. Numbered as A1 in Diels-Kranz, this testimony comes from Diogenes Laertius, *Lives of Eminent Philosophers* 9:21–23. See also Kirk, Raven, and Schofield, *The Presocratic Philosophers*, 241f.

the poem begins makes it manifest that the discourse that follows is not to be construed as the opinion of a mortal, nor even as words set forth autonomously by a mortal, but rather as the mere sounding forth of a discourse coming from beyond, from an origin that exceeds the mortal sphere no less than does the abode of the gods.

The goddess entreats him to learn of truth and of opinion. These are the words of the goddess: "It is necessary that you learn all [things], both the unshaken heart of well-rounded truth and the opinions of mortals in which there is no true belief. Nevertheless, you shall learn these [opinions] also, how the appearances, which pervade all things, had to be acceptable" (B1). The ontological theme broached in the *Theaetetus* is here introduced in the most succinct form: it is "the unshaken heart of well-rounded truth." This expression is supplemented by Fragment B2, which again is presented as coming from the goddess, who implores the initiate to listen receptively to her tale (μῦθος). She describes the appropriate way in these terms: "that it is and that not to be is not the way of persuasion, for persuasion follows upon truth." This way thus conjoins being, persuasion, and truth. According to the teaching of the goddess, "being is ungenerated and imperishable, whole, unique, immovable, and complete." Furthermore: "It was not once nor will it be, since it is now altogether, one, continuous" (B8). Thus, being is no less detached from temporality, from the flow of φύσις, than it is from space, or, more properly, from χώρα.

The conjoining of being, persuasion, and truth does not at all amount to simply equating them. In particular, it is not as though being were the truth, nor as though being were a truth among others. Neither is the conjunction of being and truth simply a matter of recognizing that statements such as "being is ungenerated" are true in the sense of adequately describing their object. Rather, they are conjoined in a manner quite different from the relations of identity, attribution, and predication characteristic of modern philosophical theories.

If, as has been proposed, ἀληθές is taken etymologically, then it can be rendered as *not concealed*, and *unconcealed*.[39] The truth conjoined with being would not be something apart from being; it would not be located in a thinking or speaking that would represent being, that, over against being, would duplicate it, that would issue in a representational double within the thinking or speaking. Any such duplication is excluded by the character of being as one, as whole, as complete.

---

39. Kahn, *The Art and Thought of Heraclitus*, 121f. (discussed in chap. 3, above).

The well-rounded truth would occur, rather, as the unconcealment of being, the unconcealment in which being would offer itself as manifest. Through its manifestness it would be persuasive. In its manifestness it would shine forth in its brightness; it would come to light without itself becoming in any way other than itself.[40]

The thinking and saying of being would not, then, fall outside of being as involving representational doubles of being; for being is whole, is complete, and whatever would fall outside being, that is, not-being, is not. In referring to the thinking and saying *of* being, the genitive would be as much subjective as objective (if such categories are at all appropriate). In other words, the thinking and saying of being would belong to being, responding to its unconcealment, in which it would be persuasive, for "persuasion follows upon [or: attends to, accompanies—ὀπηδεῖ] truth." Such is the sense of Parmenides' most celebrated Fragment: "For it is the same to think and to be"[41]—construed as: For thinking and being are the same, are one.

The goddess entreats the initiate to learn not only about the truth of being (a learning that, like the thinking of being, would belong to being) but also about the opinions of mortals, in which there is no true belief, and in this connection to learn also about the acceptance of all-pervasive appearances. The word δόξα (opinion) corresponds to the verbal form δοκέω, which signifies both *to suppose* (or *opine*) and *to appear*. The word translated as *appearance*, δοκοῦντα, is also a form of δοκέω. The linguistic connections make it evident that opinions are correlative to appearances: one has certain opinions on the basis of how things appear, and, conversely, the guise in which things appear depends to a degree on the opinions held in advance

Already the connection with the corresponding analysis in the *Theaetetus* begins to come to light. Because it moves at the level of opinion rather than mere perception, the Parmenidean account is less reductive. Unlike the sheer flow resulting from the interaction of perceptual organs with perceivable things, appearances display a certain stability, a certain determinate character. In this way they match much more closely what

---

40. In place of the expression εὐκυκλέος (well-rounded), there are two variant readings, both of which are even more transparently appropriate: εὐφεγγέος (bright, with clear light) and εὐπειθέος (persuasive). See Diels-Kranz, *Die Fragmente der Vorsokratiker*, 1:230n.

41. τὸ γὰρ αὐτὸ νοεῖν ἐστίν τε καὶ εἶναι (Fragment B3). See also B8.

is commonly taken to be φύσις. To this extent the second part of Parmenides' poem advances an account of φύσις.

In the second part of the poem, the goddess instructs the initiate about opinions in their correlation with all-pervasive appearances. In mortal opinions, she declares, "there is no true belief [πίστις ἀληθής]"— or, as this can also be rendered: no true reliance. True belief or reliance would be a belief or reliance warranted by truth, that is, a belief or reliance responsive to—and ultimately belonging to—the unconcealment of being. In opinion there is no such responsiveness or belonging to being in its unconcealment. The result borders on an impossible opposition: opinion, in which there is no true belief or reliance, falls outside being in its unconcealment, and yet, outside being there can be only not-being, which is not.

At this point the Parmenidean account virtually coincides with the analysis in the *Theaetetus*, specifically, with the analysis by which, within the realm of φύσις, there is a thoroughgoing reduction of being. Like the flow on the Protagorean scene, appearances in their correlation with opinion are bereft of being, and, as Socrates the ventriloquist says, "'to be' must be removed from everywhere" (*Theaetetus* 157b). In the *Theaetetus* there remains, however, the provisional strategy of relegating appearances to the sphere of becoming, whereas for Parmenides even becoming, in falling outside being (which indeed has no outside), is condemned to not-being, which is not.

The question is, then: How, if opinions fall outside being, can they maintain even the possibility of being? The threat of not-being extends also to appearances, since they are correlative to opinions. How can they be other than being and yet somehow, in some sense, still lay claim to being? How can they escape not-being, so as, in some manner, to cling to being?

The origination of mortal opinions as such and, correlatively, of appearances occurred in what has been termed "a primordial event."[42] This event is described as having taken place through mortal decision, through a positing[43] that, as such, escapes the alternatives on which Parmenides otherwise insists most strongly, the alternatives of being

---

42. *Eine Begebenheit der Vorzeit*, which can also be rendered as: *an event of prehistory* (Karl Reinhardt, *Parmenides und die Geschichte der griechischen Philosophie* [Frankfurt a.M.: Vittorio Klostermann, 1959], 26).

43. In this connection Parmenides uses the verb κατέθεντο, an aorist middle form of κατατίθημι: to place, lay down, posit. See B8.

or not-being. Fragment B8 describes this event: "for they [mortals] decided to name [or: posited names for—κατέθεντο] two forms, a unity of which is not necessary—in which they have wandered about—and they divided form contrariwise and established characters apart from one another." The word rendered as wandered about, πεπλανημένοι, is a passive participle of πλανάω. It is often translated as *have gone astray*, which implies that this decision is simply in error. And yet, since it is precisely what brings forth the entire sphere of appearances, it cannot be simply an error. In its translation as *wandered about*, account is taken of the connection between πλανάω and the noun form πλανήτης (*planet*). Planets do not go astray, as if their orbits were erroneous; rather, they wander, and it is precisely because they wander that they are named as they are.

It is, then, in the decision to name—that is, in positing—two forms that mortals went wandering about, as planets go wandering about the perfectly revolving sphere of the fixed stars. It is evident how this decision results in wandering: since being is *one*, to posit *two* forms is precisely to go wandering away from being. Thus it is that mortals come to situate themselves, instead, in opinions, which are correlative, not to being in its truth, but rather to appearances for which the two forms posited are constitutive. This is why, as Fragment B6 declares, "mortals ... wander, double-headed," for the appearances to which their opinions are entirely oriented are constituted by the two forms that once were posited, and, accordingly, mortals are suspended between these two forms—that is, they wander, double-headed.

This primordial positing of forms marks the origination of what, in the *Theaetetus*, is called, among other names, φύσις. Also, as in the *Theaetetus*, appearances are taken as correlative to the senses, though not only to the senses. Thus Parmenides contrasts the way of the "aimless eye and ringing ear and tongue" with that of thought (νοεῖν) and λόγος (B7).

The goddess names—that is, names once more what was once named in the primordial event—the two forms that were posited. One is named "the ethereal flame of fire, gentle and very light, everywhere identical with itself but not identical with the other." The other form, contrary to ethereal fire, is "obscure night, dense in body and heavy" (B8). The description of fire as "everywhere identical with itself" indicates how, on this wandering way, on this wandering away from being, there is nonetheless an affinity with being. It is by being identical with itself while not being identical with the other that the forms that are named escape the mere opposition or alternatives of being and not-being.

Fragment B9 also names the two forms, substituting light for fire, though clearly the relation between light and the fire that radiates light is such that this is no mere substitution but rather two ways of naming the same form. The Fragment reads: "But once all things have been named light and night and these according to their own powers [δυνάμεις] have been attributed to these things and to those, all is full at the same time of light and obscure night, of both equally, since there is nothing which does not belong to either." Here again an affinity with being is identified: just as being is whole and complete, so appearances (all things) are full of the two forms, light and night. Yet, in that there are two forms, appearances are other than being. In succinct terms: appearances are both the same as being and other than being. It is for this reason that they belong neither to being nor to not-being.

In all things, then, there are in equal measure the two forms. As one commentator expresses it: everything "appears to us, at once, as light and shadow."[44] Yet, there are other "elemental opposites"[45] that are subordinate to light and darkness, or, as the two basic forms are also named in more cosmological terms, fire and earth. The opposites, thus named otherwise, are also to be found mixed in things and elements, as testified by Aristotle in *On Coming to Be and Passing Away* (330b13–15; also Parmenides, Fragment A35): "Those who make [the elements] two from the outset, as Parmenides fire and earth, make the intermediate elements, such as air and water, mixtures of them." It is on the two primary forms, variously named, that all appearances and the mixtures that comprise them are based.

Thus, the more cosmological Fragments enumerate various elemental appearances. It is precisely in this connection that the word φύσις occurs. Fragment B10 begins: "You will know the nature [φύσις] of the aither and all the signs in the aither." To nature, to the expanse of appearances, there belong also "the pure torch of the resplendent sun," "the revolving works of the round-faced moon and of its nature [φύσις]," and "the heaven which embraces all." With the elements and the things they illuminate and encompass, there appear all the mixtures

---

44. Reinhardt, *Parmenides und die Geschichte der griechischen Philosophie*, 22.
45. Ibid., 21.

and processes that belong to nature: "coming to be and perishing, being and not-being, change of place, and exchange of bright color" (B8).

In addition to the affinities to the *Theaetetus* that are displayed in Parmenides' poem, especially in the second part, there are also affinities with Heraclitus and Empedocles.

As Parmenides thinks being as one, so with Heraclitus there is also a thinking of one. Heraclitus' Fragment B10 declares: "From all, one; and from one, all." With Heraclitus, everything beyond the thinking of the one depends on differentiating within the one. It is through these differentiations that Heraclitus' thought is led to nature and its manifold appearances and concealments. With Parmenides, too, thinking progresses from one to nature, but it does so by identifying a positing that suspends nature between the one, that is, being and not-being. Here, too, there are differentiations, not *within* the one but rather *from* the one.

In one significant respect, Empedocles' thought coincides with Parmenides'.[46] For Parmenides the truth of being demonstrates that "coming to be is quenched and perishing unheard of" (B8), though among appearances these do occur. Empedocles goes still further and completely excludes such processes. Fragment B12 declares: "For from what in no way is, it is impossible to come to be, and for what-is to perish cannot be fulfilled or known, for it will always be there wherever one puts it at any time." For both Parmenides and Empedocles, it is necessary to begin with being and to insist on its perdurance. Only on the basis of being would there come about what mortals call coming to be, which, however, is no more than variant mixings of what always already is. Yet, with Empedocles, nature does not fall outside being or between being and not-being; rather, it is the very scene on which being perdures in the mixings of the elemental roots.

---

46. Diogenes Laertius reports what various other commentators are supposed to have said about the relation between Empedocles and Parmenides. For instance, "Theophrastus says that Empedocles was an enthusiast of Parmenides and an imitator of his poetry." Or again, "Alcidamas says ... that Empedocles studied with Parmenides." Yet these sources are by no means in complete agreement. For example, "Hermippus says he [Empedocles] was an enthusiast, not of Parmenides, but of Xenophanes, with whom he associated" (*Lives of Eminent Philosophers* 8:51–69; in Diels-Kranz: A1).

In the *Theaetetus* it is the Heracliteans, each on his own, and Parmenides who are juxtaposed. Once these have been brought onto the scene, the stage is prepared for Socrates to depict his and Theodorus' situation as like that which occurs in a gymnasium when people play at a tug-of-war in which they stand in the middle between two opposing teams and are pulled, in turn, in both directions. So, likewise, Socrates and Theodorus are pulled in both directions, now toward those who set everything flowing, now toward those who arrest all things. It is between these two, between limitless flow and absolute stasis, that the ensuing discussion, the most decisive in the entire dialogue, will prove to be stretched.

Yet before launching this discussion, Socrates addresses one side directly, leaving aside the other, the Eleatic, on the grounds that the λόγος needed to address the awesome and strange (δεινός) figure of Parmenides would overwhelm the entire present λόγος on knowledge.[47] In order to address critically the Heracliteans, Socrates effectively radicalizes their position: since there are two species of motion, alteration and locomotion, and since in all things both species must be engaged (lest there be rest in one respect, hence both rest and motion), it will not be possible even to say that all things flow. For as they flow in locomotion, they also simultaneously undergo continual alteration, so that each will always be changing into something else. Thus, even more rigorously than earlier in the dialogue, Socrates shows that unlimited flow renders speech impossible. The advocates of the flow could not even say *so* (οὕτω) or *not so* (μὴ οὕτω), for even these words would arrest the flow. Socrates concludes, not without a tinge of irony: "But those who speak this λόγος must posit another voice [φωνή], since now at least they do not have the words for their own hypothesis, unless, after all, *nohow* [*in no way whatsoever*—οὐδ' ὅπως; or (Burnet) οὐδ' οὕτως] would most particularly fit them, since it is spoken without limit [ἄπειρον]" (183b). It goes without saying that speech without limit is no speech at all, but, at most, consists of utterances like those from the raving voice of the Sibyl. To speak is to articulate, to delimit, that to which the speech is directed; it is to determine something as something, to bring determinacy to bear upon it. To withdraw all determinacy, to dissolve it into the unlimited

---

47. See note 37 above.

flow of becoming, can only leave the speaker bereft of words, reduced virtually to silence, capable only of words that, denying determinacy, are dissipated the moment they are uttered.

With the silencing of his comrade and teacher, Theodorus, too, withdraws from the conversation, and, again engaging Theaetetus, Socrates returns to the thesis that knowledge is perception. With this return and the reentry of Theaetetus into the conversation, Socrates launches an extension of the discourse only remotely foreshadowed up to this point in the dialogue. The passage in which this extension is carried out is the most decisive in the entire dialogue.

In the passage Socrates examines the comportment by means of which and in which one comes to apprehend things perceptually. Though he begins by considering the apprehension of that which is seen through the eyes, heard through the ears, and so on for the other senses, his analysis moves almost immediately to a consideration of what is involved in the apprehension of things as such. His intent is to distinguish a moment that exceeds what is yielded through the various senses but that is necessary for the full apprehension—and ultimately for the knowledge—of things. The result is, on the one hand, that Theaetetus' thesis identifying knowledge and perception is definitively refuted; but, on the other hand, it is shown precisely what must be brought to supplement mere perception so as to yield knowledge. The passage thus reclaims and distinguishes the theses expressed in Theaetetus' initial statement (at 151e): on the one hand, his thesis that "knowledge is nothing else than perception" is refuted once and for all; on the other hand, his thesis that "whoever knows something perceives that which he knows" is to an extent vindicated and completed by the identification of that which, in addition to mere perception, is required for knowledge.

Setting aside Theaetetus' initial supposition that it is by our eyes that we see white and black things (and correspondingly for hearing), Socrates induces his interlocutor to acknowledge a basic distinction that will govern the entire remainder of the passage: the eyes are that *through which* we see (δι' οὗ ὁρῶμεν), not that *by which* we see (ᾧ ὁρῶμεν). In other words, the eyes and the other senses are merely instruments (ὄργανα) by which various perceptions come to us. In order to see what is yielded through the eyes, a power other than the mere sense of sight is required, a power *by which* we perceive, for instance, the color that comes to us through the eyes. And yet, the operation of this power by which is grasped the manifold perceptions gained through the senses does not suffice for the perceptual apprehension of something perceptible. The decisiveness of the further move that is required beyond the manifold perceptions Socrates marks by the word δεινόν: "Strange [or: wondrous, even monstrous] it would be, my boy, if many perceptions sat in us as if in wooden horses, but all these did not stretch together into [or: toward] some one look [ἀλλὰ μὴ εἰς μίαν τινὰ ἰδέαν ... πάντα ταῦτα συντείνει], regardless of whether it is soul or whatever it must be called by which, through these as if they were instruments, we perceive perceptible things" (184d). Filled with unseen Achaian soldiers, the wooden horse stands before the gate of Troy waiting for the moment when it will be drawn through the gate and those who previously were concealed will suddenly appear in the open. As long as the manifold perceptions simply lie in us, like soldiers in the wooden horse, nothing is seen. Only when those within are drawn through the gate and can behold the look of Troy itself, only when there is an opening for vision beyond, do things come to light, come to be perceived.

Perception thus requires the transition in which the manifold of perceptions conveyed through the senses stretch together into or toward one look. In this extension they will necessarily be drawn together themselves; and thus, in accord with the alternative senses of the preposition εἰς, it can be said that in stretching *toward* some one look they are themselves drawn *into* a certain togetherness, a certain accord. Yet neither their differences among themselves nor their separation from the one look will be entirely abolished. The one look must, in some measure, be set apart from the manifold perceptions as that toward which they stretch together. Furthermore, since what these perceptions, taken alone, would present is precisely the Protagorean scene of radical becoming, that is, the scene of ever recurrent generation of singularities, their stretching together toward some one look would have the effect of limiting their sheer disordered dispersal. In being drawn together and stretched toward some one look, the radical singularity would be cancelled and a certain determinacy would be instituted. The flow would be limited by the relatedness enacted toward the look. In the case (to which Socrates will soon refer) in which the one look is that of being as such, the limit and the consequent determinacy are most directly evident; for in this case moments of *becoming* are, in effect, being stretched together toward *being*.

By marking the submission of the scene of becoming to such stretching together toward one look, Socrates tacitly renews the schema that was already outlined earlier in the discourse on the wonderful and laughable things. For in that discourse, too, it was a matter of two opposed ways of construing the scene of becoming: one way left the scene discontinuous and indeterminate, that is, construed it as radical becoming, while the other way clung to continuity and determinacy. In the earlier discourse these two ways remained apart, but now, by introducing the extension of the moments of becoming toward one look, these are brought together, though in such fashion that the strange logic that appeared in the earlier discourse is still retained.

The logic is one of excess, and at the present juncture it proves even more manifestly than before to be the very logic of φύσις. For, taken merely as the scene of becoming, φύσις is now submitted to being extended in every case—in the case of each and every natural being—toward some one look. On the one side, the look must be regarded as set apart from φύσις; indeed, this apartness will soon be confirmed by Socrates' further inquiry regarding the character of the look. And yet, while exceeding φύσις, the look cannot but be, nonetheless, the look *of*—or at least a look that in some measure belongs to—perceptible things set within nature. The determinacy that the look brings to bear on φύσις must come from beyond and yet must, at once, belong precisely to φύσις.

Socrates proceeds to determine the character of the look, contrasting it with the perceptions that stretch toward it. Ascertaining that what is perceived through one sense instrument cannot be perceived through a different power, he turns first of all to a question concerning numbers, to a question of ones and of two. Referring to sound and color, he declares that both are two and that each of the two is one. His question to Theaetetus concerns the numbers that different perceptions (through different powers) can have in common, as well as other determinations such as the same and the other, being and not-being, any of which can be had in common by different perceptions. Specifically, the question concerns that through which such commons are apprehended, granted that they cannot be apprehended through any power of sense. He asks: "So through what do you think [διανοεῖ] all this about them? For it is possible neither through hearing nor through sight to grasp what is common to them [τὸ κοινὸν λαμβάνειν περὶ αὐτῶν]" (185b). After a brief interlude, Theaetetus answers that there is no instrument of the sort they have discussed that would be capable of grasping the commons—"but"—swearing "By Zeus"—he concludes, "the soul itself through itself, it appears to me, looks upon [ἐπισκοπεῖν] what is common to them all" (185d–e).[48]

The look toward and into which the manifold perceptions stretch together thus has the character of the common (τὸ κοινόν); and, to take—as Socrates does—the cases most remote from the perceptions, it may assume the form of number, of same and other, of being and not-being. Asked specifically about being, Theaetetus places it among those kinds "which the soul by itself stretches itself toward" (186a). His answer serves to establish a primary connection: the manifold perceptions stretch together toward the common look because the soul by itself stretches itself toward the look, drawing the perceptions along—as if they were Achaian soldiers in a wooden horse being drawn through the gate of Troy. In order to stretch itself toward the common look, thus drawing the perceptions along, the soul must, through itself, think the look, coming to look upon it. It is by all that belongs together with this thinking that perception of things is achieved.

Yet, what exactly—if anything—is it that belongs together with this thinking (διανοεῖν) and with this looking upon (ἐπισκοπεῖν) the common look? Or is it only a matter of a higher, non-sensible mode of vision that supervenes upon perception? What is it that allows the soul to apprehend the look in advance such that it can stretch itself toward the look? What is it that guides and enables the soul's stretching toward the look?

It is to these questions that Socrates and also, if unintentionally, Theaetetus allude in the brief interlude that is enacted between Socrates' query about that through which one thinks the commons and Theaetetus' answer that it is "the soul itself through itself." Socrates marks the start of the interlude by mentioning that there is still something else that is a sure sign regarding what they are saying. As he continues, there is reference to the preceding examples of color and sound: "If it were possible to examine whether both are salty or not, you know that you will be able to say by what you will examine this, and it appears as neither

---

48. In the *Cratylus* the corresponding connection is made to φύσις. Socrates says: "Therefore it would fit beautifully to give to this power that sustains and upholds nature [φύσις] the name *nature-holder* [φυσέχην], and this may be refined and pronounced *soul* [ψυχή]" (400b). This passage cannot, however, be read as a straightforward assertion, since it occurs in the midst of an etymological comedy. See my discussion in *Being and Logos*, 232–45.

sight nor hearing but something else" (185b–c). The interlude will be an exercise in saying: Socrates assures Theaetetus that he knows he will be able to say that which Socrates is inviting him to say, and which indeed he will say. What is to be said concerns the pair, color and sound, as they are conveyed through the powers of sight and hearing, respectively. It concerns specifically whether both are salty or not, or rather, more precisely, the means by which to examine whether or not both are salty. Socrates' assurance to Theaetetus is that he knows he will be able to say what this means is. And yet, what exactly is it that would be examined by that means that Theaetetus momentarily will name? It could hardly be a question of whether a certain color is salty or whether a certain sound is salty. As a question of whether both are salty, it could only refer to something, some perceptible thing, that is of a certain color and that emits (or in some other way possesses) a certain sound. For such a thing to be salty would mean, then, not only that it tasted salty but also that this perception of saltiness stretched, together with the color and sound, toward a common look. Hence, the means that Theaetetus is to say—that Socrates assures him he knows he will be able to say—is twofold: it is not only the sense of taste but also the means—whatever it may be—by which the taste of saltiness is stretched, together with other perceptions, toward a common look.

The word by which Theaetetus says this means expresses perfectly this twofold: it is "the power through the tongue [ἥ γε διὰ τῆς γλώττης δύναμις]" (185c). While indeed it is through the tongue that a salty taste is conveyed, it is also by the practiced use of the tongue that one speaks. The word γλῶττα (Attic for γλῶσσα) means tongue not only as the organ of taste but also as speech, as language. What the brief interlude thus discreetly indicates through its exercise in saying is that speech—that is, λέγειν, λόγος—belongs together with the thinking by which the soul orients and stretches itself toward the common look.

Socrates' response is also to speech, to the speech with which Theaetetus has concluded the little exercise in speech. Socrates declares: "You speak beautifully" (185c). Theaetetus has spoken beautifully because through his speech he has let something beyond the range of sense be manifest, has let it shine forth.[49] Socrates says not only that Theaetetus speaks beautifully but also that he is beautiful, not ugly, as Theodorus, in comparing him to Socrates, had insinuated. Not only in

---

49. See note 12 above.

his speech but in deed, in his deed of speaking of speech, of the soul, and of being, Theaetetus lets these shine forth from beyond. Socrates adds that Theaetetus is also freeing him of a "very long λόγος," one that concerns the soul and the body and that which is examined through the power of each. Need it be said that this λόγος has proven to be much longer even than Socrates could have envisioned, extending, as it has, throughout the history of philosophy as a story told again and again in ever new guises?

Socrates repeats what beautiful Theaetetus has spoken beautifully, but now in more schematic form: "the soul itself through itself examines some things, and some things through the powers of the body" (185e).

Thus gathering the means for envisioning or looking on (ἐπισκοπεῖν) into two kinds corresponding to the soul and the body, respectively, Socrates sets the stage for appropriating—here at the highest pinnacle of the entire dialogue—the mathematical schema outlined earlier in relation to Theaetetus' mathematical research. Now there has been carried out a double gathering into two ones. On the one side, there are (1) the soul's perception through the senses and (2) its envisionment through itself of the common ones toward which it stretches itself. On the other side, there are also two: (1) the flow of becoming as conveyed to us through the senses and (2) the common looks, which from beyond the flow bestow on it a measure of determinacy. Because the flow of becoming receives its measure of determinacy from the ones (the common looks) that remain apart from it, the dissolution of oneness into the flow will never simply be halted and oneness restored; thus, this one, in which there are no ones, corresponds to the incommensurables in the mathematical schema.

Yet, what decisively differentiates the schema of knowledge from the mathematical schema is that the flow of becoming and the common looks are not simply related as two ones. Their relation is not arithmetical—though, translated into the sensible and the intelligible, they have all too often been mistaken this way in the history of philosophy. Rather, their relation is such that the common looks *exceed* the flow of becoming, while yet they remain the common looks *of* the perceptible things that belong to this flow. The common looks are, like Theaetetus' wonder, ὑπερφυής, and theirs is a logic of excess.

This decisive passage with which the long first discourse of the *Theaetetus* concludes demonstrates that perception alone—in the narrow sense of "seeing, hearing, smelling, feeling cold, feeling hot"

(190d)—does not yield knowledge. It shows that knowledge requires more than the soul's mere receptions through the bodily senses, that it requires also that the soul, through itself, stretch itself toward the common looks, toward such common looks as being, sameness, and difference. Near the end of the passage, Socrates expresses this twofold in another manner: he says that knowledge requires not only what "is present by nature [πάρεστι φύσει]" for perception but also a considering or calculation (ἀναλογισμός) that reaches out to being. The former lies, then, on the side of nature, taken merely as correlate of sensibility, while the latter reaches beyond nature so construed.

And yet, it is not necessary—in the end not even quite possible—to construe nature in this way. For if nature is taken as nothing more than the correlate of sensibility, then it will prove to be such that it reverts to mere flow. It will turn out again that natural things flow away (even to the point of no longer being things at all); and it is only through the soul's stretching itself and its perceptions toward the common looks that things can be made to return and to acquire the stability bestowed by determinacy. Nature lies neither merely in sensible things nor in the common looks to which sensibles are made to stretch. Rather, nature consists in the complex in which the looks exceed sense and yet belong to sensible things.[50] To be sure, nature does not ultimately lie in a nature beyond nature, but neither does it consist of natural things alone. The figure of nature includes both what is thought and what is sensed, drawn together through the logic of excess.

Monstrosity as such—as in monstrous wonder—takes place as an exceeding of nature within—or from within—nature. In the figure of nature itself the same schema of excess is displayed, yet in such a way that the moments of exceeding and belonging no longer occur with respect to—in relation to—nature (as an exceeding of nature in which the excessive also belongs to nature). Rather, these moments take place in the very constitution of nature, such that its defining figure is outlined by these opposed moments. In the figure of nature there occurs, not just monstrosity, but hypermonstrosity.

To express the soul's reaching out beyond, Socrates also uses the word συλλογισμός. Here the word does not yet have the specific logical

---

50. This is the juncture where the Parmenidean pattern of separation between being and appearances and between thinking and opinion (or sense) is rewoven into the complex texture governed by the logic of excess.

or analytical sense that it will be given by Aristotle. Rather, its sense is determined by that of the corresponding verb συλλέγω: to gather, collect, bring together. Συλλογισμός thus designates a thinking or reckoning that brings together, that gathers. Clearly it says in another way the soul's stretching itself toward the common look, says it with emphasis on the way in which this stretching has the effect of gathering the disparate perceptions.

To be sure, Theaetetus' thesis that "knowledge is nothing else than perception" is refuted, as Socrates finally declares and Theaetetus, in turn, acknowledges. Knowledge does indeed include something else above and beyond perception; Socrates has described it as the soul's stretching itself toward the common look, but also, as the first part of the dialogue comes to an end, he has designated it by the words ἀναλογισμός (consideration that reaches out to being), συλλογισμός (thinking that gathers), and simply διάνοια (thinking). However, Theaetetus' alternative thesis "that whoever knows something perceives that which he knows"—that is, that perception belongs as a moment to knowledge—has not been refuted; rather, it has been determined precisely what else, beyond perception, is required for knowledge. That there might be forms of knowledge not linked directly to perception is a possibility that is silently left open at this juncture.

Therefore, contrary to the view that the first discourse of the *Theaetetus* simply ends aporetically, that it accomplishes nothing more than the refutation of Theaetetus' identification of knowledge with perception, this discourse achieves a definitive determination of the twofold structure of knowledge, at least of knowledge insofar as it issues in the apprehension of perceptible things. Socrates himself acknowledges that an advance has indeed been made and that further progress will require considering "that name, whatever the soul has, whenever it alone by itself deals with beings" (187a). The entire remainder of the dialogue, the second and third discourses, is devoted to such considerations. These discourses undertake a more precise determination of the thinking of beings. Thus, rather than being simply coordinate with the long first discourse, they merely supplement it with further considerations of what it has definitively established. To the second and third discourses, one could apply—if more straightforwardly—the word that Socrates used, not without irony, to designate the entire passage in which was sketched the scene of philosophy.

(E) PARERGA

The first word of the *Theaetetus* is echoed throughout. Yet there is something paradoxical about these echoes, a certain opposition between what they echo and their very occurrence. For the first word of the dialogue, ἄρτι, bespeaks confinement to the just-now, to the present moment, whereas to echo this first moment, to repeat in the echoes that which is said—namely, the moment—in the first moment, is precisely to escape confinement to this moment and to what is said in it. Its repetition extends it beyond the just-now, while, in echoing it, the repetition recalls it, brings memory into play across the expanse stretching back to—and from—the first moment.

The just-now is correlative to the singular perceptions. In the present moment one has momentary perceptions; perceptions come to be present in the present. If there were no further means, no extension beyond the moment and the momentary, one would be confined to the just-now, borne along in the flow from one moment to another without any opening beyond the moment. In declaring that knowledge requires a thinking capable of drawing the perceptions together toward a common look apart from their flow, Socrates is marking a way in which the just-now is exceeded, a way opening beyond the present moment. Another way in which the moment can be exceeded is by means of memory, by which the just-now is opened up to a long-ago (πάλαι), and the long-ago is rescued through its repetition in the just-now. In the second discourse the operation of memory will be brought under consideration; in this consideration its relation to the thinking of the common look will figure significantly. Still a third way of escaping confinement to the just-now is offered by λόγος, which, as such, posits determinations that exceed the singular perceptions of the moment. This way beyond the just-now will be thematically treated in the third discourse, though it will turn out to have been broached long before it becomes thematic. This way, too, will prove to be intrinsically related to that provided by the thinking of the common looks. It is through these references back to the primary result of the first discourse that the subsequent two prove to supplement it and thus can appropriately be termed parerga.

At the end of the first discourse, Socrates has declared that any further advance with the question of knowledge will require considering "that name, whatever the soul has, whenever it alone by itself deals with beings" (187a). The name by which this power of the soul was initially designated is διάνοια (thinking). But now, launching the second discourse, Theaetetus proposes another name: δοξάζειν. The word can mean *to opine, to have, hold,* or *form an opinion*. This sense of the word clearly plays a role at certain points in the second discourse, perhaps most notably in the scene in which Socrates speaks of the skill with which public speakers and lawyers can make others opine what they want them to opine, and indeed can do so within the time allotted by the water clock (201a–b). And though the word drifts more than once into this sense, even in its most prosaic form, the discourse that has prompted its introduction—the discourse on the stretching of the soul toward the looks—precludes its having only this sense. As the corresponding noun δόξα is not limited to *opinion* (and certainly not in the modern, subjective sense), so even less is δοξάζειν limited to *opining*. At the very least it can also mean *to believe, to suppose,* or even simply *to think*.

Marking as correct the name that Theaetetus has proposed for the soul's distinctive power, Socrates then instructs him: "But wipe out everything before, and now [begin] once more from the beginning" (187b). Beyond simply indicating that a new discourse is being launched, Socrates' instruction is double-edged. On the one hand, the discourse will soon become a discourse on memory, on precisely that which makes it impossible simply to "wipe out everything before"; for memory is precisely the power to bring back what was before, to rescue it from oblivion, to let it return. In fact, it will immediately become evident that there is at least one thing that Theaetetus has not wiped out. Asked to say again what knowledge is, he observes that not all δόξα is knowledge, since there are false δόξαι. Thus, he betrays that he remembers one of the main points established in the criticism of Protagoras: that not all thoughts or opinions are true, but some are false. On the other hand, it will turn out that in the second discourse there are certain respects in which everything before is wiped out. Specifically, there are passages in which something that should be evident is disregarded to such an extent that the discourse tips over into comedy.

Socrates does not dispute that there are false δόξαι but says only that he is perplexed (ἐν ἀπορίᾳ) concerning this πάθος of false opining, of making a false supposition, of coming to hold a false view. So, he and Theaetetus adopt a strategy, a kind of reverse strategy: they will undertake to determine what false δοξάζειν is in order then to determine what constitutes true δοξάζειν and whether it can be identified as knowledge.

As this strategy is carried out in the course of the second discourse, it will not be possible to prevent it from circling back on itself. Even if, at least at the outset, it has a certain remote legitimacy, it proves to be ever more thoroughly undermined—or self-undermining—as the discourse proceeds.

Socrates launches, in succession, three attempts to say what false δοξάζειν is. He begins: "Is it not necessary now in opining [δοξάζοντα] to opine [δοξάζειν] either something one knows or something one does not know?" (188a). He continues by proposing that to opine falsely is to suppose that the things one knows are not these things but some others of the things one knows. More generally, he proposes that to opine falsely is to suppose some things (known or not known) to be other things (known or not known). As soon as he goes on to state the first of the four alternatives, Socrates already identifies the peculiar opposition that it harbors. To suppose that something known is some other thing that is known is impossible, for, if both are known, one cannot be mistaken for the other. As Socrates says: "though he knows both, he is, in turn, ignorant of both" (188b). Socrates runs through the other three alternatives, rejecting each; in response, in particular, to the two mixed cases (something known mistaken for something unknown and conversely), Theaetetus declares: "It will be a monster [τέρας]" (188c)—something contrary to human nature, if not to nature as such.

This initial venture also displays the circularity that will haunt the entire undertaking. Knowledge is to be determined as true opining. Yet true opining is, in turn, to be determined through its opposition to false opining. But then, in this initial move, false opining is being determined in terms of things known or not known, that is, as a certain kind of supposition made in regard to things known or things not known. Thus, in order to determine knowledge, knowledge is being presupposed. Knowledge would—if the venture otherwise succeeded—be defined in terms of knowledge.

Since the first approach has collapsed, Socrates next proposes to search for false opining, not in terms of knowing and not knowing (thus tacitly acknowledging the circularity that undoes the first attempt) but in terms of being and not-being. His proposal is that false opining consists in opining that which is not. Socrates then poses—in highly significant terms—this question: "Will any human being opine that which is not [or: not-being—τὸ μὴ ὄν], either about any of the things that are [or: about beings—περὶ τῶν ὄντων] or [that which is] itself by itself [αὐτὸ καθ' αὑτό]?" (188d).

By this strange juxtaposition of terms, Socrates, in effect, recalls that the opining here under consideration is but another name for what initially was termed διάνοια. Furthermore, he indicates that, as διάνοια, opining—even if false—is, as such, directed toward beings, indeed toward beings each of which is apart from the flow of perceptions, that is, as he now formulates it, is itself by itself. The juxtaposition constitutes the refutation of this second venture: it is manifestly absurd to speak of opining or thinking the not-being of beings; that such being is also declared to be "itself by itself" only underscores the absurdity all the more forcefully. It is as a consequence of the juxtaposition—and not simply as a formalistic reversal of terms—that Socrates concludes that whoever opines not-being opines nothing and so does not opine at all.

Socrates moves on to a third proposal: "We say that false opinion is a certain kind of opining otherwise [or: interchanged opinion—ἀλλοδοξία], when someone makes an exchange in his thought [διάνοια] and says that some beings are some other beings" (189b–c). Theaetetus responds with an example: when anyone opines that something beautiful is ugly instead of beautiful or that something ugly is beautiful instead of ugly, "then truly he is opining falsely" (189c). Socrates does not hesitate to point out the strangeness of this juxtaposition of truly and falsely, comparing it to the opposition between slow and swift, heavy and light, or, more generally, to what would occur if something became opposite to itself, set into accord not with its own nature (φύσις) but with the nature of its opposite. Though he forgoes doing so, Theaetetus could, in view of such a violation of nature, again have responded that it would be monstrous.

Here again there is circularity in play, and it is to this that Socrates' remark gestures. In their venture, Socrates and Theaetetus are undertaking to say the truth about false opining, to determine and say what it truly is. Yet such a venture must already be oriented to truth and to true opining: in order to undertake to opine or think truly about something—even about false opining—one must already know, in some measure, what true opining is; otherwise one would have not the slightest inkling of how to set about it. And yet, the entire inquiry into false opining was undertaken in order to determine what true opining—and hence knowledge—is. As the dialogue continues, this circle will be drawn ever tighter.

In the elaboration of this third proposal regarding false opinion, there is a subtle shift in the diction. Perhaps most notably, when Socrates describes false opining as "to set down one thing as another in his thinking" (189d), the word he uses is no longer δοξάζειν or δόξα but διάνοια. When he then reiterates the description in slightly different terms, he twice repeats forms of the word διάνοια. The substitution of this word serves to recall that the thinking at issue is that in which the soul itself, by itself, stretches toward the common looks. And then it is as if the repetition of the word spins the discourse off in another direction, interrupting the preoccupation with false δόξα.

Socrates launches into a discourse on διάνοια in which it is, in turn, determined as discourse. The passage is the most decisive in the two parerga. It is addressed to the question of what thinking is to be called; in it Socrates states what it is that he calls thinking (διανοεῖσθαι—the middle voice form of διανοεῖν): "Speech [λόγος] that the soul itself goes through with itself about whatever it is considering." Before going on to elaborate, Socrates interjects a remark that, both in form and in content, reflects the tension to which, as midwife, he is exposed in declaring what thinking is, or rather, what it is that he calls thinking. He says: "As one who does not know, I am showing it to you." The passage continues: "It seems to me that when it is thinking, the soul is doing nothing else but conversing, asking itself questions and answering them itself, and affirming and denying. But whenever it has come to a determination, whether more slowly or with a swift bound, and it asserts the same thing from that time on and is not in doubt, we set this down as its opinion [δόξα]. So I call opining [δοξάζειν] speaking [λέγειν] and opinion a stated speech [λόγος]; it is not, however, before someone else any more than it is with sound [φωνῇ], but in silence before oneself" (189e–190a).

The consequences of this remarkable statement reach well beyond what it explicitly says. The statement also makes explicit certain connections that were only tacitly suggested up to this point in the dialogue. Here it becomes evident that thinking—at least, what Socrates calls thinking—is not antecedent to λόγος, that it does not first occur independently and only then come to be expressed in λόγος. Consequently, λόγος cannot be regarded as merely secondary; speech is not simply an instrument or a means of expression or communication. Rather, thinking is a kind of λόγος; it is the silent speech that the soul carries on with itself. When in such conversation with itself the soul comes to a determination, when it establishes a boundary or limit (ὅρισμα) by which that which it is considering comes to be delimited, then something decisive happens: the determination reached, the delimitation established, becomes its opinion. Just as thinking or opining is silent speech, so opinion is simply the outcome of such speech; it is the determination reached in the soul's silent conversation with itself. Opinions are not first formed and only then expressed in speech; rather, they originate from—as the outcome of—the silent speech of the soul with itself.

The equivalences that this remarkable passage establishes tie together several dominant strands of the dialogue. Reiterating in a sense the transition from the discourse on διάνοια as the soul's stretching itself toward the looks to the proposal by Theaetetus that this be called by the name δοξάζειν, this passage declares the equivalence of διάνοια and δοξάζειν. Thereby Socrates makes it clear once and for all that the discussion in the second part of the dialogue bears primarily on the soul's thinking the looks, however repeatedly the discussion may drift off into questions about mere opining.

The other overarching equivalence between thinking—whether it be called διάνοια or δοξάζειν—and silent speech serves to introduce into the discourse a remarkable convergence. What begins to emerge is an incipient identity between what, up to this point, seemed to be two very different ways in which surpassing the just-now of perception could occur, namely, by thought's stretching itself toward the common looks and by the passage to λόγος. Now it is evident that these two ways—if they can be called *two* ways—belong intimately together: when, in thinking, the soul stretches itself toward the common looks, it will—precisely as thinking—have engaged itself in λόγος.

The identification of thinking as silent speech renders it all the more evident that the third of the three proposals regarding false opining must be dismissed. If the soul, in thinking or opining, converses with itself about what it is considering, then it will never take the beautiful as ugly or the ugly as beautiful. Implicit in Socrates' dismissal of this proposal is the characterization of thinking as directed at being, at that which is itself by itself, which could never, then, be confused with or mistaken for what it is not.

Confronted with the breakdown of all three attempts to discover what false opining is, Socrates declares that if they cannot locate false opining, they "will be compelled to agree to many strange things [ἄτοπα]" (190e). Socrates does not say what these strange, out-of-place things are. Yet, assuming that, in fact, not everything before has been wiped out, it is quite clear: if there are no false opinions, if all opinions are true, then they will have returned to the Protagorean scene. Furthermore, since opining is now identified as a kind of speaking, it would follow that all λόγοι—at least of this kind—are true. Any answer at which one would arrive in silent conversation with oneself would be just as true as that reached by others.

Confessing their perplexity, Socrates declares nonetheless that there may be a way ahead for their inquiry. The further search that they launch culminates in two discourses on memory, discourses in which Socrates proposes, respectively, two images as paradigms by which to represent memory. The first image, that of a wax block, seems to suggest itself almost naturally as an image of memory, and it has persisted in various guises up to that of Freud's mystic writing pad. The other image, that of a dovecote, aviary, bird cage, is of an entirely different sort.

The first of these discussions is launched when, prompted by Socrates, Theaetetus portrays a scene in which false thinking would, it seems, occur. The scene is one in which, knowing Socrates, he sees from a distance someone else whom he does not know and comes to suppose this person to be Socrates. This scene calls, then, for the image, which Socrates proceeds to sketch in the following words: "Then please set down for the sake of the λόγος a wax block [ἐκμαγεῖον] in our souls, larger for someone and smaller for someone else, of purer wax for someone and more fouled for someone else, and harder for some and more fluid for some, and for some it is in a measured condition" (191c).[51]

This is, says Socrates, the gift of memory (Μνημοσύνη), the mother of the Muses. One could ponder for a long time on the relation between gift and memory. Memory is a gift, a power that is not procured but given with our very being. What memory presents is a gift, something gone that is given back, the vanished past brought back into the present. The free giving or free acceptance of a gift may require, on the other hand, an inhibiting of memory, a forgetting of obligations incurred in the past that would otherwise install the gift in an economy of exchange. As mother of the Muses, memory also conveys the gifts of the arts, and in this regard, at least, is not confined to mere recovery of the past.

---

51. The word ἐκμαγεῖον (in the expression κήρινον ἐκμαγεῖον: wax block) designates something on or in which an impression is made or a seal is stamped. The word plays a very important role in the *Timaeus*, where it is put forth to name one of the images of what finally comes to be called the χώρα. Not insignificantly, it is interwoven with the word φύσις. What it names is designated as "the nature [φύσις] that receives all bodies"; and it is introduced in this statement: "it is laid down by nature [φύσει] as ἐκμαγεῖον" (50b–c). See my discussion in *Chorology*, 98–113, esp. 108–9.

Socrates describes the working of memory: "Whatever we want to remember of the things we see or hear or think to ourselves [αὐτοὶ ἐννοήσωμεν], we press [or stamp an impression—ἀποτυποῦσθαι] into this by holding it under the perceptions and thoughts, as if we were putting in the seals of signet rings. And whatever is imprinted, we remember and know as long as its image is in it, but whatever is wiped out or cannot be impressed, we forget and do not know" (191d–e).[52]

In Socrates' way of casting memory as a wax block, there are two implications that need to be stressed. The first is that memory holds and gives not only perceptions, not only what we would have seen or heard in a just-now that is now long ago, but also what we think to ourselves. Memory holds and gives the thinking in which the soul itself stretches itself toward the common looks. Memory holds in a certain readiness this stretch and that to which it is stretched, and memory gives it when, for instance, one happens to perceive disparate things that have the look in common. The span of memory spans the distance across which the soul, in thinking, stretches itself, and in spanning that distance, it holds the soul in proximity to the common looks.

The second implication is that of the affiliation of memory with λόγος. When Socrates first mentions the wax block, he tells Theaetetus: "Please set it down for the sake of the λόγος." The phrase λόγου ἕνεκα can mean "for the sake of the argument," as we say, or "for the sake

---

52. It would be impossible to overestimate the enormous role that this image of stamping an impression on a wax block has had in the history of philosophy. It is—even still perhaps today—the most common way of conceiving of memory: that memory is something on which perceptions and thoughts leave a reminder, a trace, an impression, which then allows us to remember. Among the Stoics this image came to be used also in reference to perception: their view is that something is perceived when, through its effects on the senses, it produces an impression in the soul. This represents a decisive shift away from the earlier Greek view of perception (as presented in the *Theaetetus*), a shift toward what would eventually become a subjective conception. This view persists throughout much of modern philosophy (for example, in the image of the *tabula rasa*); it remains entangled in the aporia involved in the attempt to explain how impressions in the mind can constitute knowledge of things outside the mind. The phenomenological concept of intentionality effectively cuts through this aporia and, if radicalized, calls this view thoroughly into question. Concurrent with these developments, the image of impressions stamped on wax was extended to the workings of the unconscious. See Sigmund Freud, "Notiz über den 'Wunderblock' (1925)," in Freud, *Studienausgabe* (Frankfurt a.M.: Fischer Verlag, 2000), 3:363–69, together with Jacques Derrida, "Freud et la scène de l'écriture," in *L'écriture et la différence* (Paris: Éditions du Seuil, 1967), 293–340.

of the present discussion," but it also alludes to the affiliation between memory and λόγος. This affiliation is built into the image by virtue of the similarity between writing and stamping an impression on something like a wax block. Still more decisively, inasmuch as thinking is silent speech and thinking is held and given by memory, λόγος lies near the core of memory's workings. But then, this is to say that there is complicity, if not convergence, between all the dimensions in which awareness is stretched beyond the just-now of perception. Memory holds and gives the thinking, that is, the silent speaking, in which the soul stretches itself toward the common looks.

Three further developments lead from the depiction of the wax block to the image of the aviary. First of all, Socrates and Theaetetus apply the model of the wax block in a renewed effort to seek out cases where false opining could occur. They systematically run through all possible combinations of knowing, perceiving, and possessing memory, along with the privative forms of each. Most combinations are eliminated, but a few turn up in which false opining is possible. For example, Socrates considers the situation in which he has memory impressions of both Theaetetus and Theodorus and sees both of them at a distance and so not adequately. In such a situation he will try to match each perception with its memory trace so that recognition might occur. But—like someone who puts his shoes on backwards—he may apply the sight of each to the seal of the other. He mentions two other similar cases where a crossing or interchanging between perceptions and memory traces can produce false opining.

Secondly, Socrates launches into a discourse concerning the condition of the wax in the soul, describing it as, for example, pure, deep, and well-spaced in those who learn easily and have good memories. Yet in the course of these descriptions, there emerges a subtle yet decisive shift from regarding false opining as the mismatching of perceptions and memory traces to regarding it as the mismatching of perceptions and thoughts. Thus, he comes to declare that false opinion occurs "in the conjunction of perceptions with thought [διάνοια]" (195d). The effect should be to turn the discussion away from the level of prosaic opinion to that of the thinking oriented to being. Though indeed the discussion does turn in the direction of thought rather than perception, it does so in such a way that it is diverted from what would be its proper theme.

The third development will thus prove to exemplify a form in which the false opining being sought can occur. At its outset an imaginary interrogator comes to expand the dialogue between Socrates and

Theaetetus. His question is posed as follows: Could we ever suppose that the number eleven, which is merely thought of, is the number twelve rather than the eleven that is thought? The point of the question is clear: if false opinion occurred only in the conjunction between perceptions and thoughts, then, since perception is not involved, there could be no false opinion in reference to numbers; and yet, it is possible to have the false opinion that 7 + 5 = 11. The interrogator's conclusion draws conspicuously—though without mentioning it—on the transition current at the time in Greek mathematics from the conception of number (ἀριθμός) as a number of things, which could be counted, which therefore also could be perceived, to the conception of number as a number of ones, of pure units intended in thought. But what is decisive is that the discourse has now been diverted from a consideration of ontological thinking to one of arithmetical thinking. It is the aporia posed by the interrogator's question that prompts Socrates to introduce another image in place of the wax block.

A comedy has now been prepared, one so comedic that it will finally devolve into a kind of burlesque.

How has it been prepared? Precisely by the way in which, throughout the second part of the dialogue, the discourse has gotten ahead of itself, that is, has inadvertently taken for granted precisely that which it takes itself to be seeking. This is one of the prime recipes for Platonic comedy, failing to take notice or account of something and then playing things out to the point where comedic awareness of what has been overlooked is engendered.

What is it that gets overlooked? In the most general terms, it is the entanglement inherent in the pursuit of the question "What is knowledge?" There is immediately a double entanglement. As with every such question regarding what something is, there is the entanglement of having already to know what it is in order to go about inquiring about it. But in the case of the question of knowledge, the entanglement is compounded: for in this case knowledge not only is that about which one would inquire, but also is that which would be carried out in inquiring. In this case one sets out to know what knowledge is and thus must know in advance what it is, not only in order to aim at the proper theme of the inquiry, but in order to set about it at all.

The second part of the *Theaetetus* is replete with indications of such entanglement, subtle and oblique indications in the beginning, more and more open declarations as the discourse continues. Following the discussion of memory as a wax block and of the problems encountered in trying to account for falsity in pure—in this instance mathematical—thinking, the entanglement is openly declared, Socrates suggesting that their entrapment in it is something shameless (ἀναιδής). For, while claiming not to know what knowledge is but to be searching for it by searching first for false thinking, they have described this false thinking as mistaking something unknown for something known. Socrates says: "And then does it not seem shameless if we do not know knowledge to declare what sort of thing it is to know? But as a matter of fact, Theaetetus, we have been infected for a long time now by our conversing impurely, for we have said thousands of times 'We recognize' and 'We do not recognize,' and 'We know' and 'We do not know,' as though we somehow understand one another while still being ignorant of knowledge" (196d–e). Theaetetus answers: "But, Socrates, in what manner will you converse if you abstain from them?" Socrates' response suggests an inevitability of such entanglement, infection, contamination: "In none, for I am who I am."

Socrates signals the start of the comedy by momentarily impersonating one whom he calls an ἀντιλογικός, a refuter, one might say. He is one who would abstain from the entanglements and rebuke those who do not. This refuter presides over the comedy that now ensues.

Since if one knows something one cannot, it seems, mistake it for something else that one knows, for instance, eleven for twelve, Socrates distinguishes between possessing knowledge, having it stored in memory, and having knowledge present to one's thought. This distinction prompts the fanciful construction, in every soul, of a bird cage. The birds in the cage are knowledges possessed, held in store in memory, whereas the bird one reaches in and catches is knowledge that one has present to one's thought. False thinking occurs when, as the birds are all flying about, one reaches into the cage and seizes one instead of another, getting hold of eleven instead of twelve.

Socrates is not long in exposing how ludicrous this solution is: in having a knowledge of something—eleven—one is ignorant of this very thing—mistakes it for twelve—not by ignorance but by one's very knowledge. It is as if in the presence of knowledge—with the eleven present to one's thought—the soul came to know nothing.

Theaetetus responds by putting some more birds in the cage: he proposes that they should also put non-knowledges in the cage as well as knowledges and have them all fly about there in the soul. False thinking would occur when one happened to seize the wrong kind of bird, getting hold of a non-knowledge instead of a knowledge.

The profusion of birds now in the soul provokes the reappearance of the refuter, who not only rebukes Socrates and Theaetetus but now—even despite his abstinent character—actually *laughs*. Then he—given voice, of course, by Socrates—mockingly asks how—as the catcher of a non-knowledge would—someone could mistake a non-knowledge for a knowledge. Certainly not if one had it, that is, knew the non-knowledge, but only if one merely possessed it in memory without having it present. Now the tangle is set in motion, the refuter tracing in the following question the sole recourse that remains open: "Or will you tell me once more that there are in turn knowledges of the knowledges and non-knowledges, which their possessor confined in some other ridiculous bird cages or wax molds and knows as long as he possesses them even if he does not have them ready at hand in his soul?" (200b–c). In this question the refuter is in effect declaring the following: in order for the non-knowledge taken from the cage so as to be present to one's thought to be mistakable for a knowledge, that is, in order for this non-knowledge not to be known as such, it must still be contained in a cage rather than being simply present to one's thought. Thus, in being taken from the cage, it must have been brought into a second cage rather than being made simply present as such to thought. Thus a second bird cage would need to be set in the soul, and then, as the same problem would recur in it, still a third, and so on. As the comedy comes to its conclusion, the entire entangled discourse is set whirling around endlessly, as, in a tone no doubt of mockery as well as laughter—though still in the voice of Socrates—the refuter exclaims: "If it is in this way, will you not all be compelled to run around to the same point thousands of times and get nowhere?" (200c).

Socrates does not answer the question that he, ventriloquizing the refuter, has posed, but only goes on to reiterate the circle in which the search cannot but move in response to the question as to what knowledge is. Speaking now in his own name, he declares: "we do not correctly seek for false opinion prior to knowledge and let knowledge go. It is impossible to come to know it before one grasps knowledge adequately as to what it is" (200c–d). This, at the very least, the comedy has demonstrated.

At the very end of the second discourse, the sense of δοξάζειν drifts toward, indeed conspicuously shifts to, the mundane, prosaic sense of opining, which throughout has vied with its sense as διάνοια. Socrates refers to public advocates, who have the ability to make jurors opine whatever they want them to opine; they can even do so—here is a decisive indication of the shift—while the water clock is running. In particular, they are able to persuade jurors about the truth of something to which the latter were not present and so to instill in them true opinion without knowledge. In light of this example, the identification of knowledge with true opinion must be put aside.

The shift to the mundane level thus allows Socrates to draw a distinction between knowledge and true opinion. On the other hand, as long as δοξάζειν retains the sense of διάνοια, which it was initially proposed to name, the distinction cannot be maintained. For if the transition to knowledge occurs with the advent of διάνοια, in which the soul stretches toward the common looks, then true δοξάζειν—true to this sense and thus opening to the true—and the δόξα in which it issues will suffice to constitute the transition to knowledge. To the extent that this sense remains in play, even if in oscillation with the mundane sense, the conclusion of the second discourse is not simply aporetic.

Theaetetus launches the third discourse by enacting in deed the working of memory, to the account of which much of the second discourse was devoted. Affirming the distinction Socrates has drawn between knowledge and true opinion, Theaetetus draws on his memory in order to add a third, distinct term, which—so he once heard—if combined with true opinion, transforms the whole into knowledge. He says: "Yes, Socrates, this is what I heard someone say but forgot, but now I have it in mind [ἐννοῶ]. He said that true opinion with λόγος was knowledge, but without λόγος [ἄλογον] was outside of knowledge. And of whatever there is not a λόγος, that is not knowable—these are the names he used—and whatever admits λόγος is knowable" (201c-d).

It is a question of memory, of whether, having forgotten and only now remembered what he once heard, Theaetetus may also have forgotten and not—at least not yet—remembered what he heard Socrates say in the second discourse. If the sense of δόξα (and, correspondingly, δοξάζειν) falls entirely on the mundane side, then the threefold distinction between knowledge, true opinion, and λόγος is not unfeasible; neither is the supposition that the first is compounded from the other two. But if, on the other hand, δόξα (and δοξάζειν) has the sense taken over from the first discourse and reaffirmed at several junctures in the second discourse, then knowledge is not distinct from δόξα but rather eventuates precisely in and through δοξάζειν. Furthermore, δοξάζειν in this sense, as διάνοια, has been identified as a silent λόγος; hence, Theaetetus' proposed addition of λόγος to δόξα—so as allegedly to transform true δόξα into knowledge—is indeed *no addition at all*. Thus, in place of the distinction between the three terms, there is: knowledge *as* δοξάζειν *as* λόγος.

These are the two poles between which the entire third discourse oscillates: between, on the one side, knowledge as compounded from the distinct operations of opining and λόγος and, on the other side, knowledge as eventuated in the operation of opining (that is, of thought) in the form of λόγος. Much of the third discourse consists of a kind of double speech about speech, addressed ambivalently to both sides, to the mundane construal of λόγος and to λόγος as integral to opining and hence to knowledge.

The ambivalence appears in deed as soon as Theaetetus has given his report on what he has remembered. To this remembrance Socrates responds by saying to Theaetetus that he "speaks beautifully." This response alludes to the capacity of the terms Theaetetus has gathered, their capacity to let something shine through from beyond the mundane level to which the specific formulation largely adheres. But then, rather than simply voicing approval of what Theaetetus has remembered, Socrates asks about the point at which the division is to be made between knowable and unknowable. He is curious—so he says—whether he and Theaetetus might have heard the same thing about this division.

Socrates then proceeds to tell what he has heard. Yet the way in which he recasts the discourse seems designed to call Theaetetus' memory into question. Not only does he cast what he has heard as something heard in a dream, but also—as he introduces his narration—he says to Theaetetus: "Hear, then, a dream in return for a dream" (201d). What is implied in Socrates' recasting Theaetetus' remembrance as a dream? Is this simply a way of casting suspicion on Theaetetus' remembrance, suggesting that, rather than remembering, Theaetetus may have merely dreamed—even daydreamed—what he reports? But in this case it would seem strange indeed that Socrates goes on to cast what he says as something heard in a dream. Is it, then, perhaps a matter of emphasizing the ambivalence, which in dreams is still more conspicuous than in memory?

Socrates narrates his dream: "I dreamed that I heard some people say that the first things were just like elements [στοιχεῖα], out of which we and everything else are composed, and they do not admit of λόγος; that it is only possible to give a name to each alone by itself [αὐτὸ ... καθ' αὑτό], but it is impossible to address it any differently" (201e). Socrates goes on to elaborate, detailing various ways in which the elements cannot be addressed (for instance, by applying being or not-being to them), for in every case they would then be addressed as something other, whereas each is alone by itself, that is, selfsame. He repeats that the elements can only be named, not stated in λόγος. Only when the names are interwoven is there λόγος: "For the interweaving [συμπλοκή] of names is the being of λόγος" (202b). He concludes: since the elements are without λόγος, they are unknowable, as someone who has true opinion but is unable to give a λόγος about that regarding which he opines is without knowledge.

In the content of Socrates' dream the ambivalence is evident, the incipient oscillation between the two valences at which the discourse operates. Socrates speaks of elements (στοιχεῖα) in a way that extends the word beyond its original application only to letters of the alphabet to the elementary components of things;[53] yet in this passage the elements under consideration are clearly the letters belonging to λόγος, not to φύσις. Nonetheless, as letters, they can be considered simply as units, sounded or written, that can be interwoven into a λόγος, no consideration being given to the signifying capacity of λόγος, which renders it more than mere sounds or marks. To the extent that the elements are considered in this manner, the mundane valence prevails.

And yet, in Socrates' narration of his dream, there is much that serves to lift the discourse to the level of διάνοια as determined at the end of the first discourse. Regarding the looks toward which the soul stretches itself, it must be said—and is said again and again—that each is itself alone by itself (αὐτὸ καθ' αὑτό). In this connection it must also be said that since each is simply itself, it cannot be addressed as if it were also something else, something other; rather, it can only be named. Yet these names can be interwoven so as to form a λόγος. Such a λόγος—which perhaps could be called true λόγος, true to what λόγος in this superior valence is—is not simply a series of letters, sounded or written; it is, rather, that which says—which signifies—the looks in such a way that

---

53. The extension of the range of the word στοιχεῖον so that it came to cover not only the elements of λόγος (that is, the letters) but also the elements of things (their elementary components) first gained currency through Plato. In addition to the passage in the *Theaetetus* (201e), which, though it affirms this extension, is nonetheless addressed to elements in the sense of letters, there is a passage in the *Timaeus* (48b) in which, though the extension is broached, there are also reservations or at least hesitation about it.

it belongs to—even animates—the thought that reaches out to the looks in their aloneness by themselves.

Speaking now directly without enclosing what he says within a dream, Socrates declares that there are paradigms of λόγος and that these need to be put to the test. The two paradigms that he proceeds to introduce are formulated in terms of the elements (or letters) and the syllables composed of them. The first of these is the phonetic paradigm: the letters are the elements, and with them alone there is no λόγος, no speech; only with the advance to the syllable does λόγος come into play, and hence, in accord with Theaetetus' proposal, knowledge also. The paradigm rests on the conflation of λόγος with the mere sounding of speech: whereas the syllable SO (ΣΩ) can be said, the sigma is voiceless and the omega has voice but cannot be said. Socrates loses no time in disposing of this paradigm. Referring still to the syllable composed from the two letters, he asks: Can one be ignorant of each and yet know both? Theaetetus responds that this would be strange (δεινόν) and devoid of λόγος (ἄλογον). In the double speech of this discourse, Theaetetus is (unknowingly) saying that this paradigm of speech would, in a double sense, in both valences, be no speech at all.

Socrates proceeds to introduce an arithmetical paradigm according to which "the syllable comes to be one look out of those several elements that fit together" (204a)—as twice three or thrice two or four and two all amount to six. Number thus comes to represent the elements and syllables of λόγος. Socrates launches into an extended discussion of whole and parts, which leads to the conclusion that if the syllable is without parts—if, in the discourse of διάνοια, it corresponds to a single look—then it is no more sayable and knowable than an element. But, in fact, in actual learning it is primarily the letters that one learns to recognize. Socrates concludes: "And if anyone says that a syllable is knowable and that an element is by nature unknowable, we will be convinced that, willingly or unwillingly, he is being playful [παίζειν]" (206b).

Ostensibly drawing the discussion back to the main topic, the addition of λόγος to true opinion, Socrates poses the question as to what λόγος signifies (σημαίνειν). In other words, by determining what λόγος signifies, it would presumably be possible to discover what is involved in and what is accomplished by the addition of λόγος to true opinion. Yet already from the outset of the third discourse, it is evident that—at least in the superior valence of the discussion—this alleged addition is no addition at all. To say nothing of the peculiar circularity in which the question "What does λόγος signify?" cannot but get entangled. For it is not only that λόγος signifies something (in the sense that the word has a meaning), but, quite beyond this, λόγος is precisely that by which everything is signified. Whatever signification λόγος has will have been signified through its own signifying power. The signification of λόγος will have been signified by λόγος itself.

These entanglements that inevitably go unacknowledged as long as the discourse adheres to the mundane valence cannot but prompt the expectation that the three significations of λόγος that are now to be introduced will display more than a bit of ironic playfulness bordering on comedy.

Such is the tone with which Socrates introduces the first signification: λόγος is that by which "one makes one's own thought [διάνοια] evident through the voice with names and phrases, as if it were into a mirror or water that one were setting one's opinion in relief into the flowing stream [ῥοή] through one's mouth" (206d). Socrates promptly dismisses this conception of λόγος as expression, since it would, in fact, render the addition of λόγος to true opinion no addition at all, not even in the mundane valence; for anyone who has a true opinion will be able to express it, and its expression will add nothing whatsoever.

It is remarkable how readily Socrates puts aside this conception, for as the thesis that language is (merely) the expression of thought, it has been put forth again and again and indeed remains operative even in many sectors of modern linguistics (in Saussure, for instance). Yet, within the context of the *Theaetetus*, λόγος as the mere expression of antecedent thought could accomplish nothing that would contribute to the soul's drawing itself beyond to the common looks. Λόγος as expression would presuppose thought rather than contributing to its formation and movement.

Much the same can be said regarding the second signification, according to which λόγος consists in the capacity to enumerate the elements of that about which one has true opinion. A citation from Hesiod allows Socrates to construe these elements in the most mundane form, as analogous to the parts of a wagon. Yet then Socrates has only to put in question whether enumerating the parts of a wagon amounts to knowing what a wagon is; and, in the case in point, he has only to show that whereas enumerating the elements (the syllables) of Theaetetus' name requires true opinion, doing so does not advance it to the level of knowledge. And yet, what Socrates says in this connection is less than fully conclusive; in particular, he does not state what it would mean to have knowledge of Theaetetus' name. One can only presume that this striking omission is prescribed by the level at which the discussion here proceeds: to speak of knowledge and of the role of λόγος in it would require a decisive shift away from the mere discussion of names in terms of the syllables into which they are partitioned.

The third signification Socrates takes to coincide with what the many (οἱ πολλοί) would say: "to have some sign to say by means of which that which is asked about differs from all things" (208c). The formulation already borders on circularity: to give a λόγος, to speak about something, is to say a sign that signifies something. In other words, to speak is to say something of a certain sort; to give a λόγος is—almost tautologically—to signify. Socrates is specific about what the sign is to signify: it is to be a sign of difference, of that by which each thing differs from everything else. Alluding by way of ironic denial to that which λόγος truly signifies, Socrates declares that the sign must in no way touch on what is in common (κοινόν). Then, as he turns to the refutation of this conception, he declares: "Now suddenly, Theaetetus, I do not understand [ξυνίημι] it at all, not even a little, since I have come too near to what is said" (208e). The point is that understanding requires taking distance from particulars in their differences; it requires precisely what has been prohibited in what has been said, namely, touching or stretching toward the common.

Socrates moves quickly to dispose of the third signification proposed for λόγος. He points out that true opinion must turn away from the common and must, instead, concern the difference; to have true opinion about Theaetetus requires reference to his snub nose and bulging eyes, even in their difference from Socrates' similar features. True opinion must be about difference, and thus the addition of a sign of difference would add nothing at all and would not advance true opinion to the level of knowledge. In stating a λόγος, one would only be doing again what in true opinion one would already have been doing—as in the proverbial twirling of a pestle. If, on the other hand, giving a λόγος means coming to know the difference, then the circularity is obtrusive: "For to come to know is surely to take knowledge, is it not?" (209e–210a).

The entire third discourse has thus proceeded on the basis of a detachment of λόγος from διάνοια; that is, it is conditioned by a forgetting or a disregarding of the identity of λόγος and διάνοια that was established in the second discourse. It is this disregarding that renders the third discourse comedic, for in effect it merely plays out the consequences of this disregarding. Once speech is detached from thinking, it is deprived of its capacity to signify and thereby is reduced to a mere sequence of signs, which, lacking their signifying function, are, in turn, reduced to mere elements. Thus, the third discourse has commenced with Socrates' telling of his dream about the elements of λόγος, which are taken to consist of letters regarded simply as units, the signifying capacity of which is entirely disregarded. The phonetic paradigm then specifies the character of the elements, describing them as the sounds that become possible with the advance from letters to syllables. The arithmetical paradigm carries the reduction still further by regarding the λόγος as resulting simply from a fitting together of elements that is analogous to the addition of numbers. Nothing could be more appropriate than that at precisely that point Socrates raises the question of the signification of λόγος, for it is precisely the signifying power of λόγος that the entire discourse up to this point has disregarded. This reduction sets the stage for the three conceptions of λόγος that constitute the comedic passage that brings the dialogue almost to its end. The first conception, that of speech as the expression of thought, directly announces the detachment by which the signifying capacity of λόγος is stripped away. The analogy then drawn between λόγος and the enumeration of the parts of the wagon is simply a comedic exemplification of the reduction of λόγος to a mere sequence of elements, that is, of signs that are not signs of anything, and thus ultimately not signs at all. While the third conception allows that the signs that constitute λόγος are signs of something, that which they signify, namely, difference, is precisely the opposite of the common look that λόγος in its conjunction with διάνοια would signify. Throughout the entire discourse, the detachment of λόγος from διάνοια has the effect of engendering a disregard for the intrinsic capacity of λόγος to stretch beyond the mere signifying element to the common looks that would be signified.

    Asked by Socrates whether they have now given birth to everything, Theaetetus responds: "Yes, by Zeus, and I have said even more on account of you than I had in myself" (210b). While each of the determinations of knowledge that Theaetetus has proposed are, as Socrates declares, wind-eggs unworthy of nurture, through them something has shined through from beyond, the common looks and the thought that, stretching itself toward them, would at least advance toward knowledge. Thus has Theaetetus given birth to more than he had in himself, thus has he exceeded himself, as he did most manifestly in the moment of wonder, imaging in deed the ascent of philosophy itself. And yet, the draft toward the beyond, if never entirely lost sight of, is ever again drawn back toward the mundane, which ultimately means toward φύσις, toward the earthly—and toward the limit of all limits, death. As the *Theaetetus* ends, Socrates goes off to the portico of the King to confront the indictment that has been brought against philosophy.

6 EARTHBOUND. THE RETURN OF NATURE

(A) THESEUS

It is never the first word. Always there will have been others that inform it in advance, that let it say much more than, as a mere word, it would say. At its very inception these other words set it in motion, not a motion that would carry it away but one that lets it exceed itself in the very moment when it is first sounded, while also letting its echo be heard across all that is to come. Before the would-be beginning, there will have been deeds as well, deeds that will be recalled though hardly mentioned at all. Above all, there will have been words about these deeds, about the deeds of extraordinary mortals but also about the deeds of legendary heroes, frightful monsters, and the immortal gods. The words about the deeds of mortals are recalled in narratives often given voice by those who say or hear what seems the first word; in most instances the narrator will be one who witnessed the deeds, one who was present and now, later, recalls and tells of what he saw and heard. The words about the deeds of heroes, monsters, and gods make up what the Greeks called μῦθοι. From the would-be first word, certain of them, even primarily one that is all-informing, are recalled, though almost in silence.

At the outset of the *Phaedo*, Echecrates speaks to Phaedo: "You yourself, Phaedo, were you present with Socrates on that day when he drank the potion in the prison, or did you hear from someone else?" (57a). The word first spoken is αὐτός, *you yourself*, or, more literally, just *yourself*. The opening statement not only is a question but also, in the word first spoken, raises a question that reaches across the entire dialogue. What is spoken of when, addressing Phaedo, Echecrates says *yourself*? What is the self of Phaedo?—of any mortal? Is it identical with what the Greeks called ψυχή, which we can justifiably translate as *soul* only if the history of the word ψυχή (in its various translations) that began in late antiquity is set aside and its sense—hence also that of *soul*—is rigorously determined by reference back to the Platonic texts? Or is the self—of Phaedo and of everyone—something of the body, something composed from and reducible to bodily elements? Or does it somehow belong to both the soul and the body? Does it have its proper locus in the yoke that conjoins the soul and the body? It is to this question of the self that, in one way or another, much of the *Phaedo* is devoted. The single word first spoken, with all that it sets in play, thus encapsulates one of the primary questions of the dialogue.

But, more extensively, what does it mean for something *to be itself*? In the most rigorous sense, it means not being anything other than itself, being identical with itself, being the same as itself, being selfsame. Correspondingly, the word αὐτός can also mean *same*. Thus, the word first spoken alludes to a kind of being that is the same as itself. Taken in the strictest sense, it is a kind of being that in no way whatsoever varies from, differs from, is other than itself. It is a kind of being that harbors in itself nothing other than itself, nothing that could, as in a simple assertoric proposition, be ascribed to it. It is a kind of being that, in this precise sense, is absolutely selfsame. This kind of being—which will prove identical with being as such as well as with kind as such—will be called by various names, among them ἰδέα and εἶδος, both of which can, with sufficient precautions and reservations, be rendered as *look*. Interrogating this kind of being and the comportment to it of which humans are capable will—to say the least—be a primary concern in the dialogue.

Yet, in the *Phaedo* the orientation to being as such does not by any means exclude consideration of φύσις and of its modes of return. In a distinctive sense the repeated return of nature in the very midst of ontological discourses is what draws the conversation along. It keeps the discussion under way by repeatedly drawing it down, by proving to limit the ascent to being. This movement of ascent and descent continues throughout the dialogue, even in what seems to be a turn from nature initiated in a second sailing; it continues until finally the discourse is about nothing but nature and its return.

This defining movement will, however, come into view only gradually, even if a remote echo can be heard already in the first word spoken by Echecrates. Phaedo's answer to Echecrates' opening question repeats—and thereby intensifies the focus on—the word first spoken.

He says simply "αὐτός—myself—Echecrates" (57a). Entreating Phaedo to tell him about Socrates' death, Echecrates then reveals that he is a citizen of Phlius and that the present conversation is, in fact, set in this location. Phlius was a small πόλις on the Peloponnesos. It was almost completely surrounded by very high mountains, and hence was rather isolated. Travelers did occasionally pass through, since it lay on the route from Athens to Elis; but since it was allied with Sparta, very few of these travelers were Athenians or persons who had connections with Athens. Echecrates remarks that no one from Phlius any longer visits Athens and that no Athenians had arrived in Phlius who could report the details about Socrates' death. Having heard nothing except that Socrates drank the potion and died, Echecrates is eager to hear the full story from Phaedo.

Phlius was one of the mainland centers of Pythagoreanism, one of the places where Pythagoreans took refuge when, after the death of Pythagoras himself, the order suffered persecution. There was also a tradition that directly connected Pythagoras with this πόλις: he was said to have first assumed the name φιλόσοφος while in Phlius.[1] Aristoxenus, who began as a Pythagorean and later became a student of Aristotle, compiled a list of the last Pythagoreans, among whom were several from Phlius, including Echecrates.[2]

The site of the conversation and its initiation by Echecrates could hardly be more appropriate. For the dialogue will barely have gotten under way before it becomes evident that it is engaged with certain beliefs and theories of the Pythagoreans, most notably those concerning the deathlessness of the soul. There is also an appropriateness in Pythagoras' having reportedly taken on the title φιλόσοφος at the very site where the *Phaedo* takes place; for the dialogue's engagement with the question of immortality will be constantly oriented to the question of the relation of philosophy to death and to deathlessness.

Phaedo is presumably just passing through Phlius on his way to Elis. Ancient doxographers report that he came from an aristocratic family in Elis. But—so the report goes—in a brief war between Athens and Elis (which was allied with Sparta), Phaedo was captured and then brought back to Athens as a slave and probably forced into male prostitution. Yet,

---

1. Iamblichus, *The Life of Pythagoras*, in *The Pythagorean Sourcebook and Library*, comp. and trans. Kenneth Sylvan Guthrie (Grand Rapids, MI: Planes Press, 1987), 70.

2. Diogenes Laertius, *Lives of Eminent Philosophers* 8:46. Also Nails, *The People of Plato*, 138.

eventually he had the good fortune of meeting Socrates, who induced some wealthy friends to buy back Phaedo's freedom. Thereafter—so it is said—he pursued philosophy.[3]

When Echecrates asks Phaedo whether he was himself with Socrates on that day when Socrates drank the potion or whether he heard about it from another, he poses two alternatives: either actually being present so as to witness the deeds that were enacted or hearing someone who did witness them tell about them. After Phaedo reveals that he himself was there, Echecrates poses again the same alternatives, but now transferred to the scene itself where Phaedo had been present. He asks: "Well, so what is it the man said before his death? And how did he meet his end?" (57a). Here again the focus is on the same pair: speeches and deeds (λόγοι and ἔργα). In the *Phaedo* a great deal turns on this pair, on the relation between deeds, to which one may be present, and discourses, in which the deeds can be reported to someone at a remove from them.

In the dialogue there are, strictly speaking, only the two characters Echecrates and Phaedo. Beyond the brief opening scene, almost the entire dialogue consists in Phaedo's narrating to Echecrates the story of Socrates' last day. There are, however, two junctures where Echecrates interrupts the narrative, and the exchange between him and Phaedo is briefly resumed. While punctuating the dialogue, these interruptions also serve as reminders that the entire representation of the words and deeds on Socrates' last day is itself a narrative that, from a distance, recalls those words and deeds. The dialogue does not itself dramatize, does not directly present, the events leading up to Socrates' death; rather, it inscribes a λόγος that represents these events, a λόγος that, presented in Phlius some time after Socrates' death, is separated from these events both by a time span and by spatial distance. It will turn out that in the single most decisive passage in this λόγος, Socrates will describe philosophy as properly recommencing in and through a turn away from deeds and things *to* λόγοι. Thus, the very form of the *Phaedo*—as a λόγος set at a distance from the events on Socrates' last day—will prove to exemplify the account that will be given of philosophy itself.

In his opening question Echecrates asks Phaedo whether he was present with Socrates "on that day when he drank the potion." The word translated as *potion* is φάρμακον. It can mean *poison*; but it can

---

3. Diogenes Laertius, *Lives of Eminent Philosophers* 2:31. Nails, *The People of Plato*, 231.

equally well mean *drug, medicine, remedy*. For example, φάρμακον νόσου means: a medicine or remedy for treatment of an illness or disease (νόσος). Though it is usually assumed that Socrates drank hemlock, and though it is known that in Greece hemlock was often used for executions, the *Phaedo* consistently refers to what he drank as φάρμακον. The word itself poses one of the most significant and difficult questions regarding the *Phaedo*: Does the dialogue present the φάρμακον only as poison or also as medicine, as a remedy—perhaps for the illness of embodiment, as a Pythagorean might well suppose, or perhaps for the illness of arrogant presumption (ἀκολασία, ὕβρις [in one of its various senses]—see *Apology* 26e, *Phaedrus* 238a).

Confined to the isolation of Phlius, remote from Athens, Echecrates has heard very little about Socrates' last day. He tells Phaedo that he knows only that Socrates "drank the potion and died." He reports, however, that he and his fellow citizens had heard about the trial and that, knowing that it took place long before Socrates' death, they had wondered why his death occurred so long after the trial. Asked then by Echecrates why there had been this long delay, Phaedo answers that it was a matter of chance (τύχη), that by chance—as a matter of good fortune, good luck—Socrates' trial occurred on the day after a certain significant public event. Such chance conjunction, such mere coincidence, occurs whenever there is no causal or intelligible connection between two events that nonetheless come to be related. More generally, chance is precisely what does not submit to generality; it is what falls outside any noetic order. Such occurrences, resistant to any noetic account, belong especially to the domain of fables and myth, that is, to what the Greeks called μῦθος. Phaedo's reference to chance provides, then, the appropriate connection through which to bring his discourse into relation to what will prove to be the primary μῦθος of the *Phaedo*.

This μῦθος concerns certain events that took place in a legendary, indefinite past on Crete, in Athens, and in the dealings of each with the other. On Crete, King Minos received a beautiful white bull as a gift from Poseidon, who expected that Minos would, in turn, sacrifice the bull to him. But Minos could not bear to kill the bull, and rather than sacrificing it, he kept it for himself. As punishment for this misdeed, Poseidon brought it about that Minos' wife Pasiphae fell madly in love with the bull; thus she came to give birth to a monster, half bull and half human. This monster was the Minotaur. As soon as the Minotaur was born, Minos engaged Daedalus to construct a place of confinement for the monster. Thus it was that Daedalus came to build the Labyrinth. He constructed it in such a way that once within it one would continue endlessly along its twisting pathways without ever finding an exit. Even for the Minotaur, escape from the Labyrinth was impossible.

The scene shifts then to Athens, where Androgeus, son of King Minos, came for a visit. But rather than being properly received and entertained by the Athenian King Aegeus, Androgeus was drawn into a series of events that led to his death. In retribution, Minos launched a war against the Athenians; his forces brought destruction and despair upon them. In addition, the gods laid waste to the land, bringing famine and pestilence and causing the rivers to dry up. Consulting with the Delphic Oracle, the Athenians were told that if they came to be reconciled with Minos, the anger of the gods would cease and the miseries the gods had inflicted on them would end. Thus the Athenians sent envoys to Crete, and eventually they settled on an agreement with Minos. The agreement was that Minos would halt his attack if every nine years the Athenians would send him a tribute of seven maidens and seven young men. Yet, when the Athenians then sent the first tribute, the seven maidens and seven young men were put in the Labyrinth, and lacking all means of escape, they were eventually devoured by the Minotaur.

Those sent nine years later as the second tribute suffered the same fate. But then, just before the third tribute was due, Theseus, the only son of King Aegeus, arrived in Athens. The circumstances of his birth and upbringing as well as the course by which he had journeyed to Athens had been quite unusual. When, longing to have children, Aegeus had consulted the Delphic Oracle, he had received a response so ambiguous that he could not interpret it. So he set out for Troezen, a small πόλις in southern Greece, in order to confer with the leader Pittheus. By cleverly construing the Oracle's message in a certain way, Pittheus contrived to entice Aegeus to lie with Aethra, Pittheus' daughter, and she then gave birth to Theseus. When, prior to his son's birth, Aegeus returned to Athens, he left a sword and sandals for his son hidden under a large stone. Theseus was brought up in Troezen by his mother, Aethra, and his grandfather Pittheus. They carefully concealed his true parentage, claiming that he had been begotten by Poseidon.

When Theseus came of age, his mother took him to the stone where his father had hidden the sword and the sandals. Easily lifting the stone, he took the sword and the sandals and set out for Athens. Though Pittheus urged him to take the easy and safe route by sea, he refused and instead took the land route, on which there were many dangerous monsters and bandits. Theseus was eager to follow the example of Heracles and become a great hero. Indeed, on his way to Athens, he encountered and killed many dangerous beings. In imitation of Heracles, he inflicted on each of them the same violent treatment they had inflicted on others. For instance, when he encountered Sinis, who was notorious for killing passersby by tying them to two adjacent pine trees bent to the ground and then releasing the trees, Theseus saw to it that he met his end in the same fashion.

When Theseus arrived in Athens, the situation was chaotic. But after surviving all the intrigue and sorcery directed at him, there came an occasion when, threatened by the sorceress Medea, he drew his sword; seeing the sword, Aegeus recognized him and then gladly welcomed him to Athens.

Shortly thereafter, the time came for the third tribute. Theseus stepped forward and volunteered to go along on the ship to Crete. Only to his father did he reveal that his intent was to kill the Minotaur. He told his father also that if he succeeded, then the returning ship would fly a white sail in place of the black one that otherwise signaled the ill fate of the voyage. So, the ship set sail for Crete with the tribute of fourteen persons aboard. But this time there were, not seven, but nine young men, two of whom were girlish in appearance and had been taught by Theseus to imitate the voices and gestures of girls.

When the Athenians arrived in Crete, they were paraded before the Cretans on their way to the Labyrinth. Among the spectators was Minos' daughter Ariadne, who, catching sight of Theseus, immediately fell in love with him. Summoning Daedalus, she had him explain the way in which one might be able to escape the Labyrinth. Then she summoned Theseus and offered to aid him in escaping, provided he would agree to take her with him back to Athens as his bride. Then, when he agreed, she explained the means of escape that Daedalus had revealed to her: she told Theseus that he should take a ball of thread, fasten one end to the inside of the entrance, and then unwind it as he went into the Labyrinth. Theseus did just as she had instructed and, coming upon the Minotaur asleep, killed the monster with his bare hands. Then, following the thread back to the entrance, Theseus and the others escaped, and, taking Ariadne with them, they boarded their ship and sailed for Athens. There are various accounts of just what happened when, along the way, they stopped on the island of Naxos; but all reports concur that when they sailed on, Ariadne was left behind on Naxos. They stopped also on the sacred island of Delos, birthplace of Apollo; there they engaged in a dance, which commemorated their escape from the Labyrinth and which with its twisting and turning imitated the Labyrinth.

When the ship approached Athens, Theseus—either because of his joy over his victory or because of his grief over the loss of Ariadne—forgot to hoist the white sail. Spying the black sail, Aegeus was overcome with despair and threw himself from the rocky heights down into the sea. Though grieved over the death of Aegeus, Athenians were joyful at the news Theseus brought them. He became their leader and established Athens as a πόλις in the affairs of which all citizens participated. Afterwards the Athenians preserved the ship in which Theseus had made his fateful journey.[4]

Socrates' own fate came by chance to be linked to this ship. His death had been delayed because the ship had just left for Delos—the very ship, so the Athenians say, "in which Theseus once went off leading those twice seven to Crete and both saved them and himself was saved" (58a–b). At the time when Theseus had set out on his journey to Crete, the Athenians had made a vow to Apollo—so it is said, according to Phaedo's report—that if they were saved from Minos' vengeance, they would send a mission every year to Delos. It was required that once the mission was under way, the πόλις must remain pure, and so no executions could take place until the ship has gone to Delos and returned.

Socrates' death is thus delayed by the mission carried out in gratitude to the very same god who—as Socrates revealed at his trial—had originally sent him on his way of questioning. During this time of delay, of deferral, there is imposed—by νόμος (law or custom), says Phaedo—a requirement of purification, or rather, a semblance of purification, as though Athens could free itself of the guilt of condemning Socrates to death merely by deferring his execution. But during the time of deferral, as it is coming to an end, other forms of purification will come to be discussed, until, finally, Socrates goes off to take his bath. In this discussion, carried out in the prison as the time of Socrates' death approaches, it comes to light that even that very coming to an end, death, can—whether truly or not—be considered a form of purification, even one to which the philosopher has a special affinity.

---

4. The main source of the Theseus story is Plutarch, *The Lives of the Noble Grecians and Romans*, "Theseus"; also Apollodorus, *Bibliotheca* 3:216f.

Taking place in Phlius some time after the death of Socrates, Phaedo's narration is set at a distance from the events that took place in Socrates' prison on his last day. And yet, it is precisely because Phaedo was indeed present at those happenings that he can—if now from a distance—tell Echecrates and his Pythagorean companions about them. It is, in fact, striking how, from the very beginning of the dialogue, the opposition between distance and presence comes into play, that is, the opposition between a λόγος set at a distance from that of which it tells *and* presence to those events themselves, to the persons, things, and deeds. While the dramatic setting brings distance into play and sustains it, it is presence that is most obtrusive in the opening discourses, in the very texture of their diction. A form of the verb παραγίγνουαι occurs at the very outset: "Yourself, Phaedo, were you present . . . ?" It is not long then until the conversation turns to the question as to which of Socrates' companions were present on his last day. The same verb, along with its near-synonym παρεῖναι, recurs again and again in the opening passages of the dialogue. The prevalence of presence in the diction and its opposition to the discursive distance secured by the dramatic setting can be regarded as anticipating the decisive point in the dialogue where Socrates describes his philosophical practice as having first begun in engagement with the things present in φύσις, but then, in the wake of failure, having recommenced in a turn from presence to λόγος.

Echecrates asks Phaedo: "And who, Phaedo, chanced to be present?" (59b). The formulation, a question of presence, indicates that, like the coincidence of Socrates' trial and the mission to Delos, chance played some role in determining who was present with Socrates on his last day. Phaedo names, first of all, the locals, the Athenians, who were present. There was Apollodorus, whose name says how this day and this conversation eventuated; he will prove most passionate in his reaction to the approach of Socrates' death. There was Critobulus, who was among those who at Socrates' trial offered money to pay his fine. And there was Critobulus' father, Crito, who, though unnamed (designated simply as Critobulus' father), was perhaps closest of all to Socrates; he was of about the same age as Socrates, and it is to him that Socrates' final words are addressed. There was also Hermogenes, who appears as an able interlocutor in the *Cratylus* but does not speak in the *Phaedo*. Epigenes and Aeschines were also there; both had been present at Socrates' trial. Also there in the prison with Socrates on his last day was Antisthenes, who later became the founder of the Cynic school. So, the Athenians who were present were Apollodorus, Critobulus, Crito, Hermogenes, Epigenes, Aeschines, and Antisthenes—seven in all. Then two more Athenians are conspicuously added to the list: Ctesippus and his cousin Menexenus, both of whom appear in the *Lysis*. In addition to these nine, Phaedo mentions that there were some other Athenians present, but he leaves them unnamed and their number indefinite.

Then he adds: "But Plato, I think, was ill" (59b). In this regard there was perhaps an element of chance: Plato chanced to be ill—and illness is, it seems, never entirely free of chance—and so was unable to be present. But aside from this allusion, the mention of Plato's name is highly significant. This is one of the few places in the dialogues where Plato's name occurs; the only other passages where he is mentioned are found in the *Apology*, where Socrates mentions him as being present there at the trial (34a) and as being one of those who—along with Crito, Critobulus, and Apollodorus—were willing to pay Socrates' fine (38b). It goes without saying that in the dialogues Plato says nothing; never is he presented—that is, never does he present himself—as the speaker. Always he maintains the reticence of the writer and keeps himself withdrawn from the text. For everything he writes, he forges the signature of someone else. Thus, for everything said in the dialogues there is a kind of double authorship. This doubling is irreducible, since there is no basis for assuming that any speaker is just the mouthpiece for the silent Plato. In the *Phaedo* Plato's absence serves to amplify the separation between the deeds (to which Phaedo was, but no longer is, present) and the λόγος that at a distance he offers to Echecrates. In this case both authors, Plato and Phaedo, produce their λόγος—almost the same λόγος—in separation from the deeds (including those of speech) and the other persons told of in the λόγος. Phaedo is separated by time and space. Plato was always separated, since he was not present at the scene of Socrates' death.

Echecrates asks whether there were any foreigners present, and Phaedo continues then with his recitation of the names of those who were present. Among the foreigners were three from Thebes: Simmias and Cebes, who are the chief interlocutors in the *Phaedo* and who had brought money from Thebes to help Socrates escape; and Phaedonides, listed by Xenophon (along with Simmias and Cebes) as one of the true Socratics.[5] Like Phlius, Thebes was a city of refuge for the Pythagoreans; Philolaus, of whom Simmias and Cebes were disciples, had come

---

5. Xenophon, *Memorabilia* 1:48.

to Thebes after the Pythagoreans were expelled from southern Italy.[6] Fourth among the foreigners was Euclides of Megara, the one who, in the *Theaetetus*, is presented as having preserved in a book the memory of Socrates' conversation with the young Theaetetus. The fifth of the foreigners was Terpsion, who, in the *Theaetetus*, is associated with Euclides. So, the foreigners who were present were Simmias, Cebes, Phaedonides, Euclides, and Terpsion—five in all. Echecrates' further questions let Phaedo underscore that the list of names is complete. He asks whether Aristippus and Cleombrotus were present, and Phaedo answers that they were not, since they were in Aegina. Then Echecrates asks: "Was anyone else present?"—to which Phaedo answers: "I think these were pretty much the ones who were present" (59c).

So, there are fourteen people who are named as having been present in the prison on Socrates' last day. Divided into two groups, nine Athenians and five foreigners, they correspond to the nine young men and five maidens that Theseus took with him on his voyage to Crete. Judging from the depictions of Ctesippus and Menexenus in other dialogues, especially the *Lysis*, they were very young, perhaps even with faces still girlish in appearance. They correspond to the two extra men that Theseus took along disguised as maidens. At the end of his list of Athenians, Phaedo adds: ". . . and some other locals." The mention of these could perhaps be taken as a way of stressing the significance of precisely nine Athenians being named; even though some others were present, Phaedo names only nine. These indefinite others could, of course, also be associated simply with those on the ship other than the ones sent as sacrificial tribute.

It is striking that Phaedo does not include himself among the fourteen who are named, even though in the first word he utters in the dialogue he makes it known that he was there at the scene of Socrates' death. Yet there are some indications of his role. Later he will tell Echecrates that at a crucial point in the conversation, Socrates caressed his head and gathered up his hair, for—says Phaedo—"he was in the habit, on occasion, of teasing me about my hair" (89b). In this context Socrates himself speaks of Phaedo's "beautiful locks." Furthermore, the thread of Phaedo's narrative in the dialogue runs through what might be represented as a labyrinth of questions raised, answers proposed, and objections stated. So it would not be out of the question to associate Phaedo

---

6. See *The Pythagorean Sourcebook*, 37f.

with Ariadne. With Socrates playing the role of Theseus, death—or the fear of death—would represent the Minotaur.

Thus, the scene presented in the *Phaedo* reenacted in word and deed the μῦθος of Theseus' voyage to Crete to kill the Minotaur. Furthermore, the *Phaedo* is set dramatically in relation to the Athenian reenactment of the voyage, now as fulfilling the vow to Apollo rather than in the guise—and disguise—of a tribute to ward off retribution by Minos. Just as Theseus sailed to Crete and the Athenian mission has now sailed to Delos (in the same ship as Theseus, so it is said), so Socrates and his interlocutors will speak of—and enact—their sailing. Simmias, for instance, will speak of having to let oneself be carried upon the best human λόγος as upon a raft as long as a godly λόγος is lacking. Most decisively, at the heart of the dialogue there is Socrates' description of the recommencement of his philosophical practice as a second sailing. Operative in the recourse that sets the second sailing under way is a radical transformation of human comportment both to λόγος and to φύσις.

Even before Phaedo names those who were present at the scene of Socrates' death, he is asked directly by Echecrates: "What were the things said and done?" (58c). When Echecrates requests that he give a full report, Phaedo grants that indeed he has the leisure to do so. Echecrates assures him that he will have for listeners others who, like him, will find it pleasant to remember Socrates; clearly, then, the audience will consist of several others in addition to Echecrates, though they neither speak nor are named.

Phaedo begins, not directly with the narrative of Socrates' last day, but rather by describing the condition in which he found himself on that day. He says: "For my part, being present I was affected [ἔπαθον—from πάσχω] by wondrous things [θαυμάσια]" (58e). In other words, Phaedo is attesting that, as he was present there, there were wondrous things that evoked in him a passion, that called forth such wonder as that with which philosophy begins. He continues: "For no pity overcame me," no compassion such as would be expected when someone is present at the death of a friend, because "he seemed to be happy both in his bearing [τρόπος] and in his λόγοι" (58e). Phaedo adds: "So I thought that he was not going to Hades without divine warrant [ἄνευ θείας μοίρας]" and that he would "do well there, if anybody ever did" (58e-59a). This is the first mention of Hades, and hence of the conception of death as going to Hades. Yet already here there is something strange, something out of place, something utterly contrary to the customary Greek belief; for that belief was that in Hades, where one persisted only as a mere bloodless shade, no one did well. There could be no question whether "anybody ever did" do well, for indeed no one really was capable of doing anything at all.

While, on the one hand, Phaedo by his own testimony was not overcome by pity, there was not, on the other hand, the usual pleasure at being engaged in philosophy. Instead, he says, "a very strange pathos was present in me." This pathos, Phaedo explains, was an unusual mixture of pleasure and pain. He adds that all who were present were in the same condition, "sometimes laughing, sometimes weeping" (59a).

The *Phaedo* has many of the features of tragedy. A great man—"the best, the most thoughtful, and the most just," to cite the last words of the dialogue—pursues the course ordained to him yet thereby comes into an irresolvable conflict that is to lead to his death. In the course of the dialogue there will be allusions to tragedy and the tragic hero, and their texture and context must be carefully gauged. However, one response that tragedy does not evoke, that would be strange, out of place, in tragedy, is laughter, which belongs rather to comedy. Yet all those present at the scene of Socrates' death were "sometimes laughing, sometimes weeping." It appears, then, that the *Phaedo* is not simply a tragedy but rather a strange, unusual, out-of-place mixture of tragedy and comedy.

(B) DOWN TO EARTH

It is by directing attention to such a strange pathos, to such an unusual mixture of pleasure and pain as that which affected those who, as Phaedo says, were "sometimes laughing, sometimes weeping," that Socrates begins the conversation on his last day, on the day that he knows will be his last day.

Phaedo tells how, having heard the evening before that the ship had returned from Delos, Socrates' friends came to the prison even earlier than usual. They could not enter immediately, for, as the jailor told them, the Eleven (the officers who superintended prisons) were releasing Socrates from his fetters and arranging for him to die that day. After a while, Phaedo continues, "we went in and found Socrates just released from his fetters." His wife, Xanthippe, was there with their little boy. But as she became hysterical, Socrates turned and looked at Crito. Such gestures often recur in the course of the dialogue; they provide a kind of punctuation in the discourse and the deeds. Here the directed look marks a beginning, for it introduces Socrates' very first words: "Crito, have someone take her home" (60a). Socrates' final words will also be addressed to Crito and again will take the form of a request. Here at the beginning his words not only refer to a return to the place where someone belongs but also set the tone for the comportment that throughout the conversation Socrates will maintain in himself and insist on from others. Whenever any of those present tend toward a kind of pathos that, as in tragedy, would amplify the pain and suffering brought on by the imminence of death, Socrates shames them or, as in the case of Xanthippe, sends them away. In an even more exemplary manner, Socrates restrains his own behavior, keeping his distance from tragic pathos.

Phaedo's narrative continues: once Xanthippe had been taken away, "Socrates sat up on the bed [or couch—κλίνη]" (60b). Attention is thus directed to his position, his posture: he had been lying down and now is sitting upright on the bed. Phaedo reports that after sitting up, Socrates bent his leg and rubbed it with his hand. So, at the moment when he has just been released from his fetters and freely sits up, his very first deed is directed to his body. Furthermore—Phaedo continues—as he then begins to speak, his speech has to do with his body. He says: how strange, how out of place (ἄτοπος), is that which humans call "pleasant." It is out of place because it is not just opposed to its opposite but also is peculiarly related to, conjoined with, it. Or, as Socrates is reported to have said: "How wondrously related it is by nature to its seeming opposite" (60b). In other words, the way in which, in and by nature (πέφυκη), pleasure is related to its opposite is so out of place that it is provocative of wonder, with which philosophy—and here Socrates' final discourse—begins. Socrates explains just how strange this relation is: pleasure and pain will not come to one at the same time, and yet if someone gets one of them, he is usually going to get the other, too. Here Socrates is putting into words what he has himself just felt: after the painful fetters have been removed, he now feels pleasure. So, here too, as with Phaedo and the others, there is a strange mixture of opposites; yet Socrates' description stresses that it is not simply a mixture, since opposites cannot simply be mixed, but rather a deferred mixing, a mixing mediated by time. Socrates invents a little story (μῦθος), the story that—so he says—Aesop would have composed had he noticed this strange relation between pleasure and pain. The story is that since the god could not reconcile pleasure and pain in their war with one another, he fastened their heads together at the same point, so that when one comes, the other follows after.

Speaking for the first time in the dialogue, Cebes interrupts, swearing, "By Zeus, Socrates." Then he remarks that what Socrates has just said reminded him of something about which Evenus (a teacher, rhetorician, and poet from Paros) and others had inquired. What they had asked about were the poems that Socrates had been composing while in prison, in particular, the discourses (λόγοι) of Aesop that he had set to verse and the hymn to Apollo. In response, Socrates refers to a certain dream he had often had in which he had been told: "Socrates, make [or: compose—ποίει] music and work at it" (60e). For the Greeks, music [μουσική] included anything presided over by the Muses; but in the narrower sense here intended, it meant lyric poetry, especially as sung along with accompaniment on the lyre.[7] Thus, what Socrates had been composing in the prison were verse renditions of Aesop's stories and a hymn to Apollo, to whom he owed gratitude both for originally setting him on his way and for the deferment of his execution. Socrates offers an interpretation of his dream, or rather, two interpretations, the earlier one and the one on the basis of which he had undertaken his present compositions. Previously Socrates thought that in the dream he was simply being urged to continue the philosophical practice in which he was engaged, since philosophy he considered the greatest kind of music. But now, just in case the dream meant that he should compose ordinary, demotic music, he thought he should do so. So, he says, he composed a poem "to the god the sacrificing to whom was present" (61b)—referring to Apollo in such a way as to allude to the mission to Delos, because of which his death had been deferred. He continues: "And considering that a poet, if he is to be a poet, must compose stories [ποιεῖν μύθους], not discourses [λόγοι], and that I myself was not a storyteller, therefore after the god, I turned to the stories of Aesop, the ones I had at hand and knew—whichever I chanced on first—and made them into poetry" (61b).

A question is prompted by Socrates' report of his dream and of the poetic, musical activity that he has undertaken in response to it. The

---

7. Diogenes Laertius reports regarding Socrates: "Moreover, in his old age he learned to play the lyre, declaring that he saw nothing strange in learning a new accomplishment. As Xenophon relates in the *Symposium*, it was his regular habit to dance, thinking that such exercise helped to keep the body in good condition" (*Lives of Eminent Philosophers* 2:32).

question is whether, now that Socrates has been released from his fetters and faces imminent death, this activity is abandoned; or whether, on the contrary, in the conversation on his last day, he continues—even if in another manner—to compose music. Does Socrates, in what he says in the face of death, remain, in some manner, a poet? To be sure, he denies that he is a storyteller, a μυθολογικός, one who invents, composes, or tells mythic tales. And yet, despite this denial, he has just invented such a tale and even made it clear that he was inventing it, namely, the little story about how the god fastened together the heads of pleasure and pain. His engagement here in storytelling is only slightly mitigated by his claim that this is the tale that Aesop would have invented. But Aesop did not invent it; it is Socrates' tale.

Considerable prominence is thus accorded to music in Socrates' description of his practice both before his imprisonment, when he regarded philosophy as the greatest kind of music, and during his time in prison, when he took up demotic music. In affiliating philosophy with music, Socrates is, in effect, drawing Pythagoreanism into the conversation. Already it has come to light that the *Phaedo* has a double Pythagorean context. The outer conversation is situated in Phlius, the Pythagorean center where, it seems, the title *philosopher* was first used and philosophy thus acquired both its name and the semantic unity correlative to the name. Here Phaedo speaks with the Pythagorean Echecrates and others presumably with Pythagorean connections. In the inner conversation in the prison, Socrates' two primary interlocutors are Simmias and Cebes, disciples of Philolaus, the most prominent Pythagorean after Pythagoras himself; they hail from Thebes, one of the mainland havens for the Pythagoreans.

While bestowing on the practice that had originated in Miletus its proper name by appropriating this name to himself, the philosopher Pythagoras is credited with having discovered the mathematical basis of musical accord or harmony. Thus, from the time when philosophy took on its proper name, it was affiliated with music. In his *Life of Pythagoras*, Iamblichus relates that Pythagoras was born on the island of Samos (c. 570 BC) and that after years of traveling he settled in Croton in southern Italy (c. 531 BC). Here he established his school, a community centered around the Muses and their leader Apollo; thus from the beginning they gave place of honor to the immortals who, like themselves, were engaged with music. The Pythagoreans practiced asceticism, abstaining from wine and from many foods and holding in contempt such things as fame and wealth.⁸ A generalized asceticism will surface repeatedly in the *Phaedo* in the responses that Simmias and Cebes give to Socrates' proposals, and also in Socrates' own words, though in a manner that becomes increasingly interrogative.

In the Pythagorean community there was a rule of secrecy; anyone found guilty of divulging Pythagorean doctrines to the uninitiated was subject to severe punishment. Because of this secrecy no Pythagorean writings were disseminated prior to those of Philolaus at the end of the fifth century BC. Iamblicus reports: "Admirable too is the careful secrecy with which they preserved the mystery of their writings. For during so many generations, prior to the time of Philolaus, none of the Pythagorean writings appeared publicly. Philolaus first published those three celebrated books that, at the request of Plato, Dion of Syracuse is said to have bought for a hundred minae."⁹

Yet at the heart of Pythagoreanism there was the original discovery of the mathematics of music. It is likely that by measuring the appropriate lengths of a vibrating string, Pythagoras discovered that the chief musical intervals are expressible in simple numerical ratios between the first four integers, the octave corresponding to the ratio 2:1, the fifth to the ratio 3:2, and the fourth to the ratio 4:3. The Pythagoreans took special note of the fact that expressing the musical intervals required only the first four integers, the tetrad; and that the tetrad generates (by the addition of the four numbers) the number ten, the decad. Aetius writes of the significance that the Pythagoreans ascribed to the tetrad and the decad: "Ten is the very nature of number. All Greeks and all barbarians alike count up to ten, and having reached ten, revert again to the unit. And again, Pythagoras maintains, the power of the number ten lies in the number four, the tetrad. This is the reason: if one starts at the unit and adds the successive numbers up to four, one will make up the number ten. . . . And so the Pythagoreans used to invoke the tetrad as their most binding oath."¹⁰ The number ten, as generated from the

---

8. Iamblicus, *The Life of Pythagoras*, in *The Pythagorean Sourcebook*, 58–64, 73–76.

9. Ibid., 105. In antiquity there was a rumor that it was from these books by Philolaus that Plato copied out—plagiarized—his *Timaeus*. Diogenes Laertius reports: "Hermippus says that according to one writer the philosopher Plato went to Sicily, to the court of Dionysius, bought this book from Philolaus' relatives for forty Alexandrian minae, and from it copied out the *Timaeus*" (*Lives of Eminent Philosophers* 8:85). See my discussion in *Chorology*, 147f.

10. Diels-Kranz, 58 B15.

tetrad, they represented by a configuration of dots arranged as an equilateral triangle.

$$
\begin{matrix}
& & \bullet & & \\
& \bullet & & \bullet & \\
\bullet & & \bullet & & \bullet \\
\bullet & \bullet & \bullet & \bullet
\end{matrix}
$$

This figure they termed the tetraktys.

Many of the Pythagorean theories and beliefs were related to the discovery of the mathematical basis of harmony. Foremost was their concern with the accord or harmony in the constitution of certain things. The soul, in particular, was regarded as comprised of, or at least as exhibiting, a certain harmony. This is a conception that will be proposed in the course of the *Phaedo* and that will be critically addressed by Socrates.

The Pythagoreans focused on the opposites, to which, it seems, they applied the term ἀρχαί. Some of the later reports, as, for instance, in Aristotle's *Metaphysics*, give lists of the opposites with which the Pythagoreans were concerned: for example, limit/unlimited, even/odd, light/darkness.[11] In the *Phaedo* the opposites living/dead play a major role; engagement with them serves to open up a thorough interrogation of opposition as such. Even at the outset of the dialogue, as already noted, the opposition between presence and distance is embedded in the dramatic context; this opposition will return in various guises in the course of the dialogue.

In the developments that were introduced into Pythagoreanism by Alcmaeon and Philolaus, special emphasis came to be placed on the accord or harmony of opposites. Alcmaeon, for instance, developed a theory of health based on balance between opposites. Aetius reports: "Alcmaeon maintains that the bond of health is the equal balance of the powers, moist and dry, cold and hot, bitter and sweet, and the rest, while the supremacy of one of them is the cause of disease; for the supremacy of either is destructive."[12] If this theory of health as the balance of the opposites is extended from the body to the soul, then it can provide the basis for an account of the excellence of the soul. It is in this guise that it will emerge in the course of the *Phaedo*.

---

11. Aristotle, *Metaphysics* 986a17–30.
12. Kirk, Raven, and Schofield, *The Presocratic Philosophers*, 260.

The Pythagoreans were devoted to contemplation (θεωρία). The supremacy of the contemplative life is expressed in a parable that Diogenes Laertius attributes to Pythagoras: "Life, he said, is like a festival; just as some come to the festival to compete, some to ply their trade, but the best people come as spectators, so in life the slavish men go hunting for fame or gain, the philosophers for the truth."[13] The Pythagoreans engaged especially in the contemplation of the order and harmony of the heaven. It was in this connection that they extended the word κόσμος to the heaven (οὐρανός) and the universe at large (τὸ πᾶν). Previously, in Homer, for instance, the word had designated an ordered array, as in the array of troops going into battle. The Pythagoreans extended it precisely because of their belief in the order and harmony of the heavenly array. The contemplation of the order in the heaven and its reflection back upon the soul was later described in a celebrated passage in Plato's *Timaeus*, though not without a certain limit or breach being marked.[14] Contemplation of higher things is also proposed and submitted to interrogation in the *Phaedo*, though the dialogue also sets over against it a discourse oriented to the earth.

Both Pythagoras and the later Pythagoreans took over a great deal from Orphism; there were legends that linked Pythagoras with Orpheus, ascribing to him, for instance, the capacity to tame wild beasts, as Orpheus was said to have done through the power of his music.[15] According to Orphic belief, the soul is bound to the body (σῶμα); it undergoes a cycle of incarnations until it is released through purifications and rites. The Pythagoreans did not take over such beliefs without adapting them to their own outlook. In particular, they maintained that purification was to be accomplished not by cultic rites, but by contemplation and by the installation of harmony in the soul that contemplation was capable of effecting. Music also, its harmonies akin to those of the heaven, had the capacity to instill its harmony in the soul. An ancient fragment attests to this capacity: "The Pythagoreans, according to Aristoxenus, practiced the purification of the body by medicine, that of the soul by music."[16]

---

13. Diogenes Laertius, *Lives of Eminent Philosophers* 8:8.
14. Plato, *Timaeus* 47a–e; see my discussion in *Chorology*, 89f.
15. Iamblichus, *The Life of Pythagoras* 70f.
16. Kirk and Raven, *The Presocratic Philosophers*, 1st ed., 229. Aristoxenus was a pupil of Aristotle and an expert on musical theory.

In the *Phaedo* there is much that derives from Pythagoreanism, as its double Pythagorean context already suggests. Yet, there is nothing taken over that is not, in one way or another, brought under interrogation. This is preeminently the case with the theme of purification, especially insofar as it is conceived as a means by which the soul would free itself of embodiment and of the attachment to nature and the earth that embodiment entails. In this interrogation what is fundamentally put in question is the bond of the human to φύσις and to the earth as the receptacle of φύσις.

At the moment when he has just finished portraying himself as engaged with music, Socrates introduces an abrupt shift in the discussion. He suddenly instructs Cebes to tell Evenus—who had inquired about Socrates' music making—that if he is sound-minded (σώφρων) he should follow him, should follow Socrates, as quickly as possible. When Simmias exclaims, "How can you exhort Evenus in this way, Socrates?" (61c), Socrates goes on to make the even more outrageous remark that all philosophers should take this same advice. This is the first reference—still indirect—that Socrates makes to his death. It is of the utmost importance—indeed for the dialogue as a whole—that what follows is a distinctive deed, for at such a crucial juncture deeds are more significant than words. Before Socrates' friends are admitted, he has been lying down; and again, at the end, when he has drunk the φάρμακον, he will be lying down. But immediately after he turned and looked at Crito and said his first words, he sat up on his bed or couch. Then, after the initial storytelling and the self-portrayal, and at the same time (ἅμα) that he utters his outrageous remark tacitly referring to his imminent death, there comes the deed that will echo throughout the entire dialogue: "And as he spoke, he put his feet down on the earth [ἐπὶ τὴν γῆν] and for the rest of the time conversed sitting in this way" (61d). Putting his feet down on the earth, Socrates plunges into the conversation that will conclude with a great μῦθος about the earth. With his feet on the earth, he practices music to such an extent that he comes finally to give voice to a song of the earth.

In this abrupt turn in the conversation, marked both by word and by deed, Socrates speaks about philosophy and, though without explicitly mentioning it, about death. He moderates his outrageous remark only to the extent of excluding suicide, since "they say it is not lawful" (61c). But in general Socrates reorients the entire discussion to the relation of philosophy to death, even to a certain bond or constraint that governs the philosopher's relation to his death. It is then in this connection that Socrates puts his feet down on the earth, as if in deed responding to this configuration, saying in deed that this configuration of philosophy and death has to be brought down to earth, that it has to be brought into connection with the earth.

When, along with Simmias' expression of his dismay at Socrates' remark, Cebes adds his own exclamation, Socrates responds by asking whether both of them have not heard about such things from Philolaus. Thus bringing Pythagoreanism onto the scene, Socrates announces that he is going to speak about these things, though he adds that he will speak about them "only from hearsay," from what he has "chanced to have heard" (61d). His appeal to hearsay and chance is indicative that what he is about to say is anything but what could be termed a rigorous discourse. But also the indication is that it is something he is merely passing along, something that a Pythagorean such as Philolaus might have said, but which now is to be said in the voice of Socrates. Thus, in this way he reveals in advance that that to which he will give voice does not come from himself but rather from a Pythagorean such as Philolaus, to whom he merely lends his voice. In other words, Socrates will engage in a kind of ventriloquy, lending his voice to another who is not actually present.

Nonetheless, Socrates links this Pythagorean ventriloquy to his own situation of confronting his imminent death. He says: "For perhaps it is especially fitting for someone who is about to emigrate to that place to examine and also to mythologize about the emigration there—what sort of thing we think it is. For what else would one do in the time until the setting of the sun?" (61d–e). There is an indefiniteness in Socrates' statement. He does not yet speak of dying but only of emigrating, going away as in leaving home and going abroad (ἀποδημέω). And in designating the place to which he will emigrate, he refers to it simply by means of the indefinite adverb ἐκεῖσε (*thither, to that place*), without any reference at all to a specific region or a future life. Most remarkably, despite his earlier denial that he was not a μυθολογικός, now on his final day he appears to be announcing a change; now he is proposing to pass the time until his death by mythologizing (μυθολογεῖν). Yet he does not specify whether this means that he will actually compose or tell μῦθοι or whether he will—perhaps in addition—take them up in some other manner. The only clue he provides is in the word διασκοπεῖν, *to examine* or, more literally, *to look through*. To look through something (such as the emigration thither) is to penetrate it visually. When whatever obscures it is cleared away, it is brought to display itself clearly and to open up to one's vision. The question is evident: How is such looking-through to be carried out in conjunction with mythologizing? Is it a matter of looking through the μῦθοι? What would be involved in looking through a μῦθος? What could be seen by looking through a μῦθος?

Cebes is curious about suicide and about how the unlawfulness of suicide goes together with what Socrates has said about the philosopher being willing to follow after someone who is dying. Invoking wonder ("it will perhaps appear wondrous to you" [62a]), Socrates speaks directly to the same dilemma that Cebes has just posed, but now in a different form: it appears wondrous that for some it is better to be dead (in Pythagorean terms: for those who escape the cycle of reincarnations), and yet it is not pious for them to commit suicide. The dilemma as Socrates poses it does indeed appear so wondrous to Cebes that it evokes a kind of response that would least be expected in a discussion of death and suicide: "And Cebes gently laughed" (62a). On the other hand, Echecrates might well have anticipated that there might be laughter, though perhaps not in such a context; for at the outset Phaedo had mentioned to him that those present with Socrates were sometimes laughing, sometimes weeping. Yet, Phaedo continues now by recalling that Cebes not only laughed but also was, it seems, so struck with wonder that he slipped out of proper Attic Greek back into his dialect, swearing in the name of Zeus.

This entire scene is one of Socratic ventriloquy. What Socrates is putting forth, even the dilemma that has evoked Cebes' laughter, comes from a source other than himself. It is a wondrous—and perhaps, as Cebes' laughter and verbal slip suggest, a somewhat comical—Pythagorean belief that Socrates has chanced to hear and that he now conveys in his voice. The contrast is evident: whereas Socrates lends his voice to someone like Philolaus so that it is, in this sense, not his own voice, Cebes slips back into his own dialect, that is, as the text literally says, his own voice (φωνή). The question that this curious scene poses—without its being given voice—is how, in his ventriloquizing, Socrates is (as he proposed) engaging in mythologizing. And how, furthermore, is he looking through the Pythagorean beliefs or through whatever is the theme of his mythologizing? Are these beliefs perhaps μῦθοι so that, in giving voice to them, Socrates is mythologizing? And in looking through them does he somehow discern a pertinent λόγος?

Socrates declares that what he has said seems, in the form in which he has presented it, to be unaccountable, that is, ἄλογον. And yet, he continues, perhaps it does permit of an account, that is, a λόγος. The λόγος that he proceeds to offer is, he says, the one given in the mysteries. The word for mysteries, ἀπόρρητος, means *what is not to be spoken*. But what must remain unspoken can also be designated ἄλογον. Thus, what Socrates, even more conspicuously ventriloquizing, goes on to say is suspended between λόγος and ἄλογον: "The λόγος that is spoken [λεγόμενος] about these things in the mysteries, that we humans are in a kind of garrison and that one is bound not to release oneself from it nor to run off, appears to me to be a grand one and not easy to look through [διιδεῖν, a synonym of διασκοπεῖν]. And yet this, at any rate, seems to me well said [εὖ λέγεσθαι], Cebes; the gods care for us, and we humans are one of the gods' possessions" (62b).

Here Socrates speaks with ironic deference: he says that the λόγος spoken in the mysteries is grand or great, using the word μέγας, which can also mean *excessive, presumptuous*. The reference to the mysteries indicates explicitly that what Socrates is giving voice to here is Orphic doctrine, preeminently the belief, taken over by the Pythagoreans, that the body is the prison of the soul; the elaborate prescriptions and rites of Orphism were aimed at purifying the soul so that it might escape the prison house of the body and eventually free itself from the cycle of rebirth. In describing the abode of humans, Socrates uses the word φρουρά, translated as *garrison*; but the word can also be rendered as *prison*, in which case it is a near-synonym of the word δεσμωτήριον, which occurs at the very outset of the dialogue in Echecrates' opening question. Clearly the imprisonment of which Socrates speaks here is mirrored by the setting in which he is speaking; and the theme of purification, which is implied, is mirrored in the circumstance that Athens must remain pure until the mission to Delos returns. At the end of his declaration, Socrates restates the belief somewhat differently, putting the μῦθος into what could conceivably be considered a λόγος: the gods care for us, and we are their possessions—pieces of property, goods that belong to them. It would perhaps not be too far afield to suppose that here there is a pun based on the similarity (both of the words and of their meaning) between κτῆμα, the word actually used, and κτῆνος, which can also mean *a piece of property* but is used chiefly to denote property in the form of flocks and herds. The allusion of the former to the latter would suggest that it is as if we humans were the sheep and cattle of the gods.

What Socrates has said serves to satisfy Cebes, completely so once Socrates rounds out the discussion by asking him whether, if one of his possessions were to kill itself, he would not be harsh with it. Socrates' formulation playfully alludes to the comparison that is implied between humans, on the one side, and flocks of sheep and herds of cattle, on the other. Though Cebes expresses his certainty about what Socrates has said and thus presumably remains oblivious to the comparison that it implies, Socrates conspicuously avoids saying that it is correct or true, limiting himself to declaring it "well said."

Once the question of suicide has been discussed—though also in a sense left open—there follows an interlude that serves to separate this discussion from the much more extensive discussion of philosophy and death that is to come. The interlude consists of a series of four moves or interruptions, which not only leads from one discussion to the next but also brings both to bear on the concrete situation in which they occur.

First of all, Cebes objects that there is an inconsistency between what Socrates has said about humans being the possessions of the gods and his assertion that philosophers should be ready and willing to die. The problem, as Cebes formulates it, is that those who are most thoughtful should recognize that they are better off with their rightful masters, the gods, who are the most excellent overseers; hence, they should not be prone to flee from their masters. This inconsistency exposes in effect—though without its being expressed—both the weakness of the comparison that has been drawn and the indeterminateness of the link that Socrates has posited between philosophy and death. Yet, embedded in what Cebes says is a connection, made here for the first time in the dialogue, between philosophy and thoughtfulness (φρόνησις): the philosopher is described as the most thoughtful (φρονιμωτάτος). This is the first characterization that the *Phaedo* offers of the philosopher; it will recur in various—and indeed different—connections throughout much of the dialogue.

Secondly, Phaedo reports that to him it seemed that Socrates was pleased with what Cebes had said—presumably because it had the effect of exposing the weakness of the discussion. In any case, Phaedo reports the deed that followed: "And he looked at us [καὶ ἐπιβλέψας εἰς ἡμᾶς]" (63a)—this in deed punctuating the discourse, before then paying his compliments to Cebes for tracking down λόγοι. Yet, it is evident that the λόγοι Cebes tracks down—such as that in which he has just expressed the inconsistency—are themselves situated within a context composed largely of mythical elements such as the story that humans are in a kind of prison and are the possessions of the gods.

In the third of the moves that form the interlude, Simmias brings the question that Cebes has posed to bear on Socrates himself. Simmias tells Socrates that it seems that Cebes is aiming the λόγος at him, because he is so eager to leave them as well as the gods, who, as Socrates has agreed, are good rulers. Thus accused, Socrates declares that he will have to defend himself against the accusation, just as in a law court. Referring to his trial, he says that he will try to make a better defense than he did before the judges. The very diction of this passage (he uses the verb form of ἀπολογία as well as the word itself) makes it unmistakable that the *Phaedo* is staging a trial in which Socrates will be retried, in which he will be tried again for what he insists issues directly from his pursuit of philosophy. Thus, in the *Phaedo* there is a repetition of the trial as portrayed in the *Apology*; but now it is a trial not before the "men of Athens," but before his closest friends.

The interlude concludes with an interruption by Crito, who, Socrates notices, has been trying for some time to say something. In what Crito says, he simply passes along to Socrates the warning given by the man who will administer the φάρμακον. The warning is that Socrates should converse as little as possible, for if someone talks too much, he gets warmed up, and this has a bad effect on the action of the φάρμακον. As Crito had expected, Socrates refuses to heed the warning. Thus, in deed Socrates pits speech, which brings heat and so prolongs life, against the φάρμακον, which brings on coldness and death. And yet, this deed, this gesture by which Socrates takes the side of life against death, only makes it seem still stranger than ever—or perhaps more wondrous—that Socrates has connected philosophy so intimately to death, that he has declared that the philosopher should be ready and willing to die. The stage is set for a direct confrontation with the question of philosophy and death.

In the drama that is about to begin, the stakes are extraordinarily high, perhaps higher than in any other passage in the *Phaedo*. Ever since late antiquity this passage and others parallel to it have repeatedly been put forth as attesting to the otherworldliness of so-called Platonic thought. It has been taken as a straightforward repudiation of life itself in the name of philosophy, as the basis for an asceticism that would posit another world as the true destination of the human, a higher world in relation to which this world would be denigrated. Nietzsche's invectives against this otherworldliness were direct and effective, though he realized, at least at certain junctures, that straightforward attribution was highly problematic.[17]

In taking up this passage, it is imperative to attend with the utmost care to just what is said, also sometimes to what is not said. There is need also to listen attentively so as to discern just who it is that is lent a voice by Socrates or perhaps by his interlocutors. Who it is that is behind what is said—often in the voice of another—can sometimes be as significant as what is said and in any case must be taken into account in determining the precise bearing of what is said. In addition, recalling that to some degree it is music that is here in the making, it is advisable to listen for any dissonances that may be sounded.

In the most direct and controversial statement, Socrates addresses his present judges. He says: "Others are likely to be unaware that those who chance to fasten upon philosophy in the correct way pursue nothing but dying and being dead" (64a). Socrates adds that if this is true, then it would be out of place for the philosopher to be troubled about dying, since he would have been pursuing this all along.

In this statement regarding philosophy and death, Socrates forgoes stating directly what the connection between philosophy and death truly is. Rather than simply declaring that philosophy is the pursuit of death, he sets the declaration within a syntactically complex configuration. The declaration is formulated in such a way that its direct bearing is not on philosophers in general but on people who *chance* (τυγχάνω) to fasten upon philosophy in the correct way. The reference to chance recalls the previous indications that this can in some ways determine the course of the philosophical life, for in the case of Socrates it was the intervention of chance that brought about the postponement of his execution. And as chance may bear on the end, so in Socrates' reference to

---

17. A very different approach to Platonic philosophy is exemplified by the following passage from *Twilight of the Idols*: Plato "says with an innocence for which one must be a Greek, not a 'Christian,' that there would be no Platonic philosophy at all if there were not such beautiful youths in Athens. . . . Philosophy after the fashion of Plato might rather be defined as an erotic contest, as a further development and an inwardizing of the ancient gymnastics and of its *presuppositions*. What finally grew out of this philosophic eroticism of Plato? A new art form of the Greek agon, dialectic" (Nietzsche, *Werke: Kritische Gesamtausgabe*, ed. Giorgio Colli and Mazzino Montinari [Berlin: Walter de Gruyter, 1969], VI 3: 120). See my discussion in "Nietzsche's Platonism," chap. 1 of *Platonic Legacies* (Albany: State University of New York Press, 2004), 7–25.

those who chance to fasten upon philosophy there is a hint that in the beginning, in the evocation of wonder, chance may—perhaps must—play a role.

Yet Socrates does not simply declare that those who chance to fasten upon philosophy in the correct way pursue death. Rather, having just promised Simmias and Cebes that he would try to explain the matter to them, he then refers to *others*—other than Simmias and Cebes—who, he says, are likely to be unaware that philosophers pursue death. Implicit in his formulation is the suggestion that, while others are likely unaware of the connection between philosophy and death, Simmias and Cebes are not. In this case it would appear that in his explication of this connection Socrates is expressing something of which Simmias and Cebes are aware, perhaps even a view (δόξα) they actually hold.

And yet, Socrates himself affirms neither the connection between philosophy and death nor the fact that others are unaware of it. For immediately after the statement, he continues with a conditional: "If this is true, . . ." The sequential occurrence of the word ἀληθές (*true*) after the word ὀρθῶς (*in the correct way*), used in the previous sentence to characterize the way in which philosophers fasten upon philosophy, lends credence to the supposition that in this context ἀληθές, like ὀρθῶς, designates not just an abstractly conceived correctness, but rather the appropriateness of a certain practice. To practice philosophy in the correct way is not to measure up to a preconceived conception but rather to carry it out in a way that allows some insight to issue from the practice, that lets something previously unseen be seen. If the two words have a similar bearing, then it could be supposed that the sense of ἀληθές is expressed in the word διασκοπεῖν (*to look through*), which was introduced earlier in the dialogue. In order to look through something, to penetrate it with one's look, it is necessary to clear away whatever obscures it and makes it remain impenetrable, elusive to vision. A saying would, then, be true if it served to clear away whatever obscures the matter spoken of and to open the way for a penetrating, revealing look into it. Thus, if what Socrates has said is true, then it should open the way by which to look through the connection between philosophy and death. The question that such a prospect immediately poses is whether one can look through whatever has to do with death. Can λόγος open a way by which to look through death? Though in the course of the *Phaedo* it will be said more than once what death is, the question is whether this can be said in a λόγος that truly clears away the obscurity, the concealment and its very concealment, that death poses.

In any case, Socrates says that *if* this is true, then it would be out of place (ἄτοπον) for the philosopher to be troubled about dying. Certainly the word ἄτοπον has here the sense that is evident in many other passages: it means *out of place*, *strange*. And yet, the word can also mean *absurd*, *inept*, even *unnatural*. In this case it could serve to designate a comical character who unwittingly acts in a way that is exactly the opposite of what, at the same time, he says.

Socrates himself speaks as if again on trial, addressing his friends as "my judges" (63e) and describing his statement about philosophy and death as his account rendered to them. The response to this statement is the same as that which was provoked earlier by Socrates' remark about suicide. Yet this time it is Simmias rather than Cebes who responds: "And Simmias laughed." Then he swore about his laughing: "By Zeus, Socrates, right now I am not much for laughing, but you did make me laugh!" (64a–b). So, not only does Simmias laugh, but also he calls attention to it, especially by swearing. As a result the word *laugh* (forms of γελάω) occurs three times in this very brief passage. Simmias explains that the many would agree that philosophers are ripe for death and would think that they deserve it. This of course is what the "men of Athens" thought at Socrates' trial, of which the present scene is a direct consequence. Simmias adds that "the people back home" would entirely agree; these are the citizens of Thebes, the other main refuge for Pythagoreans along with Phlius. Granting their view, Socrates insists, on the other hand, that the many fail to understand in what way philosophers are ripe for death; thus he proposes that they talk among themselves and bid the many farewell. What Socrates in effect is proposing is a kind of imitation of Pythagorean community in which the practices, beliefs, and theoretical matters shared by the community were not to be disclosed to those outside and so not to the many. At the same time, the proposal would restrict those allowed to be present at Socrates' retrial to his friends there with him in his cell; now he would not be judged by the "men of Athens," who in the final analysis represent the prejudices of the many.

It is within this context that Socrates broaches, for the first time explicitly, the question of what death is: "And is it anything but the freeing [ἀπαλλαγή: separation, deliverance, release, escape, departure] of the soul from the body? And is this what it means to have died: for the body to become separate once it is freed from the soul and is itself all by itself, and for the soul to be separate once it is freed from the body and is itself all by itself? Death could not be anything other than this—could it?"

(64c). In this passage it is striking that even before he refers to the soul as separated, Socrates refers to the body as separated from the soul so as to be itself all by itself, alone by itself. This phrase, surprisingly applied to the body, will soon be applied not only, as in this passage, to the soul, but also to such looks as the just itself, the beautiful, and the good. Whereas each of these looks *is itself*, is self-identical, by itself in the sense of admitting nothing else into the circuit of its self-identity, the body, once it is separated from the soul, is a corpse. Whatever self-identity the body ever had, it had when it was besouled, that is, as a living body. As soon as it is separated from the soul, its self-identity is breached; as a corpse it has already begun to decompose into something quite other, has begun to be reabsorbed into nature.

Thus, from the beginning there is something strange about what Socrates says about the body. There is something out of place in this peculiar somatology, just as in the passage itself the reference to the body is out of place, in a place where it does not belong. In what voice, then, is Socrates speaking of the body? It is at least a voice that is interrogative: for all three of the sentences in which Socrates speaks here about death are—literally—*questions*.

In support—or mock support—of what he has said—in roundabout ways, as what others are unaware of, as questions—about the relation of philosophy to death, Socrates proceeds to identify two respects in which the philosopher appears to strive for separation of soul from body. The first respect is that of pleasure. Speaking to Simmias, Socrates asks: "Does it appear to you that being serious about the so-called pleasures, such as those of food and drink, goes with being a philosophical man?" (64d). He poses the same question regarding lovemaking and other servicings of the body. In each case Simmias' answer is negative. Yet the way in which Socrates poses these questions determines just how they are to be heard. It is significant that all are posed *as questions*, not as assertions; here Socrates remains thoroughly interrogative. Furthermore, his language is laced with references to opinion and its correlate, appearance: in the word συνδοκέω (*to have the same opinion*) and in the root word δοκέω (*to opine* but also *to appear, to seem*), as when he asks Simmias whether it seems that the philosopher "stands apart from" the body. When he asks Simmias, "Does it appear to you that . . . ," he couches his inquiry in terms of the near-synonym φαίνεται (*appears*). Thus, the texture of the language indicates that Socrates is asking Simmias about how something *appears*, not about how it *is*. Indeed, when

Socrates finally asks him whether the philosopher excels "in releasing the soul from communion with the body" (65a), Simmias answers thus: "It appears so [φαίνεται]."

Thus, it *appears* that the philosopher—for instance, Socrates himself—strives to purify himself from bodily pleasures, to stand apart from the body, to keep himself turned to the soul. The question is whether this *is so*, whether the philosopher—for instance, Socrates himself—does in deed stand apart from the body. The fact that at the age of seventy Socrates has a very young son (hardly more than an infant), who was there earlier with his mother, as well as two other sons around ten and sixteen years of age, might provoke some wonder, even some doubt, about the appearance, about its seeming that the philosopher stands apart from such pleasures as that of lovemaking.

Socrates introduces a second respect in which it seems that the philosopher strives to separate the soul from the body, namely, through the attainment of thoughtfulness (φρόνησις). He asks whether in such striving the body is an impediment: "Do sight and hearing possess any truth for human beings?" (65b). Simmias does *not* in fact answer this question, but only the more obvious question that Socrates also poses, the question whether the other senses are inferior to sight and hearing. Socrates continues: "So when ... does the soul get in touch with truth?" It is not insignificant that in this formulation Socrates has slyly introduced a reference to touch (ἅπτω), for, even more than sight and hearing, the sense of touch is inseparably bound to the body. Hence, this very formulation in terms of the soul's getting *in touch* compromises what Socrates is just about to say. For he concludes with this assertion: "For when it attempts to look at something along with the body, it is clear [δῆλον] that then it is deceived by it" (65b). Simmias' answer to this complex question slyly—or naively—turns the assertoric part against itself. He says simply: "What you say is true." The reflexive complication is evident: if the soul is misled, deceived, by the body and thereby is held apart from truth, then how is it that this very assertion—by the embodied Socrates—can with any assurance be made? What about its truth? How can it be clear (and be said to be clear) to someone who is embodied that the body prevents us from ever achieving clarity and precision?

Next the discourse turns in an ontological direction. Now responding to his own question as to when the soul gets in touch with truth, Socrates asks: "Is it not in reckoning [λογίζεσθαι], if anywhere, that something of the things that are [τι τῶν ὄντων] becomes clear" to the soul? (65c). He continues by referring to the time when, "bidding farewell to the body," the soul "comes to be itself all by itself [αὐτὴ καθ' αὑτήν] as much as possible and when, doing everything it can to avoid communing with or even being in touch [ἁπτομένη] with the body, it stretches itself out [ὀρέγηται] toward being [τοῦ ὄντος]" (65c). At this point a decisive shift has come into play, and it becomes still more pronounced as Socrates proceeds to speak of—or rather, simply to name—certain beings, each of which is simply itself (all by itself). Quite remarkably, these beings are abruptly introduced; without any mediation at all, they are simply posited. The names are *the just itself, the beautiful*, and *the good*. Even more remarkable is the radical shift in direction that the discourse undergoes: the emigration that the philosopher, in pursuing death, would carry out has been diverted from emigration to the underworld (Hades), indeed from emigration to any place, and has become, instead, an ascent to being. The question is inevitable: Would the philosopher, in engaging the ascent to being, be following the same course as those who die? Would he have devoted himself to dying? It is hardly evident that he would have done so. Socrates continues naming the beings, completing his list with *health* and *strength*. Again the question is inevitable: Would it be by avoiding being in touch with the body that one would come to apprehend such beings? Or must it not be acknowledged that the very sense of *health* and *strength* is intrinsically related to the body? Could one who is out of touch with the body have any sense of what health and strength are?

Socrates reiterates the ontological theme. He asks about the man who, "using unadulterated thought [διάνοια] itself all by itself, ... attempts to hunt down each of the beings that is unadulterated and itself all by itself" (66a). Simmias answers again with the same performative contradiction: "Marvelous how truly you speak, Socrates!" The word ὑπερφυῶς means not only *marvelous* but also *excessive*. Construed etymologically, it means: over or above or beyond φύσις. Such is precisely the case with the beings that have been named, each of which is itself all by itself; they, as well as the soul that, itself all by itself, avoids being in touch with the body, would be above and beyond nature. All would be entirely out of touch with nature. Or, in the case of the soul, it would at least *stretch itself*—as Socrates has said—toward being, that is, it would stretch itself from nature toward the beyond of the beings themselves.

Socrates now reintroduces the self-referentiality that Simmias has inadvertently broached. But now it is enacted in a thoroughly playful and deliberate manner. Instead of asserting it himself, he puts it in the mouths of certain so-called "true-born philosophers."[18] He declares that they "would say something like the following to one another: 'There seems to be a shortcut that brings us to this conclusion—that as long as we have the body accompanying the λόγος in our investigation and our soul is contaminated by such an evil, we will never sufficiently attain what we desire. And this, we affirm, is the truth'" (66b). Whether what they affirm is the truth of what they have just said or is that which they desire to attain is unclear. What is clear is that by lending them his voice, Socrates literally lets them speak without being *bodily present*. Nothing could be comically more appropriate, since for them truth would require not being bodily present; for these true-born philosophers, truth would require their not being embodied, not being born, or at least thoroughly undoing their having been born.

Something else that Socrates puts into the mouths of these true-born philosophers is that the body "fills us up with erotic loves and with desires" (66c). Here the true-born philosophers begin to speak passionately about the need to avoid such passions as those with which the body fills us. In this regard they display their obliviousness to what is requisite for philosophers. For one can hardly be a lover of wisdom without being filled with ἔρως; and one could hardly desire the truth without being filled with desire. Lest this display of obliviousness go unnoticed, Socrates—speaking still for these bodily absent philosophers—has them openly declare it: "and this is where it is really pointed out to us that if we are ever going to know anything purely, we must free ourselves from the body and behold things themselves with the soul itself. And then, as it seems, the thoughtfulness we *desire* and whose *lovers* we claim to be will be ours" (66d–e; emphasis added). In unmistakably Orphic tones, they conclude on the note of purification: they resolve to purify themselves from the body until the god himself will release them.

In the final part of the discourse on philosophy and death, there are three further developments. The first comes immediately after the true-born philosophers finish their Orphic hymn on purification. Socrates sets about repeating what they have said, but now as a question. He even compounds the interrogative phrasing: "And purification—does it not

---

18. The word translated as *true-born* is γνήσιος. It is related to γένος (*race, kind*) and γένεσις (*origin, birth, race*). It means *belonging to the (true) race, legitimate* (as opposed to νόθος: *bastard*), *genuine*. Needless to say, the appellation is thoroughly ironic.

turn out to be this, as was said way back in the λόγος: Is it not separating the soul from the body to the greatest extent and habituating it to gather and collect itself all by itself . . . , released from out of the body just as from bonds?" (67c–d). Thus, the body is explicitly associated with bonds (δεσμός), like those that bind a prisoner (δεσμώτης), like those that until his last day had bound Socrates. In this association there is expressed the Orphic view of the body as the prison of the soul. But, in addition, there is posed, more covertly, the question whether Socrates' release is also a release from the body. One might suppose precisely the contrary: for when Socrates was released from his bonds, his first deed—rubbing his leg—was oriented to his body.

The second of the three developments begins as Socrates launches into a eulogy in praise of thoughtfulness (φρόνησις). In the course of reiterating that a philosopher should not be terrified by death—all that he says reflecting back immediately upon himself—he remarks, most curiously, that the philosopher's opinion will be that he will encounter thoughtfulness purely only in Hades. What is curious is that this opinion runs completely counter to the Greek—that is, Homeric—view that those in Hades are witless shades. This discrepancy reflects the tension between the two very different itineraries that have been projected for the soul: emigration to Hades, on the one hand, and ascent to being, on the other.

Socrates continues his eulogy by laying out an economics of thoughtfulness. The focus is on exchange, on the buying and selling of virtue (ἀρετή), and on what constitutes the rightful coin to be used in such exchanges. Some exchanges, he notes, are not quite legitimate, for example, the exchange of certain pleasures for others that are more desirable, that is, forgoing certain pleasures for the sake of enjoying others that are more desirable. Socrates observes that though such exchange is commonly called moderation (σωφροσύνη), it is not true moderation. As the right coin for which all virtues should be exchanged, the coin therefore by which the worth of each virtue would be determined, Socrates proposes thoughtfulness. In his words: "Maybe this alone is the right coin for virtue, the coin for which all things must be exchanged—thoughtfulness" (69a–b). Thoughtfulness is, then, the currency of virtue. However, this coin or currency is not merely an external token corresponding to the worth of the various virtues, as ordinary money corresponds to the worth of a horse, of a pair of sandals, etc. Rather, thoughtfulness is that worth itself; it is what bestows on each of the virtues such as moderation and courage and indeed on virtue as such its worth, its very being. Socrates explains: "Maybe courage and moderation and justice and true virtue as a whole *are* only when accompanied by thoughtfulness. . . . But when such things are separated from thoughtfulness and are exchanged one for the other, maybe such virtue is not anything but a kind of shadow-painting" (69b). The question of the unity and interrelation of the virtues is not unique to the *Phaedo* but in various guises is taken up in the *Protagoras*, the *Meno*, and other dialogues. But in the present account there is a kind of reductionism at work: all non-noetic forms are declared non-essential, for instance, the virtue courage, which elsewhere and in general is linked not to the calculative or noetic power of the soul, but to the heart or spirit (θυμός).

The reductive character of this virtue economics comes fully to light as Socrates proceeds to still another reduction. He says: "but maybe the true and genuine virtue is a sort of purification from all these things, and maybe moderation and justice and courage and thoughtfulness itself are nothing but a kind of purifier" (69c). As Socrates goes on to mention mystic rites, the mysteries, and initiation, the connection of this entire discussion to Orphism and thereby to Pythagoreanism becomes unmistakable. In effect, all virtues have been reduced to the purification of the soul in the interest of its release from the body. On this view, there would be, then, no virtue of the body, no virtue with the least positive connection to the body.

The remaining development occurs just before Socrates launches into the economy of virtue. He reiterates that if philosophy is the pursuit of dying, then the philosopher should least of all be terrified of death. He continues: "Again, many people have been willing to pursue their human loves to Hades when they have died—their boyfriends, wives, and sons—led by the hope that they will see and be together there with those they desired" (68a). What Socrates says here seems curiously out of place in this context: for those to whom he refers go down to Hades, not through thoughtfulness and abstention from everything bodily, but because of love and desire. One such person was Orpheus, who went down to Hades in search of his dead newlywed Eurydice. Yet, what Socrates says is quite obviously wrong in the case of Orpheus, and thus in its application to the master musician whose song could tame even the beasts, the song by the music-making Socrates proves rather dissonant. Orpheus went down to Hades, not in order to "be together there" with Eurydice, but rather to bring her back from Hades. His intent was not to be together with her in death, but to bring her back to life. Furthermore, contrary to what Socrates says, what was required of Orpheus was that he *not* see her, that he not look back at her until they had fully escaped from Hades. Another instance contrary to the Socratic description comes from Book 11 of the *Odyssey*. There Odysseus is depicted in Hades: by offering the black blood of the sacrificial sheep while yet guarding it with his sword, he is able to bring forth the shades and even to speak with them. And yet, precisely what he cannot do is "be together" with them; when he tries three times to embrace the soul of his dead mother, she slips through his arms "like a shadow or a dream."[19]

In the entire discussion around the question of philosophy and death, virtually every passage betrays in one way or another that the discourse does not consist of straightforward declarations, much less of what later come to be called anachronistically arguments. Throughout most of this portion of the dialogue, Socratic ventriloquy is behind the obtrusively Orphic-Pythagorean diction and gestures. Neither is there a lack of comedy and laughter, all the more striking in the context of a discussion of death that takes place as Socrates himself awaits his impending death. In addition, there are the performative contradictions, first by Simmias and then in the highly comedic episode with the true-born philosophers, which brings onto the scene characters who are filled with love and desire and yet take themselves to be escaping just such passions. Finally, in its way of depicting lovers who go down to Hades, the discourse goes entirely counter to the traditional mythic accounts.

(C) MYTHOLOGIZING

As soon as Socrates has concluded the discussion of philosophy and death by expressing his hope that he has been more persuasive than he was before the Athenian judges, Cebes intervenes and through his response informs Socrates that he is not persuaded by what has been said about the soul. This intervention sets the stage for the first of several discourses about the immortality of the soul. The question becomes that of whether the soul is deathless (ἀθάνατος).

These discourses, as recounted by Phaedo, will twist and turn like the thread of Ariadne in the Labyrinth as they move through the winding passageways. Sometimes it will be as if they lose Ariadne's thread for a time and wander into a blind passageway, a dead end, from which

---

19. Homer, *Odyssey* 11:207.

then the discourse will have to retreat. All too often these discourses have simply been construed as demonstrations for the immortality of the soul. But then the sense of demonstration is simply taken for granted rather than being gathered from the dialogue and from the dramatic context in which such demonstrations are set; neither does it take into account the sense of the corresponding Greek word ἀπόδειξις.[20] It is hardly of great consequence if, assuming a modern—or, at best, Aristotelian—sense of demonstration, one then finds those in the *Phaedo* less than perfect.

At least in the case of the first such discourse, there are ample indications at the outset as to how it is to be heard. In his intervention Cebes remarks that though the rest was beautifully stated, what Socrates said about the soul induces a great deal of distrust (ἀπιστία). People "fear that the soul, once it is free of the body, is no longer anywhere and is destroyed and perishes on that very day when a human body dies; and that as soon as it is free of the body and departs, then, scattered like breath or smoke, it goes fluttering off and is no longer anywhere." Cebes grants that if what Socrates has said were true, there would be "a beautiful hope." "But," he continues, "this point—that the soul *is* when the human body dies and that it holds onto both some power and thoughtfulness—probably stands in need of more than a little persuasive speech and assurance" (70a–b). The word παραμυθία, rendered here as *persuasive speech*, means also *encouragement* or *persuasion*, but with an implied reference to speech.[21] Taken literally, the implied reference is to μῦθος, and thus what Cebes is requesting as needful is persuasive or encouraging storytelling, that is, mythologizing. In reply Socrates asks: What should we do?—or, taking the verb (ποιέω) in a more specific sense: What should we compose (as one composes a story)? Socrates continues: "Or do you want us to tell a more thorough story [διαμυθολογέω] about these things to see whether what we are saying is likely or not?" (70b). Cebes responds that it would be a pleasure to hear whatever opinion Socrates has about them. The reference to pleasure (ἡδέως—*pleasurably*]

20. Ἀπόδειξις means *a showing forth, a display*, or, more specifically, *a showing forth or display of something from something* (as, for instance, the character of something can be shown from an appropriate paradigm [see *Statesman* 277a–278e]). The word occurs with some frequency in the dialogues. Its sense and semantic range can be gathered from the following passages: *Phaedo* 72c, 88b; *Republic* 472d; *Sophist* 261b; *Statesman* 302e; *Symposium* 179c; *Theaetetus* 158b, 183a.

21. The corresponding verb παραμυθέομαι means *to address with consoling or encouraging words*.

marks the divergence from the previous discourse that is to come; in contrast to the previous denigration of pleasure, Cebes is now acknowledging that he will listen pleasurably to Socrates' mythologizing. So the discourse to follow will be an encouraging, consoling mythologizing that will be pleasurable to hear, a mythologizing—and perhaps also a looking-through (διασκοπέω)—aimed at determining whether it is likely or not that the soul endures. The discourse is ready to begin, except that Socrates adds finally a kind of challenge to the "comic poet" (Aristophanes of course is meant): not even he could say that in the present situation Socrates is talking about things that are none of his business. In speaking about death as his own death impends, Socrates will defend himself against the ridiculous portrayal of him that, as he mentions at his trial, is not unrelated to the charges brought against him. Now he will defend himself before true judges, before judges attentive to his display of who he is. At the same time, there is perhaps here also a certain competition with the comic poet being played out, a play at composing a Socratic comedy that would outdo those of Aristophanes.

In his intervention Cebes expresses a view of the soul that in many people provokes doubt about the soul's continued endurance. The view is that the soul is like breath (πνεῦμα) or smoke (καπνός) and so is likely to be scattered by the wind as soon as it leaves the body. Both comparisons are thoroughly Homeric and like the word ψυχή as such refer primarily to the dead, departed soul, the soul as a kind of ghost.[22] The more common comparison, bordering on identification, is with breath, with the breath that one expires at death. Yet, Cebes goes on to say that people fear that when the soul is free of the body, it "is no longer anywhere and is destroyed and perishes." This fear or belief is not at all Homeric. To be sure, Homer portrays the dead as mere bloodless shadows of what they were as living beings; he depicts them as witless, insubstantial shades, incapable themselves even of passing through the gates of Hades until the appropriate funeral rites and burial are performed.[23] And yet, in the

---

22. See *Iliad* 23:104; also *Oxford Classical Dictionary*, 2nd ed., s.v. "soul." On the soul as like smoke, see W. K. C. Guthrie, *The Greeks and Their Gods* (Boston: Beacon Press, 1950), 139n2.

23. In the *Iliad* the tale is told of how the soul (ψυχή) of Patroclus appeared to Achilles and pleaded: "Bury me with all speed that I might pass through the gates of Hades. The souls, the images [εἴδωλα] of dead men, hold me at a distance and will not let me cross the river and mingle among them" (23:65–73). See also Guthrie, *The Greeks and Their Gods*, 296.

Homeric epics souls do not perish but go down to Hades.[24] Thus, the question is tacitly posed as to which, if either, of these conceptions is to be affirmed, the one reported by Cebes, that after death the soul is destroyed and perishes, or the Homeric belief that the soul continues to endure in Hades, even though as a bloodless, witless shade. Still a further question is raised in Cebes' intervention, the question whether, if the soul endures in Hades, it has there any power and thoughtfulness, or whether, as Homer portrays it, it is an insubstantial and witless shade.

Cebes' intervention, especially his expression of people's fear that at death the soul simply perishes, sets the stage for the first in the series of discourses on immortality. It will be expedient to begin by following the path of the discourse with only minimal explanatory remarks before then turning back to it with a series of broader questions.

The discourse commences with a question of simple alternatives. Socrates states it directly: "Either the souls of human beings who have met their end are in Hades or they are not" (70c). Immediately Socrates refers to an ancient λόγος, which is held in memory, "that souls *are* there having arrived from here, and that they arrive here again and come to be from the dead" (70c). This ancient story transcribes the Orphic belief in the transmigration of souls, at least of those that have not completely freed themselves by means of purification. Socrates is retelling—and perhaps will be transforming—an old Orphic tale. He draws—though interrogatively—an initial conclusion: "And if this is so, and the living come to be again out of those who have died, could anything else be the case but that our souls *are* there?" (70c–d).

Socrates extends the question to the point where it becomes the question of the generation (γένεσις) of opposites, or, more precisely, of contraries as such (ἐναντία). This extension exemplifies one form that Socrates' mythologizing assumes: he takes an old story about the wanderings of the human soul and transposes it into a λόγος about contraries as such. The theme of contrariety has been on the horizon of the conversation from the beginning. Even before he actually begins to recount the events on Socrates' last day, Phaedo tells Echecrates that on this day he and the others present shared a strange πάθος; they were affected by an odd mixture of pleasure and pain, so that they were sometimes laughing, sometimes weeping. Thus, they were subject to a kind of mixing or blending of contraries, of pleasure and pain and of laughing and weeping. Socrates' very first account concerns the contraries

---

24. See, for example, *Iliad* 7:330.

pleasure and pain. He speaks of their wondrous relation: they will not both come to a person at the same time, but if that person chases and catches one, he is likely to get the other one soon. This account constituted the little μῦθος that Socrates invented, or rather, presented as the story that Aesop would have invented, had he thought of doing so.

Focusing on contraries in general, Socrates poses the question "whether it is necessary for whatever has some contrary to come to be from nowhere else but from its contrary?" (70e)—for instance, the larger from the smaller and the smaller from the larger, the weaker from the stronger, the quicker from the slower, and, more problematically, the worse from the better, and the more just from the more unjust. Cebes agrees, and so Socrates formulates the general principle: "All contrary things come to be in this way—from contraries" (71a). Thus, the relation between contraries is extended into another sphere: it is not only a relation of opposition but also a *genetic* relation. This extension could be regarded as a transposition of the little story Socrates told earlier about pleasure and pain having their heads fastened together in such fashion that whenever one comes, its opposite is soon to arrive.

Socrates elaborates the conception of generation that, by retelling and extending the old story, he has introduced. He observes that between two contraries there are "two becomings," two directions of generation. For example, between larger and smaller, there is growing (becoming larger) and shrinking (becoming smaller). When Socrates asks about the contrary to being alive, Cebes identifies it as being dead. They conclude that the dead come from the living and the living come to be from the dead. The further conclusion at which the entire discussion has aimed is expressed then by Socrates: "Therefore our souls are in Hades" (71e).

Socrates offers a supplement to what has just been said: generation must go around in a circle, or else all things would eventually have the same form and generation would cease. Both the context and the phrase Socrates uses, κύκλῳ περιιόντα (going around in a circle), suggest the phrase κύκλος τῆς γενέσεως (circle of generation), an Orphic phrase designating the wheel of rebirth from which redemption was sought by means of purification. Socrates adds two specific references to amplify or illustrate what he has said about the circle of generation. The first includes a mythic reference: "For example, if there were falling asleep but no waking up again to correspond to and come to be from sleep, you know that all things would end up by making Endymion prove to be insignificant. He would make a poor showing, since all other things would be affected the same way he was—they would all be asleep!" (72b–c). In the mythic tale to which Socrates is referring, Endymion was a young shepherd of unsurpassed beauty. While he was guarding his flocks, the moon saw him and fell in love with him and lay beside him. And so, wondrously beautiful, he lies on the mountainside and sleeps forever. So has the moon arranged it so that every night she can visit him and cover him with her kisses. The immediate point of the reference is self-evident: if only the process of going to sleep took place and not that of waking up—that is, generation in only one direction—then eventually all would be asleep and would sleep on forever like Endymion.

The second reference is to a philosopher who will figure prominently later in the dialogue: "And if all things were combined and not separated out, then the saying of Anaxagoras—'All things together'—would quickly have come about" (72c). Here Socrates is accurately quoting the very first words of Anaxagoras' book, which are put forth as a description of the original state of things, of the primal mixture from which all things emerged.[25] The connection in which Socrates here employs the phrase does not correspond to the way it functions in Anaxagoras' discourse, since for Anaxagoras the togetherness of all things is only the beginning—not the end, as in Socrates' hypothetical instance—from which indeed there is subsequently separating out. One might suppose that there is some irony in Socrates' use of the quotation in this manner, especially in view of his assessment of Anaxagoras later in the dialogue.

If this first discourse on immortality is now considered in broader perspective, then it is to be observed that in the *Apology* Socrates dissociates himself entirely from Anaxagoras. Early in his trial he identifies the prejudices, the "old false accusations," which, though not included among the official charges brought against him, are nonetheless being

---

25. Simplicius attests that this is the beginning of Anaxagoras' book. The full sentence reads: "All things were together [ὁμοῦ χρήματα πάντα ἦν], boundless both in quantity and in smallness" (B1). It would seem that in putting all things together in the primal mixture from which they later separate out, Anaxagoras maintains the thesis of Parmenides (taken over by Empedocles) that there can be no sheer coming into being (as from not-being) nor any such perishing (as passing from being to not-being). See Kirk, Raven, and Schofield, *The Presocratic Philosophers*, 357f.

relied on by Miletus as support for the actual charges. One such prejudice is that Socrates investigates things "beneath the earth and in the heaven." Not only does he reply directly, declaring that he "does not pursue these things" (*Apology* 19b–c), but also, shortly thereafter, he counters the prejudice with the question "Do you think you are accusing Anaxagoras?" (*Apology* 26d). What is remarkable is that now—in this other trial, this trial before his friends, this trial in proximity to the death to which he was sentenced in the other trial—Socrates is indeed pursuing inquiries into things beneath the earth. Though it is in relation to death that he is pursuing such inquiries—and hence in connection with the concrete situation as he faces his imminent death—a certain shift in the orientation of his discourse is clearly marked. Though near the end of his trial Socrates mentions that death is like either dreamless sleep or migration to a place—clearly Hades—where the heroes of the past might be engaged (*Apology* 40c–41c), the discussion about Hades is quite different in the *Phaedo*, at least in the first discourse. In the face of death, Socrates does not simply present migration to Hades as one of two possibilities but now inquires about the passage to Hades where the souls of the dead would endure. Now he even ventures to demonstrate that the soul endures in Hades; that is, he undertakes—or at least appears to undertake—to show from the necessity of the circular generation of contraries that souls endure in Hades.

The entire first discourse is surprisingly silent about the body. In this regard there is a strong contrast with the earlier discourse on philosophy and death. In the earlier discourse Socrates spoke at length about the body, though nearly always negatively: he portrays the body as an obstacle to the attainment of thoughtfulness and truth, as that from which the philosopher must turn in order that the soul be alone by itself. On the other hand, rather than merely contrasting the two discourses, one could regard the present discourse as carrying out *in deed* the turn away from the body that was merely described in the previous discourse. Now the discourse itself is turned away from the body, in that it completely ignores it, remains silent about it, represses the body. As a result the present discourse also is compelled to ignore the definition of death presented in the earlier discourse, that death is the separation of the soul from the body. Now death is construed as a mere change of place on the part of the soul: souls travel from here to Hades and then from Hades back to the world of the living. They go from here to there and back—like a ship sailing off to some island such as Crete or Delos and then returning to Athens. Thus, while ignoring the body, this discourse treats the soul as if it were a body moving from here to there.

As a result, the discourse carries out a transposition from φύσις to ψυχή. The analysis of contraries and of their circular generation relies largely, if not exclusively, on contraries exemplified in nature: larger/smaller, weaker/stronger, quicker/slower. It is from the necessity of circular generation between these contraries in nature that the conclusion is drawn that there must be circular generation between the contrary states of the soul.

It is readily affirmed that these contrary states are living and being-dead. Yet is it self-evident that being alive has a contrary? Is being-dead such a contrary? Can one *be* dead? Is it not possible that being dead is precisely not being at all? In any case, could one not take the contrary of being alive to be, not being dead, but rather being lifeless, including in this kind things that are not dead because they have never been alive, things that are neither dead nor alive? A stone is lifeless; it is opposed to living, and yet it is not dead.

Toward the end of the first discourse, Socrates hints at something else, something other than the dead, from which the living are generated. The hint is a mere hypothetical: "If the living were generated from others . . ." (72d).[26] Nothing prevents this passage from being read as: If the living were generated from *other living beings*. The passage thus hints at a possibility that could have been exploited by Cebes as an objection to the alleged demonstration, the possibility that the living could be generated from others who are living rather than from the return of the dead. It is most remarkable that this possibility remains completely undeveloped and almost unmentioned, for there is nothing more self-evident than that living beings are generated, that is, born, from other living beings, that they are born directly from the body of another living being of the same kind. It seems that the utter denigration of the body expressed—though not without comedic moments—in the previous discourse has led to a complete forgetfulness—or perhaps a feigned forgetting—of sexual reproduction, of the workings of ἔρως through which living beings are generated.

26. εἰ γὰρ ἐκ μὲν τῶν ἄλλων τὰ ζῶντα γίγνοιτο. The expression ἐκ . . . τῶν ἄλλων (from others) leaves indefinite just what kind these others are. Burnet glosses the phrase as follows: "from some other source than the dead who were once alive" (*Plato's Phaedo*, ed. John Burnet [Oxford: Oxford University Press, 1911], note to 72d1).

In the mythic tale of Endymion, ἔρως has a different result: loved and embraced by the moon, the young shepherd sleeps on and on. The question is whether Endymion is not precisely an image of the philosopher as he was portrayed in the discourse on philosophy and death, especially considering the metonymic relation between sleep and death. The philosopher, portrayed as devoted to dying and being dead, would sleep on, like Endymion, alone with his thoughts or dreams, to such an extent that he would be oblivious to ἔρως and desire, as Endymion was oblivious to the nightly erotic visitations of the moon.

In the first discourse a comedy is played out, a comedy of the specifically Platonic sort, in which there is, first, an abstracting or disregarding of something indispensable, something that cannot in the end be ignored; and then there comes a playful enactment through which it gradually is revealed just what has been disregarded and that it is ludicrous to disregard it. Thus it is shown indirectly that what was disregarded is indispensable.

In the first discourse the comedy has to do primarily with the body. There are three moments in the comedy. First, there is an abstracting from the body, a disregarding of it. The entire discourse is silent about the body and thus enacts in deed the turn away from the body in the previous discourse. Second, as a result of this disregard for the body, the previous definition of death as separation of the soul from the body is also disregarded. Death comes to be regarded as a mere transport of the soul from here to Hades; it is considered a mere voyage across the water (the River Styx is implied) to Hades—like the voyages to Crete and to Delos. It gradually becomes evident how the comedy is being played out: abstracting from the body, speaking only of the soul, the interlocutors end up treating the soul as if it were a body, something transportable from here to there and back. The very exclusion of the body, that is, of nature as it belongs to the human, eventually results in a reassertion of the bodily, a return of nature within the discourse. This is only the first of such returns, which will eventually dismantle the Pythagorean excess enacted in the first discourse and beyond. Third, along with the abstraction from the body in general, there is total disregard for the fact that living beings come to be from the *bodies* of other living beings, a disregard that can perdure only if, like Endymion, one sleeps on and on, never awakening to what lies all around and to what moves the soul most profoundly.

(D) REMEMBRANCE

The second discourse on immortality is launched by Cebes. Addressing Socrates and referring to what has been declared about the dead, that they *are* in Hades, he says: "And besides, Socrates, this also goes along with that other discourse [λόγος] you are in the habit of declaring [λέγειν], which—if it is true—says that our learning happens to be nothing other than remembrance" (72e). So this other λόγος declares that learning (μάθησις), that is, coming to know, is remembrance (ἀνάμνησις), that is, being reminded of something by something. The discourse that Socrates is in the habit of setting forth identifies learning as remembrance; it declares that one comes to know by remembrance of that which one would know. Memory (μνήμη) is indispensable to knowing.

Cebes associates this λόγος explicitly with Socrates. Presumably the indication is that now Socrates will speak for himself, in his own voice, rather than continuing to lend his voice to the expression of Pythagorean doctrines. Yet, as Socrates elaborates the thesis that learning is remembrance, it is imperative to listen with the utmost care for any difference that distinguishes his explanation from that given by Cebes, who, even though he associates the thesis with Socrates, is likely to regard it through a Pythagorean lens.

Cebes rounds out his opening observation by indicating how the identification of learning as remembrance provides support for the supposition that the soul is deathless. He says: "And according to this discourse, I suppose it is necessary that we have learned at some previous time what we now remember. But this is impossible if our soul was not somewhere before being born in this human form. So, in this way too the soul seems to be deathless" (72e–73a). His point is straightforward: learning is remembering, and yet one can remember only what one once knew but has forgotten; hence one must, in some previous time, already have learned what one can now remember. Cebes assumes without stating it that this previous time must extend back before birth, since from that moment on, one is capable of remembering.

In Cebes' statement of the thesis associated with Socrates, there is a glaring circularity: learning is based on remembrance, which in turn is based on learning in a previous time. Far from accounting for the character and possibility of learning, Cebes' statement simply transfers the problem to a previous time.

This circularity is not unlike that found in the *Meno*. In this dialogue Meno is portrayed as exemplifying a kind of ignorance that is linked to a peculiar kind of memory. He simply repeats what he has heard but has not understood. In his case remembering neither results in his coming to know nor is based on his having come to know. His is a sham memory that does not produce learning.

One of the things Meno repeats is a paradox—Socrates calls it an eristic λόγος—that would render learning impossible (as in deed it is for him). He asks Socrates: "But how will you look for something when you do not in the least know what it is? How are you going to set up something you do not know as the object of your search? To put it another way, even if you come right up against it, how will you know that what you have found is the thing you did not know?" (*Meno* 80d). Socrates restates the paradox: one cannot learn or inquire "either about what he knows or about what he does not know"; for inquiry about what one already knows is completely redundant, and inquiry about what one does not know is impossible, since one will not know what is to be the object of the inquiry, and even if it is found, one will not know that what has been found is what one set out to learn. It is in response to this paradox that Socrates declares that learning is remembering. Here, just as in the *Phaedo*, he claims to speak merely from hearsay, simply to repeat what he has "heard from wise men and women who told of divine things" (*Meno* 81a). Thus, his response regarding learning as remembering is itself presented as a deed of remembering. His response is meant to cut through the paradox that Meno has himself recalled. Socrates says: "Since the soul is immortal and has been born many times and has seen all things both here and in Hades, there is nothing that it has not learned. So it is no wonder that it can remember what it already knew before about virtue and other things" (*Meno* 81c). In this statement the circularity is even more evident. The very possibility of learning is accounted for by reference back to learning accomplished in prenatal time; learning is explained on the basis of learning. Yet if learning cannot be explained in the present life, it cannot any more readily be explained how it took place in previous lives. The problem of learning, of coming to know, of acquiring knowledge, is not really solved by the identification of learning as remembrance but is merely postponed, deferred backward.

If the accounts of learning in the *Phaedo* and the *Meno*, respectively, are reformulated as simple implications, then something strange comes to light. According to the *Phaedo*: since learning is remembrance, the soul must be immortal. According to the *Meno*: since the soul is immortal, learning can occur as remembrance. The difference is obtrusive: the implications go in precisely opposite directions, and if they were combined, they would generate still another circularity. What is thus indicated is that these discourses are irreducible to the mere implications that link the soul's immortality to the thesis that learning is remembrance; rather, each discourse is situated within a unique interplay of different dramatic moments—myth, deeds, situation, as well as the specific intent and development of the larger discourse.

In response to Cebes' invocation of the thesis, associated with Socrates, that learning is remembrance, Simmias immediately asks: "But Cebes, what were the demonstrations for this? Remind me—I cannot remember very well at present" (73a). A demonstration (ἀπόδειξις) brings something to light, displays it in such a way that it becomes manifest; a demonstration shows something from something, shows it in such a manner that it and its inherent connections become evident. This word expresses the character of the discourse to come, of the second discourse as a whole. It will be—or at least will aim at being—a showing forth of learning as remembrance, a showing by which it will be made manifest that learning is remembrance. Thus it is to be a showing by which one can be brought to learn—to remember—that learning is remembrance. It is precisely this doubling that is alluded to by Simmias when he asks to be reminded.

Cebes responds by offering Simmias a "most beautiful" λόγος, one that traces the lines of the demonstration that would be appropriate. He sets forth this λόγος in these words: "When human beings are questioned, if somebody questions them well, they themselves tell everything as it is, although if knowledge and a correct λόγος did not happen to be within them, they would not have been able to do this. Further, you get the surest indication that this is so when you direct them to mathematical diagrams or something else of that sort" (73a–b). As a beautiful λόγος, this outlines a demonstration that would allow the character of learning as remembrance to shine forth in its self-evidence, that would let it be manifest. In such demonstration, questioning—if done well—elicits knowledge, brings about learning. Since the questioner does not teach, does not instruct, does not convey knowledge, it must have come from within the one questioned, that is, it must have been there within already, must have lain forgotten, and then been remembered. Cebes adds that this process of remembering is most evident when a visible trace of it is provided by something like mathematical diagrams.[27] It is *from* such a trace that the process of coming to know as remembrance becomes most openly manifest. Cebes' beautiful λόγος thus accords with the character of demonstration as showing something from something.

Cebes thus offers his description of how learning as remembrance takes place. In advance one possesses knowledge within oneself, and remembrance consists in its being drawn out. In remembrance, the knowledge hidden within oneself—hidden even from oneself, forgotten—is set out into the open. In addition, one has a correct λόγος within oneself, and thus when properly questioned, one can "tell everything as it is." The silent λόγος within is converted into a sounding λόγος, an expression. Indeed, the word *expression* says precisely what Cebes takes remembrance to be, what he takes to be decisive for it, namely, the externalization of knowledge and of correct λόγος. In remembrance, as Cebes construes it, there is transport of hidden knowledge and silent λόγος from inside to outside, so that knowledge comes to be exposed (and even traced as such in diagrams) and λόγος is sounded.

Simmias confesses that he still needs to undergo precisely that which the discourse is about, namely, remembrance. Though he acknowledges that he has begun to remember (that learning is remembering), he wants to hear what Socrates will say about it. Socrates proposes that they look at it in this way: "Whenever someone who has either seen

---

27. In the *Meno* Socrates demonstrates in deed the thesis that learning is remembrance in his questioning of the slave boy. Beginning with a square of area 4, he poses to the boy the problem of determining the length of the sides of a square of area 8. Initially the boy supposes that doubling the length of the sides of the square of area 4 will yield a square of area 8. Socrates leads him to realize that this supposition is false; that is, by the questioning Socrates lets the boy come to know that he does not know—emphasizing then to Meno that the boy has been aided rather than harmed. Further questioning then leads the boy to recognize that if a square of area 16 is constructed from four squares of area 4 and if diagonals are then drawn across each of the smaller squares so as to form a larger square, then this larger square with the diagonals as its sides will be of area 8. On the one hand, Socrates insists that the boy "had these opinions in him" (*Meno* 85c) and was led to remember them through the questions Socrates posed to him. On the other hand—though it goes unremarked—the entire demonstration proceeds by means of the diagrams that Socrates draws, that is, not only through what may lie forgotten within the boy but also by reference to something perceptible. It is not a matter merely of questions that evoke remembrance but of questions posed in reference to perceptible diagrams and of remembrance activated by reference to visible geometrical constructions.

or heard something—or has grasped it by some other sense—not only perceives that thing but also thinks of another, the knowledge of which is not the same but different, do we not justly say that he remembers that which he comes to have in mind?" (73c–d). It is of the utmost significance that Socrates' account makes no reference to expression, to transport from an interior, where there is silence and hiddenness, to an exterior, where knowledge would be set out in the open and λόγος sounded. Rather, Socrates characterizes the movement at the core of remembrance in a very different way. It is a movement of manifestation: *from* the sense perception of one thing, one comes to have in mind—that is, there becomes manifest—something else, something different, something the knowledge of which (and so that thing itself) is different. In short, remembrance occurs when, from the perception of something, something else comes to be manifest, to be shown. Yet, this is tantamount to saying that remembrance is a showing (the coming about of a showing) of something from something, a showing *from* something perceived *of* something different from what is perceived. Here it becomes evident why the reference to demonstration (ἀπόδειξις) is of such importance: the word designates not only the character of demonstration proper but also the structure or movement of remembrance as such.

One extremely significant consequence comes immediately to light. According to Socrates' account, remembrance proceeds from sense perception (seeing, hearing, or some other sense). But sense perception is not an operation solely of the soul; it requires sense organs, and thus the body.[28] Thus, the bond of remembrance to perception is a bond also to the body. That remembrance proceeds from perception and hence from an operation in which a bodily moment is indispensable entails that one who, as in the comedy of the true-born philosophers, stands apart from the body would be incapable of remembrance. Furthermore, if all learning takes place as remembrance, then those who enact dying away from the body would be incapable of learning; they would have left behind the very possibility of coming to know, of gaining knowledge. Their presumption of an ascent to being could only serve to distract them from attaining the thoughtfulness they claim to love and desire. Here, then, one observes how Socrates—still sitting with his feet down on the earth—is letting the body come back into play, undermining thereby the comedic

---

28. In the *Theaetetus* (184c) Socrates insists on the distinction between that through which we see (the senses) and that by which we see (the soul). This passage is discussed above in chap. 5(d).

abstraction, disregard, repression, of the body that the discourse on philosophy and death declared and that the first discourse on immortality enacted. To the alleged ascent in which the would-be philosopher would strive to be completely out of touch with the body and in which this figure would presume to come to know even being as such, nature in the guise of the body returns.

Socrates elaborates his account of remembrance by offering a series of examples. The first of these examples is especially significant. Socrates declares that the knowledge of a human being and that of a lyre are different. When Simmias agrees, Socrates continues: "Do you not know, then, that lovers, when they see a lyre or cloak or anything else that their boyfriend was in the habit of using, are affected in this way: they perceive the lyre, and they grasp in thought the look of the boy [τὸ εἶδος τοῦ παιδός] whose lyre it was? And that is remembrance" (73d). In this example the apodeictic structure of remembrance is quite evident: from the perception of something, namely, a lyre or a cloak, something else comes to be manifest, namely, the look of the boy, which is grasped in thought (ἐν τῇ διανοίᾳ). This example, a lover's remembrance of the look of the boy he loves, serves to underscore the bond of remembrance to the erotic and the corporeal. Rather than drawing the lover's vision away from the body, remembrance brings before his vision—at least before a certain kind of vision—the look of the boy, the look of the boy's body.

It is significant also that the word εἶδος is introduced here. It is used to designate that which is remembered, that which, on the basis of a perception, comes, through remembrance, to show itself, that which becomes manifest. In this context it does not refer to those invisibles that Socrates calls by such names as *justice itself, good itself, beauty itself.* Rather, its more concrete and literal sense here remains in force: it means simply the look of something, the look that something presents when one looks at it. This sense, this reference to sight, will remain inherent in it even when the word comes to designate such invisibles as justice itself, etc. In this connection, it should be acknowledged that there are different kinds of seeing, different ways in which the look of something can appear. In imagining, something comes before—as we say—the mind's eye. In memory in its most mundane sense, something seen in the past is brought back to mind. In mathematical intuition, something itself invisible (a triangle as such) is traced in a visible diagram. Even in the present example, that which is designated by the word εἶδος is in a sense invisible, since the lover does not actually see the boy in the sense of the boy's being present before the lover's vision. The boy is not present to his perceptual vision but rather at the moment of remembrance is not-visible, is himself invisible. And yet, in another sense, in another kind of vision, the lover does see him, does have his look before this other kind of vision, which is here designated only very broadly by the word διάνοια (hardly renderable simply as *thought*). Hence, in this example, remembrance is presented as issuing in a seeing that is also a not-seeing. This peculiar conjunction comes into play regardless of whether what is remembered is the look of a boy or that of justice itself.

Socrates mentions several other examples. Some are fairly straightforward: someone who has seen a picture of Simmias may remember Simmias himself; or someone who sees Simmias may call to mind Cebes. There is one example that is quite cryptic: someone who sees a sketch of a horse may remember a human being. Here there is an unexpressed compounding of the remembrance: someone who sees a sketch of a horse remembers the horse that is sketched; from this vision (in the mind's eye) of the horse, one remembers that this horse is ridden by a certain human being; and from the vision of the horse being ridden, one remembers the human being who rides the horse. In this example, then, there is a chain or interweaving of remembrances.

Socrates is explicit about what the examples are especially meant to show: "Then does it not follow from all this that remembrance stems from similar things and also from dissimilar?" (74a). So remembrance is not limited to cases where one is simply reminded of something by something else similar to it (as a picture of Simmias reminds one of Simmias). Rather, the relation between what is perceived and what on that basis is remembered can be one of dissimilarity (as when a sketch of Simmias reminds one of Cebes or when a sketch of a horse reminds one of a human being). Furthermore, there can be more complex remembrances in which both similarity and dissimilarity are involved (as when a sketch of a horse reminds one of the horse [similarity], and the horse eventually reminds one of a human being [dissimilarity]).

It is on such a compounded, mixed remembrance that Socrates comes to focus, and it is to this type that the remainder of the discussion is addressed. This type of remembrance involves two moments. The first is straightforward: on perceiving something, one remembers something similar. But then, as the second moment, something different occurs: one comes to have in mind (to consider, to see with discernment, to ponder discernedly—ἐννοέω) whether the thing perceived falls short of the thing remembered. Thus, it is a matter of a remembrance that moves from something perceived to something similar to it while at the same time discerning the dissimilarity, the difference, between the perceived and the remembered.

Against this background Socrates introduces his principal example, that of the equal: "We say that there is somehow some equal. I do not say stick equal to stick or stone to stone or anything else of that sort, but something other, beyond all these things—the equal itself [αὐτὸ τὸ ἴσον]. Shall we say that this is something or nothing at all?" Simmias responds: "By Zeus . . . we certainly shall say it, wondrously so" (74a–b). So, from the equality of sticks and of stones, Socrates distinguishes an other, something different (ἕτερον), something dissimilar, namely, the equal itself. On the other hand, since both are designated by the same name, since both are called *equal*, they are to some extent, in certain respects, similar. Thus, the two terms are both similar and dissimilar, same and other, and the relation between equal itself and the equality of sticks and of stones is not, then, itself an instance of equality (complete sameness); the equal itself and the equality of these things are not themselves equal. The remembrance that Socrates is about to describe will thus be a compounded remembrance involving both similar and dissimilar.

In the passage cited above in which Socrates draws the distinction between the two equalities, there is repeated reference to speech, to saying something about equality. In the passage, along with Simmias' response, forms of the word φημί (*say* or *speak*) occur three times along with an occurrence of λέγω (also *say* or *speak*, but in addition, *arrange, lay in order*). It should be observed, in particular, that Socrates does not simply, straightforwardly assert that there is some equal, that this is something; neither does Simmias make such an assertion. Rather, Socrates says only that they say there is some equal; Simmias says the same, says that they will say it, and adds emphasis by swearing "By Zeus!" and by appending the word *wondrously* (θαυμαστῶς). What is indeed most wondrous about saying something such as what Socrates says about equals is that it poses, sets up, in a certain anticipatory way orients the speaker toward, something like an equal itself. What is decisive here is precisely the connection between saying (speech) and something like the equal itself. The equal itself—whatever character it might eventually display—is, first of all, that which is meant when one says *equal*.

Socrates proceeds to outline the structure of the remembrance of the equal. Referring to the equal itself, he begins: "And we grasped the knowledge of it from where? Is it not from the things we were talking about just now: we have seen sticks or stones or some other things that are equal, and from these we have come to have in mind the equal itself, although it is other than these?" (74b). So, we have seen equal sticks and equal stones—the perceptual moment—and from these, on this basis, we have come to have in mind (ἐνενοήσαμεν—from ἐννοέω) the equal itself—the other moment, the moment of which one is reminded. And yet, the equal itself is other than, is different from, the equality of sticks and of stones, and so in this remembrance one not only will come to have the equal itself in mind but also will discern the difference. In this case, then, there is a complex remembrance: a remembrance of the equal itself, and within that remembrance a discerning of the difference.

Socrates focuses more precisely on this difference. He observes that whereas equal sticks can also appear unequal (for example, under certain conditions, from a certain perspective), the equal itself can never appear unequal. In other words, the equal itself *is* itself and always appears as itself, whereas the equality of sticks can always turn out to be in some respect unequal; it is possible for the equality of sticks not to be itself, to be not itself. In still other terms, the equal itself is always the same as itself; the equal itself is equal to itself, whereas the equality of sticks can be unequal to itself. Here one can discern the motive behind Socrates' choosing this particular example. It is an example that turns back on itself: the focus is not only on the equal itself but also on the equal's equality with itself. Socrates sums up the implications, asking as regards "equals among sticks": "Do they appear to us to be equals in just the same way as the equal itself that is [itself]? Or do they fall somewhat short of being the sort of thing the equal is—or not at all?" (74d). Simmias agrees that they fall short. This conclusion can be regarded either as a bit paradoxical or perhaps as hinting at a slightly comedic moment: the equal itself turns out not to be equal to anything else whatsoever.

There follows the most decisive move in this entire discourse. Socrates poses it as an extended question: "Whenever someone who has seen something notices that 'What I am now seeing wants to be similar to something else among beings, yet it falls short and is not able to be that sort but is inferior,' then must not the man who notices this necessarily have chanced to see beforehand that which he says it is like but falls short of?" (74d–e). Simmias answers: "Necessarily." The connection here established is to be applied to the example of equals. Then it takes this form: the act of seeing equal sticks and therein apprehending them *as* equal involves noticing, observing discernedly, that they want to be similar to the equal itself (equal to the equal) yet fall short of it. The extended question Socrates poses concerns the condition for such an act, the condition presupposed by it. This condition, to which Simmias attributes necessity (ἀνάγκη), is that one must have *seen beforehand* the equal itself. This is necessary for two reasons: first, in order to be able to observe that the equal(ity) of the sticks "wants to be similar," strives to approximate, the equal itself; and, second, in order to be able to discern that the equal(ity) of the sticks falls short of the equal itself, that is, in order to be able to discern the difference. Socrates puts it in this way: "Then it is necessary that we saw [saw in advance, saw beforehand—προειδέναι] the equal before that time when we first saw equals and noticed that 'All these things are striving to be like the equal but fall short of it'" (74e–75a).

This seeing or knowing beforehand is what in the history of philosophy will become the *a priori*. In these passages in the *Phaedo* this has one of its original—and originary—formulations. Subsequently the emphasis will usually fall on the moment of similarity or identity. What figures most prominently is that in order to recognize (see, know) something as what it is, one must already, beforehand, in advance, have seen (known) the *what*. What is especially striking in the Platonic formulation is the emphasis on difference, on the necessity that in order to recognize something as falling short of—as different from—something else, that which it falls short of must have been seen beforehand.

In his reference to the other (such as the equal itself) to which certain things (such as the equality of sticks) want to be similar, Socrates designates this other as *some other among beings*. He refers also to *the equal itself that is* (74d). As he continues, he broadens the scope of such designations: he declares that the discourse is not only about the equal and the greater and the less but also about the beautiful itself, the good itself, the just and the holy. He says: it is about "all those things upon which we set the seal 'that which is' [τὸ ὃ ἔστι]" (75d).[29] In such designations as *being* and *is*, what for the most part is stressed about the beings is that *each is itself*; thus it is that Socrates speaks of the equal itself, the beautiful itself, etc. In contrast to the equality of the sticks, which can also appear unequal, the equal itself can never be unequal, can never be

---

29. See Burnet's note to 75d2 in *Plato's Phaedo*.

different from itself, unequal to itself. To say that each is itself is to say of each that it is not—not ever, under no conditions—anything different from, other than, itself; it is to say that each is always the same as itself, that it is a selfsame being. Whether it is a being that has the character of selfsameness or it is constituted as a being by selfsameness (so that to be is the same as being selfsame) is a question that here does not come to be posed.

Toward the end of the second discourse on immortality, Socrates stresses again the role of the senses in remembrance. He observes: "So then, it is from the senses [ἐκ . . . τῶν αἰσθήσεως] that we must come to have in mind that all the things in these senses both strive after the equal that is and fall short of it" (75b). Once it is established that the seeing beforehand (of the equal itself, for example) must already have occurred before the moment we began using our senses, hence before birth, Socrates reiterates the role of the senses: "later by use of our senses we grasp again the various knowledges we once had before" (75e). There would be, then, only the slightest hyperbole in saying that recognizing equals as equals is primarily a matter of sense, granted the basic condition that the equal itself must have been seen beforehand. It is on the basis of sense that one comes to have again in mind what was once seen but has been forgotten, namely, that which is homonymous with the things of sense but, unlike them, is entirely selfsame. In any case, it is evident that, according to Socrates' description of remembrance, far from being dispensable, far from being something the philosopher would die away from, the senses belong inherently to the structure of remembrance and as such constitute a condition for knowledge. Within remembrance as bringing again to mind something forgotten, nature installs itself through the role played by the senses. To the ascent in which knowledge would be attained, nature returns, both as a moment of nature within human beings (the senses) and as the comportment of the human to nature (by way of the senses).

At the end of the discussion of learning as remembrance, Socrates returns to the question of the immortality of the soul. Since we must have seen before birth that which we now remember, he concludes that "earlier our souls also *were*, before they were in human form, and they were separate from bodies and had thoughtfulness" (76c). They did not exist as witless shades in Hades but possessed the thoughtfulness, the capacity for thought, required for the apprehension of that which after birth they would be capable of remembering. Curiously, however, Socrates does not simply let this result, this conclusion, stand. Rather, he proceeds to say something that Simmias calls "extraordinary" (ὑπερφυῶς—literally: above or beyond nature) and characterizes as a having recourse to or taking refuge in (καταφεύγω) something beautiful. The λόγος that provokes this exclamation from Simmias has to do precisely with a beyond of nature. Specifically, the result that human souls *were* before being born into human form Socrates makes dependent on the affirmation of the beings themselves that they have kept talking about.[30] More precisely, Socrates declares that the two terms, the prior being of the soul and the beings themselves, are of "equal necessity," though his formulations appear to grant precedence to the beings; he mentions the beautiful and the good and such sort of being. The beauty in which, according to Simmias, they are taking refuge is constituted by this necessity in which the connection between the soul and being begins to become manifest. In Simmias' words in response to Socrates: "Our soul *is* before we were born, just as surely as the being you spoke of now" (77a).

The second discourse thus arrives at the threshold that leads to the most decisive determination of the relation of the soul to being. As the condition of all sense perception, the soul must have seen in advance the beings themselves; but, in turn, having seen them in advance, the soul can bring them again to mind only through the apprehension of the homonymous things presented through sense. This circuit that links remembrance, sense, and prior seeing of the beings (the latter still formulated in the language of sense) constitutes the basic schema that emerges from the second discourse. It is almost as if the prior being of the soul were merely a corollary drawn on the basis of this schema. The connection thus established between the soul and the beings themselves will prove to be the primary axis on which the third discourse will turn.

(E) ASCENT

The third discourse on immortality is prefaced by three brief discussions concerning, respectively, the shortcomings of the previous discourse, the existential motivation underlying the entire undertaking, and the role that Socrates is to assume in what follows.

---

30. The word θρυλέω (*to keep talking about*) also has a pejorative sense: *to make noise, to keep babbling*. The double sense may be taken as indicative of the problematic character of this assertion, that is, that the beings are posited in λόγος, though not—or not yet—beyond.

In the first of these prefatory discussions, both Simmias and Cebes observe that the second discourse has shown only half of what was to be demonstrated. It has shown only that the soul *is* before being born in human—that is, embodied—form, but not that when we die the soul will still *be*. Thus, the demonstration based on the schema of remembrance does not suffice to dispel the fear of the many that at death the soul is scattered and this brings its being to an end. Socrates' response is that this demonstration should be put together with the previous one, which was presented as showing that the living come from the dead so that the dead must *be*. When he goes on to remark that nonetheless Cebes and Simmias might want to continue careful thought about this matter, it would seem that Socrates is offering a covert indication that he has not forgotten how problematic the first discourse proved to be, especially through the comedy played out in it.

In the second of the three discussions, Socrates leaves these questions aside in order to address another, much deeper dissatisfaction, something that remains unsettling despite what the two discourses claim to have demonstrated. His description has, however, an air of comedy, and indeed it provokes Cebes to laugh. Socrates identifies the fear that motivates the entire undertaking to demonstrate the immortality of the soul: "you have the fear of children—that in truth the wind will blow the soul away and scatter it in all directions as it leaves the body, especially whenever someone happens to die, not in a calm, but in a great gust of wind" (77d–e). Cebes admits not that they are afraid, but that "perhaps even in us there is some child who is frightened of such things." Setting this child at a distance from himself, Cebes proposes that they undertake to persuade him—the child—"not to fear death as if it were a hobgoblin" (77e).[31] The aim in the discourse to come will be to calm the fear of death, the fear borne by the child within, who is now set apart in order that the calming words of the discourse may be addressed to him. This discourse will twist and turn like a labyrinth, winding back and forth, up and down; in dramatic, mythic terms, death in its fearfulness represents the Minotaur, while Socrates assumes the role of Theseus.

---

31. The word μορμολυκεῖον (*hobgoblin*) has, through its connection to the verb μορμολύττομαι (*to frighten, scare*), the connotation that it is a figure used to frighten children—hence its appropriateness in the present context. It is not insignificant that μορμολυκεῖον κωμῳδικόν means *comic mask*.

And yet, when, in the final prefatory discourse, Socrates instructs his interlocutors as to how the calming words are to be sounded, he seems to be cast more in the role of Orpheus than in that of Theseus. For his instructions are that one must sing to the child: "What is necessary is to sing him incantations every day until you charm away his fear" (77e). Socrates enjoins Simmias and Cebes to spare nothing in their search for such a singer wherever he might be. But on this, his final day, Socrates is to play the role of such a singer, carrying on the music making in which he has already been engaged. Yet even before Socrates' appeal to song, Cebes has laughed; his laughter signals that the comedy, largely suspended during the second discourse, is now to resume. The song that Socrates will sing will be a comic song.

Socrates launches the third major discourse on immortality by referring again to the fear that when the soul leaves the body, the wind will blow it away and scatter it. He asks then: "What sort of thing is apt to suffer this affection, being scattered?" (78b). He answers: anything that is composite (composed, put together—σύνθετον) is likely to undergo such dispersion and dissolution. Specifically, he refers to things that are composite by nature (φύσει), hinting thereby that these are the things belonging to nature. On the other hand, anything that is not composite is apt not to suffer it. He then identifies the things that are most likely non-composite as those that are always selfsame and remain the same (ἀεὶ κατὰ ταὐτὰ καὶ ὡσαύτως ἔχει). Socrates notes that these are the beings about which they spoke in an earlier discourse, and he now proceeds to speak of them in several ways.

The series of descriptions (78d) is cast in interrogative form; yet Cebes repeatedly expresses his full agreement, and Socrates continues as if his questions had in effect been converted thereby to declarations with only a slight aura of questionableness. First of all, such a non-composite being he describes as "the being itself [αὐτὴ ἡ οὐσία] of whose being [τὸ εἶναι] we give a λόγος in questioning and answering." The connection here drawn between such being and λόγος (the giving of a λόγος enunciating it, speaking it out) recalls the earlier indication of this same connection in the context of the account of the equal (74a–b). The present passage reinforces what the earlier one hinted at: that λόγος serves to pose such beings, to orient the speaker and listener (in questioning and answering) to them in an anticipatory way.

The second description almost repeats the phrase with which Socrates initially identified the things likely to be non-composite. He says—still in the form of a question, the positive content of which is affirmed by Cebes—that such a being "always remains in the same way selfsame [ὡσαύτως ἀεὶ ἔχει κατὰ ταὐτά]." The insistence on selfsameness is thus doubled, intensified. Such beings are—and remain—utterly—or, in a later idiom, absolutely—selfsame. Socrates prepares the third description by invoking the equal itself and the beautiful itself and then applies to these the phrase "each that itself is [αὐτὸ ἕκαστον ὃ ἔστιν]," which is readily convertible into "each that is itself"—that is, each that is never anything other than itself, each that itself is nothing but itself, each that completely *is* and never *is not* what it is, hence each that itself *is*. Then, fourth, Socrates condenses this description into the designation *the being*, using the participial noun τὸ ὄν. The fifth description ventures further: he says that such a being does not admit any kind of change (μεταβολή). This character is, however, already implied by the utter selfsameness of such beings, since to change would be to become other, not to remain the same, hence to violate its selfsameness. Thus, it is indicated that selfsameness is the more originary character: in distinction from mere unchangingness, selfsameness involves relation to self. Finally, Socrates describes each such being as "of single look, being itself all by itself [μονοειδὲς ὂν αὐτὸ καθ' αὑτό]."

These descriptions of being itself can readily be read together with Parmenides' way of truth and set alongside what the goddess teaches about being. Both on the way of truth in Parmenides' poem and in the descriptions offered by Socrates here in the *Phaedo*, being is characterized as preeminently one. The divergence between the two accounts originates from the different ways in which the oneness of being is thought. In the case of Parmenides, being is thought as one in distinction from all else, which, as not-being cannot be and hence is not, is unthinkable, impossible. Being is one among an impossible self-vitiating plurality (hence is the whole, the all), and to this extent the Parmenidean thinking of being retains a certain arithmetic character.[32] On the other hand, Socrates' descriptions present being as one in the sense that each

---

32. The reference here is to the Greek conception of number (ἀριθμός) as a number of distinct ones. See Jacob Klein, *Greek Mathematical Thought and the Origin of Algebra*, trans. Eva Brann (Cambridge, MA: MIT Press, 1968), chap. 6. However, the Parmenidean account falls outside the arithmetic conception insofar as the one is not at all identical with, but quite the opposite of, any other ones—that is, it is unique. In counting (ἀριθμέω), on the other hand, each of the ones counted off must be identical with all the other ones.

is one with itself, is selfsame. The oneness of being is thus not thought arithmetically but in terms of relation to self. It is by virtue of this difference that a pluralizing of being can be carried out such that, in place of the one such one being, Socrates can speak of multiple one beings, of a manifold of beings each of which is one in the sense that it is one with itself. It is significant that when, in the *Sophist*, the Stranger from Elea confronts Father Parmenides, his strategy is precisely to demonstrate that being cannot be constrained to being one, to one being—that is, that the one being is necessarily exceeded—is even self-exceeding—and thus proves not to be one.[33] Being overflows into a manifold of beings, each of which is one with itself. The *Sophist* extends still further the divergence from the arithmetic conception through the account of the community of kinds.

Drawing Socrates' various descriptions together, it can be said that each being itself, of which we give a λόγος that brings it in a certain way before us, is utterly selfsame, hence admits no change; yet not only *is* each selfsame, but also each *looks selfsame*, each is of a single look, each looks always the same, each presents always the same look and *is* precisely this selfsame look. Such beings (such as the beautiful itself) Socrates contrasts with the many beautiful things, with "anything else having the same name [ὁμωνύμων] as those others" (78e). Here again the reference to λόγος is evident and indeed significant: the difference between such beings as the beautiful itself and the many beautiful things is first introduced as a difference between homonymous things. This difference is then articulated into two moments. First of all, these things with the same name as some being itself *are not* themselves; they are not utterly selfsame but are constantly becoming other than they are, are continually coming *not to be* what they are. The second moment of difference lies in their relation to the senses: they can be sensed by—or rather, through—the senses, whereas those beings that remain always selfsame can be grasped only "by way of consideration by thought [τῷ τῆς διανοίας λογισμῷ]" (79a). In this formulation the reference to λόγος is evident; it again emphasizes the evocative power of λόγος with respect to beings. Yet the word λογισμός (in verb form λογίζομαι) designates specifically *counting, calculation*, and by generalization *taking into account, consideration*. The allusion to mathematics is significant:

---

33. See my discussion in "Plato's *Sophist*: A Different Look," in *New Yearbook for Phenomenology and Phenomenological Philosophy* 13 (2013): 283–91.

a number itself, like a right triangle itself, is invisible and yet can in certain ways be brought forth into the purview of thought.

Socrates concludes: "Let us then posit, if you want, two looks of beings [δύο εἴδη τῶν ὄντων], the visible and the unseen" (79a). The decisiveness of this passage is indisputable. It calls not only for commentary but also for broader reflection on its implications.

Socrates' proposal is that they posit these two looks. *Posit* here translates a form of the verb τίθημι.[34] Positing is, first and foremost, a deed carried out in and through speech; this is the case even if what is being affirmed in the positing might hold independently of the verbal positing. It is this connection that is being maintained by their saying "Let us posit . . ." rather than simply, straightforwardly declaring that there *are* two looks of beings, two ways that beings can look. Socrates' performative utterance, his saying "Let us posit," accentuates the relation of the distinction to λόγος; it emphasizes that this difference between the two looks is not something already somehow known to be valid that is then, in Socrates' proposal, merely reaffirmed in its validity. Rather, it is in and through the proposal—doubled in his *saying* "Let us posit . . ."—that the distinction is first drawn, first brought into purview. In this differentiation between the two looks that beings can assume, the very sense of being is brought under scrutiny. Only through determination of this sense could it then be ascertained what would be meant in saying of the two looks that they *are*.

All too often this passage, along with others in the *Phaedo*, has been taken straightforwardly as a statement of a theory that Plato is supposed to have held regarding what in the dialogues are designated as beings themselves or as εἴδη, as well as by other designations in other contexts. However, in this connection it is imperative that one exercise caution and restraint rather than rushing headlong to such a conclusion. In this passage and throughout the dialogue, it is Socrates, not Plato, who is speaking, and even though it is Plato who represents him as speaking, this does not warrant simple identification. Indeed, in the dialogue in which the sense of being comes to be rigorously determined, it is not

---

34. Τίθημι has a broad range of significations. It means *to place* (as to place something in front of someone), so *to put, to set*; also *to fix* or *lay down* (as to lay down a law); also *to ordain, institute, set up*; also a number of senses geared to specific activities or objects. In the present context the word is rendered as *to posit* by Brann, Kalkavage, and Salem (*Plato's Phaedo*) and by C. J. Rowe (Plato, *Phaedo* [Cambridge, UK: Cambridge University Press, 1993]).

Socrates but a stranger from Elea who carries out the determination.[35] Furthermore, in the present passage Socrates is speaking in a very charged and dramatically complex situation. To overlook this situation and rush ahead to an all too facile conclusion is to risk getting caught up—unawares—in a kind of hermeneutical comedy.

The theory that the Platonic Socrates is alleged to be setting forth in the present passage is supposed to concern the beings themselves, the εἴδη; it would be as if it were known in advance what constitutes a theory, so that, somehow coming across these beings, one could then set about making a theory about them. And yet, there are complications that interrupt such a supposition: what is under discussion in Socrates' series of descriptions, namely, the beings, the looks, bears on the very sense of theory. The words θεωρία and θεωρέω designate a looking at something, a beholding of something. Correspondingly, the looks (εἴδη) are precisely that at which one looks in theory. In this sense the looks are what makes theory—as looking to the looks—possible. The complication is evident: that which first makes theory as such possible cannot itself simply and straightforwardly become the object of a theory.

When Socrates names the two looks (εἴδη) of beings, he calls them the visible (τὸ ὁρατόν) and the unseen (τὸ ἀειδές). In this formulation there is a complex pun. One of the two εἴδη of beings is conspicuously designated as ἀειδές, whereas the word ἀόρατον (*invisible*—hence, as the privative, parallel to ὁρατόν and used in fact in the preceding remark) could at least as readily have been used. That which is here designated as ἀειδές (*unseen*) not only is one of the two looks of beings but in more differentiated terms coincides with that which is called εἶδος, in distinction from the visible. The pun thus serves to juxtapose looks and the unseen, pointing in this manner to a kind of seeing that leaves nonetheless unseen, a seeing that is also a not-seeing. The pun extends to another connection, linking the unseen (ἀειδές) with Hades (Ἅιδης). Even at this remove from the much earlier discussion, there is allusion to the vacillation of the philosopher between two very different itineraries, one leading to Hades, the other directed at the beings themselves, the unseen.

On the basis of the distinction between the visible and the unseen, Socrates proceeds to confirm that the soul has greater affinity to the unseen beings. The entire discussion is figured by a proportion. Since the soul is unseen and the body is visible, the following proportion holds:

---

35. The reference here is to the determination of being as δύναμις (*Sophist* 247e).

soul : body :: unseen : visible

Or, in converted form:

soul : unseen :: body : visible

The conclusion is that the soul is more similar to the unseen and the body more similar to the visible. Socrates refers specifically to what they were saying "from way back": that when the soul uses the body for investigating something, then the soul is dragged down, and then it "wanders and is shaken up and gets dizzy, just as if it were drunk, because it has had contact with such things" (79c). Here Socrates appears to be recalling the discourse he voiced ("way back") in the name of the "trueborn philosophers." When Socrates then goes on to speak of the soul's ascent to the unseen beings, Cebes' response is such that it recoils on itself no less than did Simmias' in the discussion way back. He is emphatic in his affirmation of what Socrates has said: "What you say is altogether beautiful and true, Socrates" (79d). And yet, just as in the discussion way back, one cannot but wonder how Socrates, sitting there embodied with his feet down on the earth, can have evaded the very contamination he describes and thus somehow has succeeded in arriving at truth. Equally unanswerable is how Cebes has remained sufficiently uninebriated that he can affirm with such confidence what Socrates has said. Yet, in this declaration and its affirmation, there is something else that is disregarded so thoroughly that one might well suspect that still another comedy is being prepared. How is it that the discourse on remembrance has so quickly been forgotten? For that discourse demonstrated that the body, specifically the senses, rather than contaminating the soul, belongs to the very structure of learning, of coming to know. Since learning as remembrance proceeds from the senses, a soul apart from the body would never gain knowledge.

Yet Socrates races on, prolonging this forgetfulness of remembrance, posing another more extended proportion:

soul : body :: master : slave :: divine : deathbound

He expands the reiterative proportion still further:

soul : body :: divine and deathless : human and deathbound
:: intelligible : unintelligible :: single-looking : manifold-looking
:: indissolvable : dissolvable :: selfsame : never selfsame

This proportion includes, in oppositional form, most of the constitutive moments that have been broached in the discussion up to this point: selfsameness, the intelligible (τὸ νοητόν as object of thought [νόησις]), and the two kinds of looks of beings. But what is especially conspicuous and indeed provocative is that the human is made coordinate with the body, whereas the soul is set on the side of the divine—as if the human were not both soul and body. It appears that a certain self-forgetfulness is setting in—or rather, that it is about to be enacted.

In any case Socrates arrives at what seems to be a conclusion: "Well, then, since this is how things stand, is the body not apt to be dissolved quickly and the soul in turn apt to be altogether indissolvable, or something close to this?" (80b). The soul is then depicted, not simply as enduring (since, as Socrates observes, the body too can, under certain conditions, remain intact for a very long time), but rather as going off to a region that is noble and pure (καθαρόν). As once again Socrates puns, saying that this unseen (ἀειδές) place is the true Hades (Ἅιδης), it becomes apparent that the Orphic-Pythagorean theme of purification and escape from everything bodily has returned to the discourse.

The discourse that follows on the afterlife of the purified soul and on the philosopher's progression toward assimilation to unseen being as such only serves to play out more extravagantly the return of the Orphic-Pythagorean themes of purification and of ascent beyond the bodily realm. It is no less comedic than the earlier engagements with these themes. Yet its specific comedic character lies in its enacting a forgetting of remembrance, of the bond of remembrance and hence of knowing to the senses, to the body. Such forgetfulness, played out to its full comedic extent, cannot but finally provoke a certain return of the bodily, a return of the nature within the human by which there is engagement with the nature without.

The drama begins with these words: "But when the soul, itself by itself, investigates, it goes off there, to what is pure and always *is* and is deathless, and remains the same, and since it is akin to this, continually comes to be with it—whenever, that is, it has come to be itself all by itself and this is possible for it—and then it ceases its wandering and, around those things, is always selfsame and remains the same, because it has had contact with such things; and this state of the soul has been called thoughtfulness—is this not so?" (79c–d). And yet, in this rhapsodic depiction of the soul's escape, focusing finally on thoughtfulness, there is dissonance. For if one remembers—as Socrates at least pretends not to—what is required for such remembrance to bring before our mind selfsame beings such as the equal itself, then one cannot but question whether the state that Socrates has described can legitimately be called thoughtfulness. Indeed, a soul that ceases its wanderings, that remains always the same, utterly selfsame, and that no longer lets itself be transported from something seen to something else made manifest from it would have entered a state, not of thoughtfulness, but of *cessation of thought*, a state of alleged deathlessness virtually indistinguishable from death. In this depiction of the soul's assimilation to being, there is audible not so much the tone of Socratic irony as, rather, the other sense of the word φρόνησις. For the word can mean not only thoughtfulness but also arrogance, presumptuousness, overweening pride.[36] What in Socrates' depiction seems to be an ascent to pure being thus begins to look more like a presumptuous flight oblivious to human emplacement in a body on the earth.

As Socrates tells, on the one hand, about the purified souls that go off to the true Hades, he also tells, on the other hand, about the others who are defiled, who remain contaminated by what is heavy, earthly, visible: "a soul in the sort of condition we described is made heavy and dragged back into the visible region through fear of the unseen and of Hades and, as they say, circulates among the memorials and tombs, around which certain shadowy apparitions [phantoms—φαντάσματα] of souls have been seen, ghostly images produced by the sort of souls that were not released in purity but participate in the visible—which is why they too are visible" (81c-d). The unpurified souls thus remain ghosts—and as Socrates continues his ghost stories, the comedic aspect is sounded ever more clearly in his words. He tells of how these souls flit around in cemeteries and of how, dragged down by their attachment to the bodily, they are eventually imprisoned again in bodies, in bodies that correspond in a certain way to their way of living their former life: gluttons and drunkards become donkeys, the unjust become wolves, falcons, or hawks, and those who, though lacking philosophy, are moderate and just become bees, wasps, or ants—or even human. As Socrates sets forth this ludicrous bestiary, one can hardly not compare the state of these defiled souls with that of the purified ones; for even the ghosts, flitting around in cemeteries until they eventually get reentangled in a body, seem more nearly alive than those—if there were such—who are to remain forever utterly selfsame.

---

36. The word φρόνησις is used in this sense in, for example, Euripides' *The Suppliant Women* 216. The related word φρονηματισμός means only arrogance, presumptuousness.

The entire extended discourse on the exorbitant ascent reaches its climax when Socrates declares: "To enter the race of the gods is not lawful for anyone who has not philosophized and gone off from here entirely pure—but the lover of learning may" (82b–d). Yet, for a philosopher to suppose that with sufficient purification he could eventually enter the γένος—the kind and the race—of the gods would constitute the most extreme presumptuousness, the most blatant arrogance. Nothing more exorbitant, more oblivious to human embodiment and mortality, could be presumed than to suppose that one could come to be of the same kind as the gods.

There are two further passages in the third major discourse that serve to confirm that this discourse has been completely transposed into the framework of Orphic-Pythagorean beliefs. In the first passage Socrates speaks of those who turn to philosophy "and to the release and purification it effects" (82d). The passage thus announces, even more loudly than before, the return of the Orphic-Pythagorean themes of release from the body through purification. Philosophy itself is, then, to be understood in these terms, as aiming at such purification and release. Those who turn to philosophy Socrates calls by a name introduced precisely in the passage about the purified ones who enter the race of the gods; he calls them lovers of learning (φιλομαθεῖς). The name serves to recall that the discussion of remembrance was indeed an account of learning, of the character of learning as remembrance. The reference to learning within this contest in which the structure of remembrance is entirely lacking readily leads to explicit recognition that the would-be ascent is haunted by a forgetting of remembrance. It is this forgetfulness that makes possible its pretense while, on the other hand, subverting the ascent, diverting it into comedy.

One other passage extends the comedic discourse. Socrates says that the lovers of learning—who, as goes unsaid, have forgotten that learning is remembrance—"recognize that when philosophy takes over their soul, it is utterly bound within the body and welded to it, and it [the soul] is compelled to investigate the beings through it [the body] as through a cage [or: through prison bars—διὰ εἰργμοῦ] rather than itself through itself" (82d–e). So here again the Orphic-Pythagorean theme of the body as prison of the soul returns.

In the final passage in the third discourse, Socrates evokes the image of Penelope. Continuing the Orphic-Pythagorean themes he has played out throughout the discourse, he declares that once the soul is released, it will refrain from giving itself over to pleasures and pains, since this would tie it to the body and make it "engage in the unfinishable task of a Penelope unweaving the web she has woven" (84a). This final image in the third discourse is covertly an image *of* the third discourse. For, not only in this discourse but indeed throughout, Socrates and his companions have in fact been given over—as was said—to pleasure and pain, indeed to a strange mixture of these, for which Socrates invented a brief mythic tale. They are, then, tied to the body and necessarily engaged in a task like that of Penelope. In the activity of weaving, there is the most pertinent image or figure of λόγος: one weaves together the warp and the woof just as in speech one weaves together words (nouns and verbs). Penelope's "unweaving the web she has woven" is precisely what has happened in the third discourse: what is said (woven together) is undercut (unwoven) by the very saying of it. It is subverted, undone, unwoven, by being said by the embodied Socrates, who continues sitting with his feet down on the earth. Even further, what is said is already unwoven in advance by what the second discourse demonstrated regarding the bond of learning (as remembrance) to the senses and hence to the body. It is only by looking out from the cage, from the prison where they in fact are, that learning is possible.

When the third discourse ends, there is in play the pretense that the philosopher is to become of the same kind as the gods, that he is to subsist in utter selfsameness, leaving all other souls behind as ghosts flitting around cemeteries in search of a body. At the same time this discourse has—as in the final image of Penelope—unwoven itself through its forgetfulness. It is, then, highly appropriate that when the discourse has finally concluded, the dialogue continues by not continuing, marking the break with a word that is most suitable. At the very moment when the third discourse has just ended, the next word is *silence* (σιγή): "Silence came about when Socrates had said this, and it lasted a long time. And Socrates himself, to judge by looking at him, was absorbed in the previous discourse, as were most of us" (84c).

At this point in the dialogue, this silence is more significant than any word could be, and the word *silence* signifies more than could any other word. It is a word that violates what it says: to say the word *silence* is precisely to break the silence. As in the third discourse, its saying is in conflict with—that is, it unweaves, as with Penelope—what it says. Even if one forgoes actually saying the word, the tension remains; even the written word involves a tension between the fact that it signifies and that what it signifies is precisely a not-signifying, that is, remaining silent.

The appropriateness of the word extends still further. The third discourse has, in discourse, carried the ascent through to its completion. It has carried it through to the point where the soul would be assimilated to selfsame being, and humans—or rather their souls—would join the race of the gods. Beyond this point there could be no continuation, no further enactment of the ascent. There can be only silence.

The ascent would be, above all, the separation of the soul from the body, which would be left behind as the soul went off to the true Hades. Yet, if the body is left behind, then there can be no speech, no vocal utterances, only silence. Indeed, if, as Socrates proposes etymologically in the *Cratylus* (400c), the body (σῶμα) is the means by which the soul gives any sign (σῆμα) that it gives, that is, if the body is the soul's signifier, then in the true Hades there can be no signification, no λόγος—only silence.

In the third discourse Socrates enacts the stance of a Pythagorean, which is determined primarily by concern with purification and release of the soul. Yet members of the Pythagorean order were sworn to silence about their beliefs and practices; they were forbidden to reveal these secrets to anyone outside the order. Hence, in falling silent, Socrates is enacting the appropriate comportment toward what has been said. And yet, it *has been said*, and its having been said is not undone by the subsequent silence. In falling silent, Socrates—who is no Pythagorean—is parodying the Pythagorean vow of silence. On the other hand, the Pythagoreans present are the very ones who do not observe the silence: "But Cebes and Simmias went on conversing with each other in a low voice" (84c).

Turning to them, Socrates inquires whether they find something still lacking in the previous discourse. Straightaway he admits that "in many ways it is still open to suspicions and counterattacks" (84c). When Simmias hesitates—as he says to Socrates—"for fear that it might be unpleasant for you in your present misfortune" (84d), Socrates responds with an apt comparison of his song with the song that swans sing when they are about to die. He explains that it is then that they sing most beautifully in their joy that they are about to go off to the god they serve. He declares that, like the swans, he serves Apollo and from the god receives the gift of prophecy that is expressed in his swan song. And yet, he leaves unsaid just which song is his swan song, whether the third discourse is his genuine swan song (and not just a Pythagorean swan song sung by Socrates) or whether his true swan song is still to come.

The skeptical objection that Simmias expresses at this point stands in marked contrast to the third discourse. He says: "It seems to me, Socrates, perhaps as it does to you too, that to know anything certain about such matters in our life now is either impossible or very difficult"

(85c). Against the background of this suspicion, Simmias launches into a discourse shaped by the image of sailing. It is perhaps Simmias' most decisive contribution to the entire discussion on Socrates' last day. He says: "For in these matters, a man must, it seems to me, accomplish one of these things: he must learn or discover what is the case, or, if that is impossible, he must sail through life in the midst of danger, seizing on the best and least refutable of human λόγοι, at any rate, and let himself be carried upon it as on a raft—unless, that is, he could travel more safely and less dangerously on a more stable carrier, some divine λόγος" (85c–d). This says: lacking full knowledge, lacking a divine λόγος, one must sail along on human λόγοι as upon a raft. Thus, along with the other figures of transport, that of winding through the labyrinth, of ascending beyond the body and the earth, of descending into Hades in order, like Orpheus, to sing away the sting of death, or of going off to the true Hades, there is now introduced the figure of sailing on a raft of human λόγοι. As goes without saying, this figure resonates with the mythic tale of Theseus' sailing to Crete and with the Athenians' sailing to Delos. In the central discourse of the dialogue, this figure will be taken up and developed by Socrates and will shape the single most decisive passage in the entire dialogue.

Simmias discreetly informs Socrates that what has been said does not seem quite apparent to him, that the would-be demonstration that the soul, in virtue of its affinity to the beings themselves, is indissolvable and thus imperishable falls short of showing definitively that the soul is immortal. Simmias explains the reason for his skepticism by appealing to a schema of the same kind as was employed by Socrates. Again it is a matter of a proportion:

Strings and lyre: tuning:: body: soul

Thus, by using the same kind of schema that Socrates used to show that the soul is immortal, Simmias now shows that it is not immortal: just as tuning does not survive the destruction of the strings and the lyre, so the soul does not survive the destruction of the living body. Here, as with earlier Greek thinkers such as Heraclitus, the word ἁρμονία has as its basic meaning *fitting together, jointing, arranging in an order*. From this basic meaning, the musical sense and the more general sense of harmony or concord derive: when certain things are fitted together in the proper way, when they are arranged in the correct order, what results is harmony or concord; if the strings of a lyre are set together properly on the lyre, then musical harmonies can be produced. The word *tuning* suggests both the basic meaning and the more general and musical senses.

In the present context the occurrence of the word ἁρμονία cannot but serve as a reminder of its significance for the Pythagoreans, who sought to discover the ἁρμονία in all things, as Pythagoras had discovered the mathematically expressible ἁρμονία in musical intervals. For the Pythagoreans, ἁρμονία was especially associated with human well-being, with health in the body and virtue in the soul. It is not surprising, therefore, that it is the Pythagorean Simmias who introduces this theme into the discussion.[37]

Following Simmias' posing of the musical proportion, there occurs punctuation, which connects it—fits it together—with the following discussion, in which Cebes states his misgivings about what Socrates has said about the soul. The punctuation is provided by Socrates' look. The very first word following Simmias' remarks, a form of διαβλέπω, says in effect that Socrates looked straight at them, even that he looked through them.

Cebes confides that he does not accept Simmias' criticism, for, contrary to the proportion that Simmias formulated, he is convinced that the soul is stronger and more long-lasting than the body. He offers another proportion:

weaver: cloak:: soul: body

Cebes' skepticism is based on the fact that, though the weaver will survive many of the cloaks he weaves and wears, this does not entail that he will not finally perish, even as he is still wearing one of the cloaks, which will thus outlast him. Cebes' conclusion is that the soul may indeed outlast many bodies yet still may finally perish.

Even before he formulates his proportion, Cebes makes explicit what he takes to be the outcome of the entire discussion up to this point concerning the immortality of the soul. He grants that it has been adequately demonstrated that the soul *was* before it came into its present form, but, he insists, it has not been shown that the soul *will still be* after death. The demonstration that he is declaring adequate can be no other than the second discourse, the discourse on learning as remembrance.

---

37. There are significant occurrences of this theme in other dialogues. For example, in a passage in Book 4 of the *Republic* (443d), Socrates describes justice in the soul as a matter of ἁρμονία. In relation to the discussion in the *Phaedo*, it is significant that in this passage Socrates does not take the soul itself but rather the justice in it to be a ἁρμονία.

In effect Cebes is declaring that they have made no progress at all beyond what was accomplished in the second discourse. The entire third discourse with its exorbitant pretense has been merely a detour leading back to the place where it began.

(F) SECOND SAILING

When Cebes has finished explaining why he takes the survival of the soul after death not to have been demonstrated, he discreetly brings this conclusion to bear on Socrates himself. Though he avoids calling Socrates by name and casts the formulation in general terms, he speaks nonetheless of "one who is about to die" and of the necessity that he "always fear for his soul" (88b).

At just this point something happens that is unprecedented. The conversation between Phaedo and Echecrates, which frames the entire dialogue, is suddenly renewed. For the moment this conversation interrupts Phaedo's previously unbroken narrative on what was said and done on the day of Socrates' death. Abruptly the conversation is transposed to Phlius and to a date sometime after Socrates has died. The λόγος is withdrawn, removed in place and time, from the actual events leading up to Socrates' death; or rather, since all along Phaedo has been telling the story to Echecrates, this removal, this distance, is marked once more by the return of the framing conversation. A similar return to the conversation between Phaedo and Echecrates occurs immediately following the discourse that forms the philosophical center of the *Phaedo*. In the second of these interruptions or interludes, Echecrates refers to "us . . . who were absent but are listening right now" (102a). So, these two interludes, these interruptive renewals of the conversation that frames the entire dialogue, serve in turn to frame the central discourse. Framed by the two remarkings of the λόγος in its remoteness from the actual events narrated, the central discourse consists primarily of a discourse on philosophy as commencing, or rather, recommencing, through the turn to a λόγος removed from things and events. The accord is remarkable: the content of the central discourse on λόγος—this λόγος on λόγος, this λόγος on the philosophical turn to λόγος—is mirrored by the form of the dialogue, by its dramatic structure.

Framed by the two interludes, the central discourse consists primarily of an autobiographical account in which Socrates describes the itinerary by which he arrived at the second sailing. This autobiographical account is preceded by three preliminary passages leading up to it.

When the first interlude ends and Phaedo resumes his narrative of the words and deeds on Socrates' last day, what he reports is a conversation between himself and Socrates. At this point Socrates' plight is at its most extreme because of the objections that Simmias and Cebes have brought against what he said in the third discourse in enacting the attempt to demonstrate the survival of the soul after death. Socrates himself indicates the extremity of his predicament in various ways, confessing, for instance, that he risks being not a philosopher (φιλόσοφος) but a lover of strife (φιλόνεικος). It is during the time when the extremeness of his situation appears to weigh most heavily upon him that he converses with Phaedo; this is the only direct conversation with him that Phaedo reports. Yet during this short time, deeds seemed to figure more importantly than words: Phaedo reports that he was sitting on a low stool next to Socrates, and "he caressed my head and gathered up the hair on my neck, for he was in the habit of teasing me about my hair; and he said, 'Tomorrow, Phaedo, perhaps you will cut off these beautiful locks of yours'" (89b).[38] Socrates goes even further, proposing that both he and Phaedo will cut their hair today if the λόγος comes to an end and cannot be brought back to life, that is, if the λόγος on death and survival beyond death dies and is unable to survive death. In these words and deeds it is as if Socrates/Theseus were entreating his Ariadne to help him find his way, to provide a thread that might lead through the labyrinth of λόγοι. It is as if from the would-be divine, disembodied, selfsame state enacted in λόγος in the third discourse, Socrates were now *feeling* his way back with this erotic gesture and his attention to Phaedo's beautiful hair.

Yet precisely here where the Theseus μῦθος again resounds, Socrates invokes another μῦθος, or rather, he transmutes the μῦθος in such a way that Theseus metamorphoses into Heracles. He refers to the Argives, those who sailed with Jason on the quest for the golden fleece, and mentions, in particular, Heracles, who was among them at the outset of the quest. Socrates then casts Phaedo in the role of Heracles and offers to help him as his Iolaus, though Phaedo immediately reverses the roles. The reference is to the second labor of Heracles, in which he set out to kill the Hydra. This swamp-inhabiting monster had nine heads, and

---

38. The Greeks cut their hair as a sign of mourning. Burnet suggests that Socrates' words and actions indicate that he wishes to see how Phaedo will look with his hair cropped as a sign of mourning (*Plato's Phaedo,* note to 89b2).

killing it proved extremely difficult, because one head was immortal and the others were such that for every one he chopped off, two appeared in its place. In his labor against the Hydra, Heracles was aided by his nephew Iolaus, who brought him a burning brand with which he then seared the neck as he cut off each head so that it could not sprout again. When Heracles had finally chopped off all the mortal heads, he disposed of the immortal one by burying it under a rock.

But in the battle about to commence against the monstrous objections brought forth by Simmias and Cebes, there is a danger that even victory would not expel, an even greater danger than that posed by the objections. This danger is that from repeatedly experiencing the refutation of λόγοι, one might become a hater of λόγοι, a misologist (μισόλογοι). Socrates declares, without any qualification, that there is no greater evil than hatred of λόγοι; and he explains why this is paramount among evils by depicting a person who, pushing the blame onto the λόγοι, "from that moment on would finish out the rest of his life hating and reviling λόγοι and would be robbed of the truth and knowledge of beings" (90d). The evil of the misologist is paramount, because to turn away from λόγοι is to deprive oneself of the truth of beings, of the revelation in which beings show themselves as they are and thus open themselves to human knowing. This declaration is just the negative form of what Socrates will declare at the most decisive moment of his autobiography: that it is through λόγοι that one gains access to the truth of beings.

The battle is ready to begin. Socrates' words announce the beginning: "But we must get going" (91c). This marks the beginning of the second of the preliminary passages leading up to the autobiographical account. Socrates begins by summarizing the criticisms that have been aired. Then, prompted by him, both Simmias and Cebes readily express their acceptance of the outcome reached in the second discourse: that since learning is remembrance, the soul must *have been* before being bound to the body. And then, like Heracles, Socrates wages his battle against Simmias' λόγος, in which the soul was identified as the tuning or harmony of the components of the body. He fights on several fronts; it is as if, having cut off one head—by pointing out the inconsistency of this conception with the thesis that learning is remembrance—two heads now appear. On the one side, he shows that if the soul were simply tuning or harmony, then all souls would be the same, and no account could be given of the virtue or vice that distinguishes various souls. On the other side, Socrates shows that if the soul were the tuning of the bodily elements, then it would not be capable of running contrary to the inclinations of the body. Yet even the poets attest that the soul can do so, as Socrates shows with an apt citation from the *Odyssey*.

Socrates introduces the final preparatory passage by mentioning Harmonia (Ἁρμονία), referring primarily to the Theban goddess (daughter of Ares and Aphrodite), though not without also referencing the previous discussion of tuning and harmony. He declares that Harmonia has been gracious to them; in this acknowledgment Socrates is expressing his gratitude for their having been able to dispose of Simmias' objection based on the analogy between the soul and ἁρμονία. He then asks about Cadmus, the husband of Harmonia; specifically, he asks about the λόγος by which Harmonia's graciousness might be exemplified also in Cadmus. Cadmus was the legendary founder of Thebes, the home city of Simmias and Cebes. Most significantly, he was credited by Herodotus with having first brought the alphabet to Greece, hence with having first made written λόγος possible. This special connection to λόγος, along with the pairing of Cadmus with Cebes (corresponding to the pairing of Harmonia with Simmias), leads Socrates to confront Cebes' λόγος. Anticipating a battle over Cebes' λόγος, that is, over his critical objection, Socrates restates this λόγος: it says that even granted that the soul *is* before entering the body, even granted also that it may wear out several bodies, this still does not demonstrate that the soul is immortal, that it does not itself finally wear out. At this point, however, Socrates does not venture to engage Cebes' λόγος in battle. Rather, as he will propose after a lengthy pause, they must first make a detour through the question of the cause of generation and destruction. In this sense the Socratic autobiography, which is the primary speech in the central discourse and indeed the centerpiece of the entire dialogue, is treated as a detour, as a digression that must be made in order afterwards to launch the battle against Cebes' λόγος. It is a detour that turns from the ontological heights of the third discourse back to the processes that are primary, not for beings themselves (which admit neither generation nor destruction), but for the beings that have a different sort of look and that appear through the senses. The detour is a return to nature; or, at least, it is through a return to nature that it is initiated.

Socrates marks the beginning of the digression that ironically will lead to the heart of the dialogue: "Then Socrates paused for a long time and considered something within himself" (95e). In the face of his imminent death and in the face of Cebes' monstrous λόγος, which threatens even his composure in the face of death, Socrates looks within himself, looks back into his coming to be who he is. Here he engages in another kind of remembrance, a remembrance that gathers up into the present his coming to be who he is. Yet, even if its structure is quite different, it is still a remembrance through which learning occurs, though a learning in which one comes to know not beings such as the equal, but rather oneself. Here, if anywhere, Socrates puts aside the roles he has played; he desists from ventriloquy and reclaims his own voice, speaks *as* Socrates. This posture is indicated not only by his looking within but also by the way he describes to Cebes what he is about to undertake. He says that, if Cebes wishes, he will go through his own experiences, through what he has undergone, with regard to generation and destruction. When Cebes encourages him to do so, then, as he is just about to begin, he enjoins with utter directness: "Listen, then, and I will tell you" (96a).

Socrates tells, first of all, how as a young man he set about inquiring: "For I, Cebes, . . . as a young man was wondrously desirous of that wisdom they call inquiry into nature [περὶ φύσεως ἱστορία]. This wisdom seemed to me magnificent—to know the causes of each thing, why each thing comes to be and why it perishes and why it *is*" (96a). This marks, then, the beginning: looking back into himself, into his own coming to be, Socrates recalls himself as, at first, an inquirer into nature. In coming to be as a philosopher, he began with nature.

Socrates identifies some of the questions that occupied him as he launched his inquiry into nature. Among these was the question: Is it when hot and cold bring about a certain fermentation, as some people say, that animals undergo growth?[39] Or again: Is it the blood or air or fire by which we think?[40] Or: Is it the brain that produces the senses

---

39. Burnet identifies this doctrine as one held by Archelaus, a disciple of Anaxagoras and reportedly the teacher of Socrates. Burnet explains the meaning of the doctrine thus: "The meaning is, then, that the warm and cold give rise by putrefaction (σηπεδών) to a milky slime (ἰλύς) by which the first animals were nourished" (*Plato's Phaedo*, note to 96b3).

40. The thesis that it is by blood that we think can be taken as referring to Empedocles, specifically to Fragment B105, which reads, in part: "for blood surrounding the heart is human thought." The identification of the soul as air is found in Anaximenes, Fragment B2 (see the discussion above in chap. 2); a kinship between thought and air is attributed to Socrates in the *Clouds* (230). The reference to fire can be associated with

of hearing, seeing, and smelling, from which memory and opinion and eventually thought arise?[41] In each case the cause that is identified is something belonging to nature, a natural process such as fermentation, natural elements such as air and fire, or natural things such as the blood or the brain. That which is accounted for by reference to such a cause may also be something natural such as the growth of animals, or it may be something that exceeds nature as the senses are exceeded by memory and opinion and these, in turn, by thought. What defines such accounts is that in every case something is accounted for by reference back to a *natural cause*, back to something belonging to nature.

Socrates continues: "And then, in turn, I looked into the processes by which these things pass away and the affections that pertain to heaven and earth, until I ended up with the opinion that I was naturally unfit [ἀφυής] for this looking into things" (96b–c). Thus, by pursuing inquiries into nature, Socrates gained a certain insight into himself. By looking into things in the effort to discover their natural cause, he came to realize that for such inquiries he was inept by nature, by virtue of limitations prescribed for him by nature, presumably by the nature within himself. In discourse in which—as here—a natural ineptness is reported, there is a tendency (not foreign to Platonic texts)[42] to let the word *nature* undergo a decisive semantic shift: from designating the

---

the Heracliteans in view of the preeminence accorded fire by Heraclitus, as exemplified in Fragment B90: "All things are an exchange for fire and fire for all things, as goods for gold and gold for goods." (See chap. 3 above.)

41. Burnet attributes this doctrine to Alcmaeon of Croton, a pupil of Pythagoras (*Plato's Phaedo*, note to 96b5). His medical theories are related to those of the Pythagoreans in general and stress that health requires a balance or harmony between the different elements. See Kirk, Raven, and Schofield, *The Presocratic Philosophers*, 260, 338f.

42. The *Timaeus* is especially remarkable in this regard. In Timaeus' discourse on the making of the cosmos, the word *nature* (φύσις) is deployed in a way that is neither univocal nor simply equivocal; it is indeed polysemous, and yet its multiple meanings are schematically connected. At least four meanings can be discerned. (1) The word can designate natural things, the things subject to generation, which, in distinction from the "in which" (the receptacle) and the "from which" (the intelligible εἴδη), Timaeus calls "the nature between these" (50d). (2) *Nature* can designate what something is, that is, the intelligible εἶδος, as when Timaeus speaks "of the nature of the all [περὶ... τῆς τοῦ πάντος φύσεως]" (47a). (3) Timaeus speaks also of "the nature that receives all bodies" (50b), thus taking *nature* as a designation for the receptacle. (4) *Nature* is also used in reference to the traces of the elements as they were before, with the birth of the heaven, things first came to be; thus he says that they "must bring into view the nature itself of fire and water and air and earth, before the birth of the heaven" (48b).

domain of natural things (as presented through the senses), it comes to signify what something or someone is. If one were simply to follow this tendency, then it could be said that by looking into nature (in the first sense) Socrates came to a certain insight into his own nature (in the second sense). Then the discourse could expand into an account of the *nature of* things and even of the nature of nature. And yet, with this shift, one would have posited a nature beyond nature, dividing nature against itself.

But in the autobiographical account Socrates holds back from shifting straightforwardly to a nature beyond nature. Instead, he continues by describing the way in which he came to realize his natural ineptness for inquiries into nature. Both his ineptness and his recognition of it are—needless to say—to be taken as exemplary, as pertaining not just to the natural limitations of Socrates in his singularity but to a human incapacity as such for investigating nature in the way he has just described.

Socrates' insight was, paradoxically, a result of blindness. He says: "I was so excessively blinded by this looking that I unlearned even what I believed I knew before about many other things and about why a human being grows. Before I used to believe that this was clear to everyone: that a human being grows because of eating and drinking" (96c). Such presumed knowledge he came to unlearn once he undertook to look into things in the ways indicated by the questions just mentioned. This unlearning was the result of his encountering aporias that put in question what he previously believed he knew. He mentions, in particular, certain complications regarding number, especially regarding ones. One such complication is the following: when a one is added to a one, does the one to which it is added become two, or does the one added to it become two, or do they both become two by the addition of each to the other? In any case, addition is the cause of one becoming two. But then, if someone splits a one apart, then this splitting is the cause of one becoming two. Yet—and this is the major aporia—this cause (splitting, separating) is the contrary of the former cause (addition, bringing together). Thus, Socrates confesses that he no longer knows "why a one comes to be nor why, in a word [ἑνὶ λόγῳ], anything else comes to be or perishes or *is* by this way of proceeding." The significance of the arithmetic example and of the aporias it involves consists in its displaying a kind of generation that runs entirely counter to the way in which Socrates had previously taken it. The result was that he no longer knew—or rather believed he knew—at all how generation takes place. He no longer had any sure insight into generation, and it was as if he were blind to it. Yet, to have no insight into generation and perishing is to have no possibility for inquiring into nature. It is to become blind to nature. As a result, nature disappears from the purview of the philosopher.

It is highly significant that the aporias Socrates mentions concern ones, that they have to do with what happens to ones when they are treated as undergoing genesis. For what Socrates eventually will propose is to set the ones over against the generation and perishing of things. Then, instead of accounting for things by reference to natural causes, he will account for them by referring them to the ones. By means of this reference to the ones set over against nature, he will effect a return of nature.

Continuing his narrative, Socrates tells of hearing someone reading from a book by Anaxagoras, "which said that it is νοῦς that sets all in order [διακοσμέω] and causes all things" (97b–c). This book would have been, according to the ancient sources, Anaxagoras' sole book, and it was reportedly entitled *On Nature*. Socrates would perhaps have heard a passage such as the following: "Everything else has a portion of everything, but νοῦς is unlimited [ἄπειρον], autonomous, and mixed with no thing, but it is alone all by itself. . . . For it is the finest of all things and the purest, and it has knowledge about everything and the greatest power; and νοῦς controls all things. . . , all these did νοῦς set in order" (B12). Here νοῦς can be taken as the power of νόησις (as the *power of thought*, as *intelligence*, or in the Latin translation, *mens*, hence *mind*). To an extent the character that Anaxagoras attributes to νοῦς, that of being autonomous, pure, and alone all by itself, corresponds to the character that Socrates, in effect (if not by name), attributes to νόησις in distinction from αἴσθησις (*sense perception*) (see 79a).

After Socrates heard what Anaxagoras had written about νοῦς, his expectations were high. His response was to take what Anaxagoras had said one step farther and to conclude that if νοῦς is the cause of all things, then it would order all things in the way that is best; it would order them by reference to what is good. He mentions, in particular, the earth, a theme that will become much more prominent as the dialogue proceeds toward its conclusion. He recalls what he expected he might hear from Anaxagoras: "I supposed that he would tell me first whether the earth was flat or round, and when he had told me that, he would go on to take me through the cause and necessity of it, saying what is better and why, in particular, it is better for the earth to be such as it is" (97d–e). However, Socrates reports, when he obtained the book and read it,[43] he was extremely disappointed, for Anaxagoras "did not employ νοῦς at all and did not hold any causes responsible for putting things in order, but instead put the blame on air and aither and water and many other absurd things" (98b–c).[44] In other words, he accounted for things by referring them not to νοῦς, but only to natural things or elements as their cause.

Socrates ventures to illustrate the absurdity of such a kind of account by applying it in a thoroughly ludicrous manner to himself. Such an account might well regard his bones and sinews as the cause of his sitting there with his legs bent; what he says indicates that he is still—as almost from the beginning—sitting with his feet on the earth. Against such an account, he insists—with his typical oath "By the dog!"—that his bones and sinews would long ago have fled, were it not that he regards it as more just to endure the penalty the Athenians have imposed on him. In the end, what is consequential is not so much Socrates' engagement with Anaxagoras but rather the posing of νοῦς as decisive in accounting for the cause of things. In this way he broaches the schema of a different kind of account, one that would refer things not to other things or elements of nature, but to causes correlative in a certain way to νοῦς.

Against this background, Socrates asks Cebes: "Do you want me to make a display [ἐπίδειξις], Cebes, of the way by which I have occupied myself with the second sailing in search of the cause?" (99c–d). A second sailing (δεύτερος πλοῦς) is what sailors do when in the absence of wind they take to the oars. Analogously, Socrates ventured his

---

43. In this passage the plural form is used. On the other hand, Diogenes Laertius reports: "Those who wrote only one book include Melissus, Parmenides, and Anaxagoras" (*Lives of Eminent Philosophers* 1:16).

44. Socrates would presumably have read, for example, the following passage: "Together were all things, unlimited both in number and in smallness; for the small was also unlimited. And as all things were together, nothing was manifest because of their smallness. For air and aither dominated all things, both being unlimited" (B1). In the *Apology* Socrates mentions the charge against him that "he says the sun is a stone and the moon is earth." Then he asks: "Do you think you are accusing Anaxagoras, my dear Meletus?" (26d). Originally from Clazomenai, Anaxagoras spent most of his life in Athens and reportedly was close to Pericles. Like Socrates, he was brought to trial on the charge of impiety (around 450 BC). He was banished and withdrew to Lampsacus. See Kirk, Raven, and Schofield, *The Presocratic Philosophers*, 352–55.

second sailing when, in the absence of success in his previous inquiries in search of causes, he had recourse to another way of inquiry. Specifically, since inquiry that would account for things by referring them to natural things or elements broke down, issuing in aporias, Socrates took another way, ventured a second sailing, began again, made a new—a second—beginning.[45]

In response to Socrates' offer to make a display of the second sailing, Cebes replies: "I want you to . . . extraordinarily so" (99d). The word ὑπερφυῶς can certainly be rendered as *extraordinarily*, though a more literal translation would be *super-naturally*; the word thus hints at an advance above or beyond nature, that is, beyond natural causes to causes belonging to another order.

The passage in which Socrates offers his display of the second sailing constitutes the philosophical center of the entire dialogue: "Well, then, after these, since I had renounced this looking into beings, it seemed to me that I had to be on my guard so as not to suffer the very thing that those people do who behold and look at the sun during an eclipse. For surely some of them have their eyes destroyed unless they look at the sun's image in water or in some other such thing. I thought this sort of thing over and feared that my soul would be blinded if I looked at things with my eyes and attempted to grasp them by each of the senses. So, it seemed to me that I should have recourse to λόγοι and look in them for the truth of beings" (99d–e). The passage requires the most careful consideration.

It begins: "after these [μετὰ ταῦτα]." The reference is to the ways of inquiry that had been tried but had failed. These were the ways that attempted to account for things by reference to natural things or elements, to account, for example, for the stability of the earth by supposing that it

---

45. The expression *second sailing* (δεύτερος πλοῦς) occurs also in the *Statesman* (300c). The context is a discussion of ruling, of whether it should be done without laws or with laws. The Stranger declares that the best form of ruling is that which is carried out by a ruler who possesses the τέχνη of ruling, who rules by means of knowledge. Such a ruler has no need of laws; he rules without laws. In the absence of such true kingship, however, there must be recourse to laws and accordingly the demand that laws be obeyed. It is this recourse to laws in the absence of true kingship that the Stranger describes with the expression *second sailing*. The expression is also found in the *Philebus* (19c). In distinction from the wise man who knows everything, there is the man who, as a second sailing—so, in the absence of such wisdom—is not ignorant of himself. See also *Timaeus* 89a.

is propped up on a pedestal of air. These ways include also that taken by Anaxagoras, for despite his declaration that it is νοῦς that sets all things in order, he ends up—as Socrates discovered—accounting for things by referring them to natural things or elements as their cause.

Socrates continues: "Since I had renounced [or failed in or given up on] this looking to [or into] beings. . . ." Here *beings* (τὰ ὄντα) refers to things, primarily to things belonging to nature; for these are the beings that were the objects of Socrates' previous inquiries. Having renounced this looking into things, Socrates had—then, subsequently—as he says, to be on his guard against a certain danger. So, the danger was one that became threatening *after* Socrates had given up on looking to beings; it was not merely a danger incurred by looking into things but a danger that threatened only after he had renounced such inquiry, only when he moved on to something else. His advance was to a different kind of cause: instead of looking for the cause among natural things and elements, he would look for the cause beyond such things, beyond nature; he would search for a kind of cause that, from beyond things, would let things come forth in the double sense of being generated and being illuminated. But that which, beyond the things and elements of nature, is most responsible for their coming forth in this double sense is *the sun*. It is because of this connection that almost at the start the passage mentions those who look at the sun and announces the need to be on guard against the danger of blindness posed by such looking.

And yet, strictly speaking, one cannot look at the sun—not, that is, if looking requires more than a momentary glance. One can see things in the sunlight. In a certain way one can even see the light itself as it comes to illuminate things. But one cannot—for more than a moment—look directly at the sun. One cannot look into the very origin of light—*except* during an eclipse. Only then can one gaze directly at the sun—but then only by incurring the danger of blinding oneself. Even then, since in an eclipse the sun is covered over, one would not really have beheld it, or, at best, one would have beheld it only as it was withdrawn from vision. Hence, the blindness that would result could not even claim the compensation of a preceding vision of the origin of all visibility.

In the figure of looking into the sun, a proportion is implicitly operative (as at several previous junctures in the dialogue); for it is a matter not only of things being illuminated but also of their being visible as what they are. The proportion is, then, as follows: just as the sun is, from beyond things, the cause of their visibility, so something else, even more beyond things, is the cause of their being, of their being as they are and as they are called. Socrates does not quite say what it is that is the cause of things being what they are. Yet, his mention, in connection with Anaxagoras, of what is *best* for each thing, of the good of each, offers a hint—to say nothing of the explicit proportion in the *Republic* linking the sun to the idea of the good.

In any case, in the passage on the second sailing, Socrates is declaring that to look into such an original cause is just as dangerous as gazing into the sun; in both ventures there is the threat of blindness. One might well suppose that such a looking into the origin is precisely what was enacted in the third discourse. For in that discourse the soul's ascent was depicted as culminating in an appropriation of the soul to the origin such that there could result only a cessation of thought, an extinguishing of vision, that would leave the soul blind—just as it left Socrates silent.

Having marked the danger of blindness that threatens any attempt to look directly into the original cause, Socrates turns again to the danger incurred by the attempt to grasp things by sense alone: "I thought this sort of thing over and feared that my soul would be blinded if I looked at things with my eyes and attempted to grasp them by each of the senses." The blindness now referred to is that of which he spoke earlier: it is represented by the aporias that interrupted his inquiry into nature and blinded him to what previously he supposed he knew. Thus, there is a *double threat* of blindness. Danger lurks on both sides: both in looking to things and in looking away from things to their origin.

Consequently, the turn, the reorientation, that constitutes the second sailing is more complex than it might have seemed at first glance. It is a turn away from things, a renunciation of direct inquiry into nature; and it is a turn that, at the same time, holds back from venturing a direct look into the original cause of things. Rather than turning from sensible things to their origin (thus dying away from the sensible, as in the third discourse), the second sailing turns from things to λόγοι. Its course—or recourse—is like that of those who protect their eyes by looking "at the sun's image [εἰκών] in water or in some other such thing." In Socrates' words: "So it seemed to me that I should have recourse to λόγοι and look in them for the truth of beings."

The second sailing is constituted by having recourse to λόγοι. The word καταφεύγω also means *to flee for refuge*, in this case refuge from the double threat of blindness. Yet, by taking refuge in λόγοι, one also has recourse to these λόγοι as a means of looking for the truth of beings, as a means that is not exposed to the threat. The search for the truth of beings aims at disclosing things as what they truly are, and this means to reveal the look proper to such beings. Yet the look is nothing other than what has repeatedly been designated as *being* (τὸ ὄν) in the most proper sense, that is, as the selfsame being that in each case determines things so that they are called by the same name as the determining one—as the equality of equal sticks is determined by and called by the same name as the equal itself.

On the basis of Socrates' statement, it might be supposed that the λόγοι to which recourse is to be had are images of the beings themselves, like the images of the sun that can be seen in water. However, Socrates immediately excludes such a supposition: "Now perhaps in a certain way it is not quite like what I am likening it to. For I do not at all concede that someone who looks at beings in λόγοι looks at them in images any more than someone who looks at them in deeds" (99e–100a). Thus, the λόγοι are not merely images of beings that one would behold in the absence of the beings themselves or as a way of securing one's distance from them. Rather, the λόγοι serve to open up a way of access to beings, a way appropriate to human knowing, a raft of human λόγοι, as Simmias earlier called it (see 85c–d). Socrates' comparison suggests that λόγοι let beings become manifest in something like the way that a deed makes manifest something about the character of the person who performs the deed.

Yet how is it that λόγοι allow beings to be made manifest? How is it that by holding back from the look into the origin and having recourse instead to λόγοι, the second sailing advances toward the manifestness of beings? Socrates is explicit about how, in particular, the second sailing commences: "In any case, this is how I begin: on each occasion I put down as hypothesis whatever λόγος I judge to be the most vigorous" (100a). In other words, he begins by taking up a certain comportment to λόγος, a new, additional comportment and a new beginning, since humans always already live within a comportment to λόγος. This new comportment consists in hypothesizing in the precise sense of the word ὑπόθεσις, that is, laying down or setting out a λόγος so as to place it under something. In this setting out of a certain λόγος, Socrates sets out explicitly what is said in the λόγος, what is intended—or, in the modern phrase, what is meant—in and through the words that are spoken. More specifically, he sets out the one beings that are always already meant when one says, for instance, *beautiful* or *good* or *large*. As he explains, he sets out "the beautiful itself by itself and the good and the large and all the others" (100b). He sets out the beings themselves *as they are said*, as they are already operative and manifest in speech. Indeed, Socrates identifies what is set out as "the very thing I have never stopped talking about" (100b). Ostensibly he is referring to the earlier conversations in the *Phaedo*, which return repeatedly to discussion of the one beings. Yet, these are *always* the very things one will have been talking about; they are what talk is about as such.

It is only at this point that Socrates finally introduces the word εἶδος, referring specifically to the look of the cause (τῆς αἰτίας τὸ εἶδος). Thus he fashions the connection: the one beings that are operative in λόγος and that can be set out from λόγος in a certain manifestness are nothing other than the looks, the common looks, that are the true causes of things. And yet, there is no more enigmatic connection: for the one beings are said and are set out as said, whereas the common looks are manifest in their distinctive visibility. There is perhaps no saying just how the visibility of the looks comes—or can come—to be extended to the one beings that are said.

In any case, Socrates insists that, as he says, "nothing makes a thing beautiful but the presence [παρουσία] of or community [κοινωνία] with the beautiful" (100d). Something is beautiful and is called by the same name as the beautiful because it partakes of, has a share in, has something in common with, the beautiful itself. What it shares with the beautiful, what it has in common with the beautiful, is the *look* (εἶδος) of the beautiful. It has the look, displays the look, of the beautiful, looks like the beautiful. In this sense—and only in this sense—there is, as Socrates says, a presence (παρουσία) of the beautiful, of the look of the beautiful, in it. It is, then, the look that shines in and through things so as to make them look as they do, so as to make them have the look of a determinate thing. It is because the looks make things have the look of a certain determinate thing that the looks constitute the being of these things.

Philosophy begins, then—it makes a new, a second beginning—with a turn from the sensible, from natural things. It is in this limited sense that it can be called the practice of dying, that is, a withdrawing of the soul from the engagement that the body sustains with sensible things. And yet, this turn is no flight into a beyond that would leave the body and the sensible behind. Rather, it is a turn to λόγοι as they call forth the beings themselves, the looks, the original causes. Yet, through this turn there is accomplished a return to the things of nature, a return in which these things become manifest in their look, in the look that shines through them and determines them in their being. In the second sailing the soul does indeed draw itself away from nature, but only in order that there might be a return of nature in the manifestness of its being.

(G) SONG OF THE EARTH

The fourth discourse on immortality begins immediately after the second of the two interludes in which the conversation between Phaedo and Echecrates is resumed. This final discourse thus falls outside the frame enclosing the discourse centered in the Socratic autobiography. It is put forth as a response to Cebes' criticism following the third discourse, criticism that at that point went unanswered. The discourse falls into two parts: in the first part, Socrates takes up again the analysis of contraries and extends it beyond the earlier analysis; in the second part, he applies this analysis to the question of the immortality of the soul and ventures still another demonstration.

He begins by drawing a distinction between a contrary itself (corresponding to what the central discourse designated as a look) and the things that can have the contrary—as fire has the hot, which is contrary to the cold. He explains that something that has one contrary can come to have the other, but that when the other approaches, the first contrary must either flee or have perished by the time the other arrives. He illustrates with the example of largeness and smallness: "One of two things must happen: either largeness must flee and get out of the way when its contrary, the small, advances toward it, or else it must already have perished by the time smallness comes near it" (102e). Socrates adds the observation that there are things that are not contraries but that always contain one contrary and thus will not admit the other—as snow contains the contrary *cold* and thus cannot admit the contrary *hot* while remaining what it is, snow. He continues also to refer to the example of numbers, as he did in detailing the aporias that led him eventually to launch the second sailing: the number *three* contains the contrary *odd*, and though *two* and *three* are not contraries, *two* will not admit the *odd*.

Socrates applies this analysis to the task of demonstrating the immortality of the soul. The contours of the demonstration can be readily drawn. It is established, first of all, that the soul is what comes to bring life to the body. It follows, then, that the soul will not admit the contrary to life, namely, death (just as the number *two*, being *even*, will not admit the *odd*). Thus, it can be concluded that when death approaches, the soul either will perish or will have fled. But for the soul to perish would amount precisely to admitting death. Socrates concludes: "Therefore, when death comes at a human being, his deathbound part, as is likely, dies, but his undying part takes off and goes away safe and undestroyed, having gotten out of death's way" (106e). And thus: "it is the case that the soul is an undying and imperishable thing and that our souls really will be in Hades" (106e–107a).

Though Cebes has nothing else to say against the demonstration, Simmias confesses that he has "some lingering distrust." Socrates says only that it "must nevertheless be looked into for greater certainty" (107b). Needless to say, Simmias' distrust of the demonstration and Socrates' hesitation simply to affirm it are well justified. For again the soul is being treated as if it were a body that goes from here to there. Still more significantly, in this would-be demonstration it has become uncertain even what death is; previously it was construed as the separation of the soul from the body, but now that separation is said to occur only as a *result* of the arrival of death.

Yet, what is perhaps most remarkable is that Socrates moves quite directly from this alleged demonstration to a mythic tale about what happens to souls when they go away to Hades. It is as though the final would-be demonstration blends or transmutes into the final μῦθος, into the song that, most of all, can be regarded as Socrates' swan song. Indeed, once he has told the lengthy tale, concluding with the admission that all may not be exactly as he has described it, he declares that since the soul appears to be immortal, it is fitting—or at least it is a beautiful risk—to suppose that something like what he has described is the case. Then, referring to one who would risk this supposition, Socrates says: "And he should sing incantations to himself again and again; and that is just why I have drawn out the tale [μῦθος] for so long" (114d). Here Socrates discloses the sense of the entire portion of the dialogue from the outer frame where the Socratic autobiography ended up to the very final scene depicting Socrates' death. The soul appears (φαίνεται) to be immortal; the fourth discourse and in a sense all four discourses have displayed this appearance, this seeming to be immortal. Yet, since none have definitively demonstrated that the soul is immortal, it is necessary to supplement these discourses with a mythic tale, with incantations sung in order, as Socrates said earlier (77e), to charm away the fear of death that deeply disturbs the child present in each person. In his swan song Socrates sings such incantations—to himself, perhaps, but above all to those closest to him and there with him as the time of his death draws near.

The tale is indeed drawn out, twisting and turning like a labyrinth from stories of the soul's afterlife to a very extended story about the earth, about the hollows in it, about all that is pure and splendid on its surface, and about the network of channels beneath its surface. Then, finally, the tale returns to a description of the fate of the soul on the earth.

The tale begins by describing what happens to the soul of each person after death: his δαίμων leads him to a place where the dead are gathered and judged; a guide then sets them on their journey to Hades, where each will dwell in the region that is fitting. The way on which they must travel has "many branchings into two and also three ways" (108a). Again the figure of the labyrinth is drawn.

Abruptly the tale turns to a description of the earth, which will be the principal theme of the entire story: "And many and wondrous are the regions of the earth, and earth itself is neither of the sort nor of the size that it is held to be in the opinion of those who usually speak about the earth, as I have been persuaded by someone" (108c). Socrates' tale of the soul's afterlife thus turns into a song of the earth; based on an unnamed source, most likely to be taken as mere hearsay,[46] the story will tell of the look (ἰδέα) of the earth.

Near the beginning it tells that if one could see it from above, the earth would look like a twelve-piece leather ball. It is round and suspended motionless in the middle of the heaven by virtue of its equiformity.[47] It is very large, and the portion where, says Socrates, we dwell is a small part around the sea, as frogs dwell around a swamp. In the earth there are many hollows "with all manner of looks and sizes, into which the water and the mist and the air have flowed together" (109b). Humans are unaware that they dwell in the hollows, thinking, rather, that they dwell up on the earth's surface. If someone could go up to the surface—just as fish leap up out of the sea—and if "the nature in him

---

46. See Burnet's discussion, which disqualifies a number of possible candidates: Archelaus, Anaximander, the Pythagoreans. He does note, however, that the influence of Empedocles can be discerned in the details of the description (*Plato's Phaedo*, note to 108c8).

47. See ibid., note to 109a2.

were sufficient to endure seeing the sight" (109e), then he would recognize that it is up there that the true heaven, the true light, and the true earth are to be found. At this point in the story an elaborate description of the region up there on the earth's surface is launched, a description of the pure, splendid colors, of the trees, flowers, and fruits, as well as the mountains and the smooth, transparent rocks, of which the so-called precious stones in the region below are mere fragments. Socrates formulates a double proportion:

1) water and the sea: us:: air: those up there

2) air: us:: aither: those up there

The sight, hearing, and thoughtfulness of those up there on the surface of the earth exceed ours in purity; not only in the power of thought but also in that of sense perception they are superior to us. And they have "groves and temples for the gods in which the gods are really dwellers" (111b); the contrast with our groves and temples is left unsaid, that in them there are really present only images of the gods. In sum, "such is the earth's nature" (111c).

It is striking how the presentation of these descriptions reproduces the situation earlier in the dialogue when knowledge was said to require dying away from the body and the senses despite the fact that this very declaration was uttered by the embodied Socrates and affirmed by the embodied Simmias. The situation of the mythologizer is structurally much the same: how is it that someone living down in a hollow where everything is obscured by mist—Socrates himself and whoever it might be that passed it along to him—can describe the look of all the things, persons, and even gods that are to be found up above on the surface of the earth? Is it that the mythologizer somehow is capable of ascending to the surface—like a fish leaping up out of the sea? Or is it that in telling a mythic tale—in contrast to determining and expressing the requirements of knowledge—the opposition between word and deed, between what is said and the conditions of the possibility of saying it, is tolerable, that it even belongs to the very character of mythologizing? If this character injects into the tale a trace of comedy, the tale itself—unlike the earlier discourses—does not devolve into comedy.

The tale goes on to describe all that lies under the surface of the earth: passageways by which the hollows are connected underground;

EARTHBOUND 245

great rivers of water and others of fire, all flowing together into Tartarus; and the four great streams, the outermost of which is Oceanos.

As the tale approaches its end, it tells of the itineraries followed by various sorts of souls, depending on the character of their deeds while they were living. Those whose misdeeds are so great that they are incurable are cast into Tartarus with no possibility of escape. Those guilty of lesser misdeeds go also to Tartarus, but after a year they are released and sent to supplicate forgiveness from those against whom their misdeeds were committed. There are, finally, those who are freed from these subterranean regions: "But all who seem to have distinguished themselves in leading a holy life—it is they who are liberated and set free from these regions here within the earth, as though from prisons, and who, arriving at their pure dwelling up top, dwell on the surface of the earth. And of these people, the ones who have been sufficiently purified by philosophy live without bodies for all time to come" (114b–c).

Hardly anything could be more remarkable than that Socrates' final discourse is a song of the earth, considering how often in the previous discourses, especially in the third, the body, the senses, nature, and the earth as the very receptacle of nature were denigrated as the locus that the true—or true-born—philosopher would strive to die away from. As Socrates' death draws near, he speaks only about the earth, and even what he says about the destiny of the various sorts of souls is in every case described in terms of the region of the earth to which they are finally transported. In the mythic tale it is as if the celebration of the earth comes to represent also a celebration of the body. For the earth is depicted almost as if it were the body "writ large," its system of circulating rivers and streams imaging the circulatory system of the body, Tartarus, where all these come together, representing the heart.[48]

Yet what seems most remarkable of all is the depiction of the purest and holiest souls: even they, even if they become so purified that they can live (even though they are dead) without bodies—even they go to dwell up on the surface of the earth. Not even they, though purified by philosophy, would take flight from the earth.

Thus, Socrates' song is a celebration of the earth and of all that belongs to the earth. As Socrates' death comes ever closer, he sings of a return of everything that is of the earth. He sings of a return of nature

---

48. See Ronna Burger, *The Phaedo: A Platonic Labyrinth* (New Haven: Yale University Press, 1984), 194.

with the earth as its receptacle. Throughout the entire conversation, from the moment when Socrates tells Cebes that he had undertaken the practice of music until finally he sings his swan song, Socrates has sat with his feet down on the earth. Only when he has finally sung his song of the earth does he stand up and go off to his bath, cleansing not his soul but his body.

Just before he goes off to bathe, Socrates mentions tragedy. If tragedy is regarded as primarily speech that expresses tragic pathos, as speech that displays suffering in such a manner as to make it appear all the more intense, evoking corresponding pathos in those who witness it, then Socrates' mode of speech cannot be declared simply tragic, not even in the situation depicted in the *Phaedo* where he faces death. In fact, he shames those who display such pathos—Xanthippe, of course, but also his dearest friends there with him as he prepares to drink the potion. Indeed, he mocks the tragic hero when, as he is about to go off to his bath, he declares: "'But me destiny calls anon,' as a man in a tragedy might declaim" (115a). Very shortly thereafter, in response to Crito's inquiry about burial, there comes from Socrates "a gentle laugh" (115c). It is in a certain—non-symmetrical—opposition to the pathetic sounding of tragic speech that after drinking the potion and shaming his friends for their outburst, he counsels that "one should meet one's end in propitious silence" (117e). If tragic pathos is not entirely lacking, there is on Socrates' part a distancing of himself from the tragic.[49]

In Phaedo's final words to Echecrates, he calls Socrates "the best and, yes, the most thoughtful and the most just" (118). Socrates was most thoughtful, it seems, in the reserve that he maintained to the end in venturing a vision of what is to come, as in his song of the earth, while holding back from the pretense—or arrogance—of certain knowledge; in this manner he infused his thoughtfulness with his insuppressible awareness of human limits, of ignorance. If justice requires rendering to each what rightfully belongs to him, then the superlative may be taken to denote his practice of rendering more than others can rightfully claim, that is, his practice of free giving, of generosity.

But what, then, finally, about the cock owed to Asclepius? What about Socrates' final words, addressed to Crito: "We owe a cock to Asclepius. So pay the debt and do not be careless" (118)? The custom behind these words was that of offering a gift to the physician god Asclepius

---

49. See my discussion in *Platonic Legacies* (Albany: State University of New York Press, 2004), chap. 8.

upon recovering from an illness. What, then, is the illness from which there has been a recovery? It could hardly be a recovery from human emplacement in a body within nature upon the earth. Rather, the recovery—for Socrates but also for his friends—will have been from the presumption of an ascent into the company of the gods themselves, and from the danger that in venturing direct access to being itself one risks blinding one's very soul. It is a recovery that would free humans for a celebration of all that belongs to nature, that would enable them to embrace the return of nature.

ENGLISH INDEX

abode, 45–47, 94, 103; of the gods, 123; of humans, 101, 117, 180
Achilles, 7, 51, 92n18, 102n27, 194n23
Aegeus, 163–165
Aeschines, 166–167
Aeschylus, 6, 7; *Agamemnon*, 6–7
Aesop, 171–173, 196
Aethra, 163
Aetius, 21, 24, 53, 174–175
Alcmaeon, 175, 232n41
Alexander, 3
Amathus, 51
Anaxagoras, 18, 197–198, 231n39, 234–235, 237–238; and mind, 234
Anaximander, 9, 15, 17–18, 20n10, 22, 243n46; and the indefinite, 15, 17
Anaximenes, 9, 15, 17–22, 38, 49, 102n26, 231n40
Androgeus, 163
Andromache, 50
Animals, 6, 39, 45, 47, 95, 231–232
Antaeus, 110
Antisthenes, 166–167
Aphrodite, 10, 49, 51–52, 93, 230
Apollo, 5, 10, 83, 165, 169, 172–173, 224; Apollo's Lyre, 88; *Homeric Hymn to Apollo*, 54n12
Apollodorus, 165n4, 166–167
Arcadia, 5
Ares, 230
Ariadne, 164–165, 169, 192, 228
Aristides, 83
Aristippus, 168
Aristophanes, 116, 194
Aristotle, 9n15, 14, 16, 20–22, 26–27, 30n8, 39, 52, 62n3, 69n7, 137, 160, 176n16; *Generation of Animals*, 44; *Metaphysics*, 175; *Meteorology*, 49n8, 101n24; *On Coming to Be and Passing Away*, 127; *On the Heaven*, 49n8; *Physics*, 37
Aristoxenus, 160, 176
Artemis, 6–12, 27, 29, 32, 82–84, 86; light-bringing, 8; protector, 6; temple of, 9
Asclepius, 12, 246
Aulis, 6–7
aviary, 144, 146

birth, 4, 7, 45, 65, 85, 87, 92, 105, 156, 162–163, 201, 211; childbirth, 6, 8, 11, 82, 86; of Dionysus, 41; of the heaven, 232n42; rebirth, 180, 196
Boreas, 10
bow, 4, 5, 8
breath, 18, 20, 25, 54, 193–194
Burnet, John, 18, 20n11, 46n6, 129, 199n26, 210n29, 228n38, 231n39, 232n41, 243n46

Cadmus, 230
Calchas, 6
Cape Sounian, 73
chance, 116, 162, 165–167, 172, 178–179, 183–184, 209
Circe, 48
Clement, 46
Cleombrotus, 168
comedy, 11, 17, 67, 91, 95, 116, 139, 154, 170, 192, 205, 213, 222, 244; etymological, 133n48; hermeneutical, 218–219; Platonic, 147–149, 200; Socratic, 194
Condensation, 22–23
cosmos, 25; making of, 232n42; revolution of, 121n34

Crete, 48, 162–165, 168–169, 198, 200, 225
Crito, 246
Croton, 173
Critobulus, 166–167
cycle, 10, 176, 179–180
Cypris, 50, 51
Cyrene, 73, 74

Daedalus, 162–164
Delos, 5, 165–166, 169, 170, 172, 180, 198, 200, 225
Derrida, Jacques, 60n2
Diels-Kranz, 21, 22, 35
Dike, 122
Diogenes Laertius, 9, 19, 23, 26n1, 27, 42n1, 48n7, 68, 69n7, 122, 128n46, 172n7, 174n9, 176, 235n43
Dion of Syracuse, 174
Dionysus, 41
dissolution, 19, 90–96, 135, 214

earth, 41, 45–46, 48–56, 93, 101, 102n27, 110, 115–116, 127, 176–178, 198, 205, 219, 221, 223; earthly region, 101; myth of the, 92n18
Echecrates, 158–162, 166–169, 173, 179–180, 195, 227, 241, 246
Electra, 7, 102
Eleusis, 69
Elis, 160
Empedocles, 9–10, 19, 37, 42–57, 91–92, 102n27, 128, 197n25, 231n40, 243n46
Endymion, 197, 200
Ephesians, 3
Ephesus, 3, 9
Epicharmus, 91–92
Epigenes, 166–167
Erineos, 69
Erymanthus, 5
Euclides, 60–61, 68–73, 75, 100–101, 168
Euphronius, 75
Euripides, 7–8; *Hippolytus*, 4n3, 8n14, 28n4; *Iphigenia in Tauris*, 6, 7n12; *The Suppliant Women*, 221n36
Eurydice, 191
Euthyphro, 64–65
Evenus, 172, 177

Fate, 10, 163, 164–165, 243; fateful, 165
fire, 2, 17n6, 22–24, 38–41, 50, 52–53, 95, 126–127, 231–232, 244–245; firewood, 16; of heaven, 37–41; of hell, 38; of Zeus, 49
Freeman, Kathleen, 46

Gaia, 110
generosity, 246
Greece, 3, 162–163, 230

Hades, 34n14, 41, 53–54, 69–70, 169–170, 188, 190–192, 194–195, 198, 200–202, 218, 225, 242–243; true Hades, 220–221, 224
Harmonia, 230
harmony, 34–35, 173–176, 229–230, 232n41; mathematical basis of, 174; sense of, 225
heaven, 20, 24, 38, 48, 50, 51, 53, 58, 67, 101, 115–116, 127, 176, 198, 232, 243; fire of the, 37–41; heavenly bodies, 18, 38, 55; light of, 102; lord of the, 53; sign from, 98; starry, 59; true heaven, 244
Hegel, G. W. F., 18–20
Heidegger, Martin, 14n1, 35
Hellas, 6
Hephaistos, 50–51
Hera, 5–6, 52, 53–54, 92–93, 102
Heracles, 10, 110, 164, 228–229
Heraclitus, 9–10, 17, 26–30, 31n10, 33–41, 44, 91–92, 96, 128, 225, 232n40; comrades of, 120
Hermogenes, 64–65, 166–167
Herodotus, 230
Hesiod, 20, 33, 48, 54, 93n19, 102, 154
Hippolytus, 4, 54; third-century AD writer, 21
Homer, 3, 9, 16, 20, 28, 38, 48–51, 83n14, 91, 92–93, 95, 102n27, 118n32, 176, 190, 194–195; on Artemis, 29n5; Homeric gods, 10; Homeric Hymns, 5, 54; *Iliad*, 5, 20, 48–49, 50–51, 62n3, 92, 102n25, 102n27, 102n32, 194n23; *Odyssey*, 5, 48, 50, 69, 73, 192, 230
huntress, 4, 6, 8
Husserl, Edmund, 60n2, 119

ENGLISH INDEX   251

Hydra, 228–229
Iamblichus, 173
Iolaus, 228–229
Iphigenia, 6–8, 12
Iris, 101–103

Jason, 228

Kahn, Charles H., 15n2, 17n6, 20n10, 30

Labyrinth, 163–165, 168, 192, 213, 225, 228, 243
Laconia, 5
laughter, 149, 160, 179, 192, 214
leisure, 10, 70, 114–115, 120, 169
Leto, 5, 7
Libya, 73, 110
look, 2, 15, 23, 35, 81–82, 131–132, 139, 152–153, 159, 186, 206–207, 239–244; common, 133–138, 142–143, 145–146, 150, 154, 156; look through, 178–180, 184, 194; selfsame, 216, 219–220; Socrates', 226, 231–233

Magna Graecia, 3
matter, 119; Aristotle and, 16, 39
Megara, 60, 68–71, 110, 168
memory, 2, 60–62, 69–71, 107, 109, 138, 144–151, 201–202, 206, 232; and λόγος, 146, 195; span of, 145;
Menelaus, 49
Menexenus, 167–168
Meno, 202, 204n27
midwife, Socrates as, 11, 65, 82–87, 104, 105, 116, 142
Miletus, 64, 72, 82, 110, 173, 198; city of, 3, 13, 18, 19
Minos, 162–163, 165, 169
Minotaur, 162–164, 169, 213
misologist, 229
moderation, 30, 190–191
monster, 10, 58, 98, 101, 107, 109, 140, 158, 162–164, 228

natality, 7
nativity, 6
Nausikaa, 5

Naxos, 164–165
Nestis, 52, 54
Oceanos, 92–93, 102, 245
Odysseus, 7, 30, 48, 69, 111, 192
olive oil, 1, 72–74, 91–92, 96, 100, 114
Oreithyia, 10
Orpheus, 176, 191–192, 214, 225; Orphism, 176, 180, 191

Pain, 8, 84, 99, 170–171, 173, 195–196, 222–223
Paphos, 51
Paris, 49, 102n27
Parmenides, 33, 47–49, 63, 91, 121–122, 124–129, 197n25, 215–216, 235
Paros, 172
Pasiphae, 162
Patroklos, 48
Pausanias, 43, 45
Peloponnesos, 160
Penelope, 69, 222–223
Persephone, 54, 70
Phaedo, 158–162, 165–171, 173–176, 179, 192, 195, 227–228, 241, 246
Phaedonides, 167–168
Phaedrus, 10
Philolaus, 167, 173–175, 178–179
Phlius, 160–162, 166, 167, 173, 185, 227
Pindar, 115
Piraeus, 69
Pittheus, 163
Plato, 2, 15–17, 23, 33, 52, 62, 68n6, 70, 91, 152n53, 167, 182, 217; *Apology*, 65, 82–84, 116–117, 162, 167, 182, 197–198, 235n44; *Cratylus*, 11, 64–65, 92n18, 102, 133n48, 166, 224; *Crito*, 65, 116; dialogues, 10–11, 81; *Euthyphro*, 64–65; *Laches*, 83n15; *Lysis*, 167–168; *Meno*, 77, 85n16, 191, 202–203, 204n27; *Parmenides*, 33, 121n36, 122n37; *Phaedrus*, 10, 81n12, 96n22, 162; Platonic Socrates, 218; *Protagoras*, 85n16, 191; and Pythagoreanism, 174; *Sophist*, 63, 65, 73n8, 121n36, 122, 193n20, 216; *Statesman*, 62n3, 63, 65, 73n8, 74, 80n11, 121n34, 193n20, 236n45; texts, 16, 159, 232; *Timaeus*, 16–17, 38–39, 53,

83n14, 93n19, 94, 99, 121n36, 144n51, 152n53, 174n9, 176, 232n42
Plutarch, 33, 40, 165n4
Poseidon, 5, 53, 73, 110, 162–163
Prodicus, 85n16
Prometheus, 51
Protagoras, 73, 88–89, 92, 96n21, 97, 103, 105–106, 108–110, 119–120; criticism of, 139; head of, 66; Socrates/Protagoras, 109; *Truth*, 87, 105–106
Pythagoras, 13, 18, 38, 160, 173, 176, 226; death of, 160; Orphic-Pythagorean, 192, 220, 222; Pythagoreanism, 160, 173, 191; Pythagorean, 160, 162, 166–169, 173–180, 185, 200–201, 224, 226, 232n41, 243n46

rainbow, 19, 101–102
relief, 8, 85, 154
reticence, 34, 167
Rome, 21

sacrifice, 6–7, 11–12, 162
Samos, 3, 18, 173
sanctuary, 6–8
Saussure, Ferdinand de, 154
Schleiermacher, Friedrich, 29
Sciron, 109–110
second sailing, 169, 227, 235
silence, 91, 98, 100, 116, 130, 142, 158, 205, 223–224, 246
Simplicius, 21–22, 48n7, 52, 121n35, 197n25; *Physics*, 55n13
Sinis, 164
skepticism, 48n7, 224–226
sky, 7, 27, 48–51, 55–56, 102n27
Sophocles: *Antigone*, 118n32; *Electra*, 7, 118n32
Sparta, 109, 160
St. Paul, 3
Stoics, 27, 38, 145n52
Stranger (Eleatic), 63, 80n11, 121n34, 122n37, 216, 218, 236n45
Styx, 200

Tauris, 7–8, 12
Taygetus, 5

Telemachus, 30
Terpsion, 60–61, 68–70, 100, 168
Tethys, 92–93, 102
tetraktys, 175
Thales, 15, 17–18, 21, 67–68, 72, 108, 113, 116–117
Thaumas, 101–102
Thebes, 167–168, 173, 185, 230
Theophrastus, 14, 15n2, 21, 44n3, 48n7, 52, 128n46
Theseus, 10, 110, 163–165, 168–169, 213–214, 225, 228
Thetis, 51
Timaeus, 39, 93n19, 232n42
Titan, 46, 48–49
tragedy, 28, 91, 170–171, 246
Troezen, 163
Troy, 6, 131, 133
Typhon, 10–11

unlimited (Anaximenes), 22

ventriloquy (Socratic), 90, 103, 112, 178–179, 192, 231

water, 15, 17–18, 21, 23–24, 37, 40, 49, 51–52, 54, 68, 127, 154, 235, 243–245; clock, 114–115, 139, 150; sun's image in, 236, 238–239
wax block, 144–147
weeping, 170, 179, 195
wisdom, 30, 31–32, 44n4, 75–76, 82–83, 106, 109, 118, 231; high throne of, 43; lover of, 189; superhuman, 65
Wright, M. R., 46, 55

Xanthippe, 170–171, 246
Xenophon, 167, 172n7
Xenophanes, 9, 48

Zeno, 9, 27, 38
Zeus, 5–6, 10, 54, 56, 88, 93, 102n25, 179; fire of, 49; shining, 52–53; swearing "by Zeus," 10, 106, 132, 156, 172, 185, 208; Zeus' thunderbolt, 10, 41, 51

GREEK INDEX

ἀγών, 17, 18
ἀήρ, 20–21, 24, 38, 40n21, 49, 54; ὑγρὸς ἀήρ, 49
Ἅιδης, 41, 54, 218, 220
αἰθήρ, 20, 24, 38, 49
αἴσθησις, 34–36, 44n4, 60, 234
αἰών, 34, 39
ἀληθέα, 30–31
ἀναιδής, 148
ἄπειρον, 22, 129, 234
ἀπόδειξις, 106, 193, 203, 205
ἀπορία, 75, 81, 84, 117, 139
ἀρετή, 11, 30, 190
ἁρμονία, 34–35, 225–226, 230
ἀρχή, 16–17, 20–25, 27, 36, 38, 46–47, 49, 51–52, 54, 56–57, 68, 101, 103, 105

βασιλεύς, 64
βιβλίον, 26–27

γαῖα, 48, 50
γελοῖον, 10
γῆ, 37, 50, 52, 54; ἐπὶ τὴν γῆν, 177

δεύτερος πλοῦς, 16, 235, 236n45
δόξα, 76, 124, 139, 142, 150–151, 184; δοξάζειν, 139–140, 142–143, 150–151

εἶδος/εἴδη, 15–16, 23, 33, 80–82, 85, 159, 206, 217–218, 232n42, 240
εἰκών, 61, 106, 238
ἐπιστήμη, 76–77
ἔργα, 80, 161

ζῷα, 39

ἦθος, 45, 47, 117

θάλασσα, 40, 48
θυμός, 191

καπνός, 194
κατάβασις, 72, 113
καπνός, 194
κίνησις, 103
κόσμος, 38–39, 176
Κύπρις, 51

μέτρον, 39, 120, 121n34
μνήμη, 201
μοῖρα, 10, 169
μορφή, 14
μυθολόγημα, 10
μῦθος, 3, 69, 108, 123, 162, 169, 171, 177, 179–180, 193, 196, 228, 242

νεῖκος, 55; φιλόνεικος, 228
νόμος, 165
νοῦς, 234–235, 237
νῦν, 62–63

οὐρανός, 20, 24, 27, 38, 48–49, 53, 55, 176

πάλαι, 61–62, 138
Περὶ Φύσεως, 9, 26–28, 37, 42
πνεῦμα, 18, 25, 194
ποίησις, 39, 53
πόντος, 48
πῦρ, 17n6, 37, 49, 51
πῦρ ἀείζωον, 39

ῥεύματα, 105
ῥιζώματα, 37, 52

σιγή, 223
σοφία, 30, 76
στοιχεῖα, 17, 37, 52n9, 151-152
σχῆμα, 1, 56
σχολή, 10, 114, 120
σωφροσύνη, 30, 190

τέρας, 101, 107, 140
τέχνη, 28, 39, 53, 65, 82, 85, 236n25m
τὸ πᾶν, 38, 103, 176
τόπος, 94; ἄτοπος, 63n3, 171
τὸ πρᾶγμα, 119; τὸ πρᾶγμα αὐτό, 58
τύχη, 162

ὕδωρ, 17, 21, 37, 40
ὕλη, 14, 16, 20-21, 39
ὑποκείμενον, 22

φάρμακον, 85, 161-162, 177, 182
φιλία, 55
φύομαι, 4, 7-8, 86
φύσις, 33-34, 36-37, 232n42
φωσφόρος, 7-8, 32

χώρα, 94-95, 99-100, 121, 123, 144n51

ψυχή, 133n48, 159, 194, 199

JOHN SALLIS is Frederick J. Adelmann Professor of Philosophy at Boston College. He is author of more than twenty books, including *Light Traces* (IUP, 2014) and *Logic of Imagination* (IUP, 2012).

www.ingramcontent.com/pod-product-compliance
Lightning Source LLC
Chambersburg PA
CBHW030616230426
43661CB00053B/2013